SACRIFICING TRUTH

SACRIFICING TRUTH

Archaeology and the Myth of Masada

Nachman Ben-Yehuda

an imprint of Prometheus Books
59 John Glenn Drive, Amherst, New York 14228-2197

Published 2002 by Humanity Books, an imprint of Prometheus Books

Inquiries should be addressed to
Humanity Books
59 John Glenn Drive
Amherst, New York 14228–2197
VOICE: 716–691–0133, ext. 207
FAX: 716–564–2711

06 05 04 03 02   5 4 3 2 1

Library of Congress Cataloging-in-Publication Data

Ben-Yehuda, Nachman.
Sacrificing truth : archaeology and the myth of Masada / Nachman Ben-Yehuda.
p. cm.
Includes bibliographical references and index.
ISBN 1–57392–953–0 (alk. paper)
1. Masada Site (Israel)—Siege, 72–73—Historiography. 2. Excavations (Archaeology)—Israel—Masada Site. 3. Jews—History—168 B.C.–135 A.D. 4. Israel—Antiquities. I. Title.

DS110.M33 B47 2002
933—dc21   2002020808

Printed in the United States of America on acid-free paper

In memory of my parents,

Dina and Yitzhak

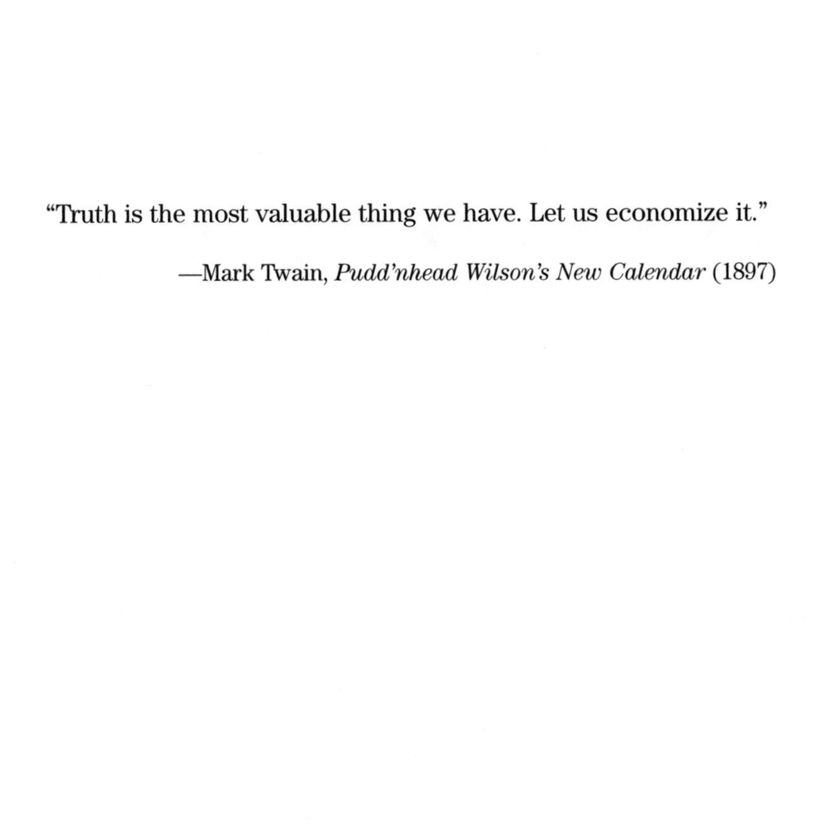

"Truth is the most valuable thing we have. Let us economize it."

—Mark Twain, *Pudd'nhead Wilson's New Calendar* (1897)

CONTENTS

LIST OF ILLUSTRATIONS

ACKNOWLEDGMENTS

First and foremost I wish to thank Etti, Tzach, and Guy, whose love, devotion, and dedication enabled me to transform this project from an idea into a book.

Much appreciation is due to the many archaeologists, some at the Hebrew University, who gave us so much of their time for interviews. I am particularly grateful to Gila Hurvitz, Gideon Foerster, and Ehud Netzer, who were always willing to listen and help, despite obvious disagreements. Professor Foerster's comments on the archaeological chapters of the book were both useful and indispensable. Both Ze'ev Meshel and the late Shmaria Guttman granted me generous interviews despite being aware of the debunking nature of this project. I feel obligated to emphasize the obvious, and that is that whatever is written in this book is my full and sole responsibility and in no way reflects (or does not reflect) the views of any of the many interviewees regarding Masada.

I want to thank the incredibly helpful staff at the Imperial War Museum in London, where I learned so much about the business of deception in war. Erich Goode, John Hagan, and Barry Schwartz should be credited with persuading me, in the course of some intense conversations in the summer of 1997 in Toronto, to write this book as a separate volume. I am particularly grateful to Eileen Barker and Stanley Cohen, who helped me spend two fruitful consecutive summers in London, courtesy of the Department of Sociology, London School of Economics, where I was able to bring this project to completion. My conversations with Paul Rock and David Downs were of great help. I am particularly grateful to Paul Rock's many useful, insightful, and indispensable detailed comments on an earlier draft. In London I enjoyed the generous, courteous, and very efficient assistance of librarians and staff from both the British Library and the Imperial War

Museum. Martin Gladman will recognize in this book the results of some of our conversations at West Finchley. I still remember with much fondness and appreciation the challenges and intellectual curiosity so characteristic of these conversations. Finally, I am grateful to John Simpson, Dennis McGill, and Nancy Howell of the Department of Sociology, University of Toronto, whose help enabled me to spend time during the summer of 1999 in Toronto to complete a revision of the manuscript.

My research assistants during the life of this project, and the one preceding it, made all the difference. At the beginning there were Einat Usant, Vered Vinitzky-Seroussi, Anat Kaminer, and Yossi Bar-Nachum. On this specific project I was assisted mainly by Dalit Rudner and Iris Wolf. I am deeply indebted to the energetic and determined Iris Wolf, whose intelligence, help, and support were unsurpassed. Without her enthusiasm, persistence, and resolution, this study would probably still be waiting to be completed.

Israeli Foundation Trustees research grant no. 032-1191, 1994–96, funded part of the work presented in this book. Part of this book was presented at the annual meeting of the American Sociological Association in Washington, D.C., August 2000, section on "The Sociology of Knowledge."

I am indebted to Ruth Rossig's tenaciously superb editing of a previous draft, to Nicholas A. Read, whose wonderful editing made this a better book, to the Shaine Foundation whose grant helped finance it, and to Uzzi Amit-Kohn for many challenging and useful comments about content and title. Professor Kohl's suggestions for a revision were extremely helpful, and I am deeply indebted to his careful and constructive review.

I am grateful to different presses for permission to use the following materials (partly adapted, partly used "as is"): from chapters 2, 3, and 9 from my 1995 book by the University of Wisconsin Press; from pages 179–180, 182–183, and 190–93 from my 1985 book by the University of Chicago Press; illustration number 15 is from pages 198–99 of Yadin's 1966e book, by Random House (I used the Weidenfeld and Nicolson edition), and illustration number 16 is from page 427 of Arye Kasher's 1983 book published by the Zalman Shazar Center.

Picture number 1 was taken by Albatross, aerial photography, Tel Aviv. I am very grateful to Albatross for their permission to reproduce it. Pictures numbered 4, 5, and 14 were reproduced from book III reporting on the Masada excavations, by permission of the 1963–64 archaeological Excavation Expedition to Masada, the Institute of Archaeology, Hebrew University, and the Israel Exploration Society. I am very grateful to professor Ehud Netzer and Professor Gideon Foerster, who were instrumental in granting access and permission to use these photos. Pictures numbered 7, 10, and 13 were reproduced from the exhibit book of Masada. I am thoroughly grateful to both Professor Gideon Foerster and Gila Hurvitz from the Institute of Archaeology at Hebrew University for being so instrumental in helping to get the illustrations and scan them. These pictures too are reproduced by permission of the 1963–64 archaeological Excavation Expedition to Masada, the Institute of Archaeology, Hebrew University, and the Israel Exploration Society. I am very grateful to Yael Barshak from the Israel Antiquity Authority who, in one simple phone call, approved using the pictures, courtesy of the authority. Pictures numbered 2, 3, 8, 9, 12, 17, 18, and 19 were reproduced by courtesy of the Government Press Office, State of Israel.

1. Masada, looking south. (Picture by Albatross, Tel Aviv)

CHRONOLOGY

To help us have a linear time line that contextualizes events mentioned in this book, a relevant chronology is presented here.

Sixth–fourth centuries B.C.E.: Nabatean culture and kingdom flourish.

Second–first centuries B.C.E.: Maccabees—a dynasty of Jewish priests, presidents, and royalty in Israel in the period of the second temple.

73(?) B.C.E.–4 B.C.E.: Life of King Herod. His reign lasted thirty-three years between 37–4 B.C.E. (peaking between 27–13 B.C.E.).

40–4 B.C.E.: Probable construction of Masada, most of it by King Herod. After his death, a Roman garrison is stationed in the fortress.

September 23, 63 B.C.E.–14 C.E.: Life of Caesar Augustus.

31 B.C.E.: Battle at Actium.

66–74 C.E.: The Jewish Great Revolt.

66 C.E.: Jewish rebels take Masada by force from the Roman garrison.

Fall of 72–spring of 73 C.E.: The Roman Tenth Legion besieges Masada. The Roman camps and siege ramp are built. Eventually, on the fifteenth of Nissan (Xanthicus) Masada falls. Following Elazar Ben-Yair's persuasion, 960 rebels commit suicide, seven survive. A Roman garrison is stationed there for at least forty years.

Autumn 131–summer 132 (probably closer to the summer of 132) Bar Kochva's revolt begins. The revolt ended in 135 C.E. when Beitar fell without survivors.

Fifth–sixth centuries C.E.: Byzantine monks occupy the upper part of the fortress and construct a church.

1800s–early 1900s: A number of non-Jewish travelers and visitors and travelers visit Masada. Most of them identify the place correctly and file reports about the visits (some reports include maps and charts).

1912: First tour to Masada by Jews from the gymnastic group of "Maccabi" in Jerusalem.

1920s: The Berdyczewski-Achad Ha'am debate in which Masada is mentioned as a case of Jewish heroism.

1923: Dr. Y. N. Simchoni provides the Hebrew-reading audience with an excellent and readable translation of Josephus Flavius from Greek into modern Hebrew.

1922–1925: First trips to Masada by various individuals and groups from Jerusalem and Tel Aviv.

1927: Yitzhak Lamdan publishes the full version of his famous and popular *Masada* (which he began writing during 1923–1924).

1933: Shmaria Guttman climbs to Masada with two colleagues and becomes convinced that Masada must become a national symbol.

1940: Lehi (better known as the "Stern Gang"), headed by "Yair" (named after Elazar Ben-Yair, Masada's last Sicarii commander), is created.

1941: Shmaria Guttman climbs to Masada again.

1942: Shmaria Guttman's seminar of guides takes place on Masada. The "plan for the North," a plan for self-defense of the Jews in Palestine in case Rommel's Afrika Korps overcomes Allied resistance, is debated (between 1940 and 1942).

1942–1948: Masada is visited more frequently by youth movements; members of the prestate underground Hagana/Palmach visit there regularly.

1948: The Israeli army, mostly recruits to the armored units but others too, climb regularly to Masada. Youth movements and schools make Masada a preferred site for their annual trips. This situation lasts into the 1970s.

1949: Masada is under Israeli sovereignty. A new path to Masada is paved by the Israeli army (Nahal units blast the way through rocks).

1953: Snake path to Masada is exposed.

1955–1956: First archaeological excavations at Masada. First exposure of Herod's palace.

1950s: The Sodom-Ein Gedi road opens (the road from the Dead Sea beach to Masada was paved in 1956).

1958: The snake path is widened by volunteers from youth movements.

1960: Shmaria Guttman excavates and restores one of the Roman army siege camps.

1962: A new road to Masada is opened.

December 1964: *Sela Metzada*, a large-scale fund-raising campaign for Masada, is launched.

1963–1965: Yigael Yadin's main excavations and reconstruction of Masada:

November 6, 1963, first discussions about the finding of a synagogue on Masada.
October 17, 1963, finding of skeletal remains in locus 2001–2002.
November 10, 1963, David Ben-Gurion visits Masada.
October–November 1963, Byzantine church is excavated.
November 14, 1963, first report of finding skeletal remains in locus 8.
December 1963, excavations of locus 113 begin.
January 1964, first discussions of archaeologists of the Nabatean findings.
February 6, 1964, animal horns found on Masada.
February 1964, the southern Mikve is found. On February 11, 1964, a group of Orthodox rabbis visits Masada and inspects this Mikve.
1964, Israel issues a series of Masada stamps.
January 6, 1965, an ostracon with the inscription "Ben Ya'ir" is reported to have been found in locus 113.
January 1965, discussions of the discovery of the Columbarium.
April 1, 1965, David Astor and son visit Masada.

1966: Many activities about Masada, including a Masada exhibition in the Israeli Museum and the publication of Yadin's books.

March 1967: First time the issue of a Jewish burial for the skeletal remains found on Masada is raised in the Israeli Knesset.

1967: The *Jewish Spectator* maintains that there was no suicide on Masada.

1967–1968: The building of the cable car to Masada is debated.

1968–1969: The debate regarding the burial of the bones from Masada rages.

July 7, 1969: The bones of twenty-seven humans found on Masada were brought to burial in an official state ceremony.

1969: Israel Eliraz and Joseph Tal's opera is presented on Masada.

1970: The building of the cable car to Masada begins. The Arad-Masada road is completed. A huge ceremony of 2,500 Jewish students on Masada is held as an act of identification with Soviet Jews.

1971: The cable car to Masada is operational.

1971: *Newsweek* commentator Stewart Alsop accuses Golda Meir of having a "Masada Complex."

1972: The beginning of an inspiring sight-and-sound show at Masada.

1973: A few official ceremonies are held on Masada, including a 1,900-

year commemoration ceremony of the fall of the fortress. The debate about the "Masada Complex" continues.

1981: The movie *Masada* is shown by ABC.

March 21, 1917–June 28, 1984: Lifetime of Yigael Yadin.

1988: The Israeli Philharmonic Orchestra plays Mahler's Symphony no. 2 on Masada as part of a social extravaganza.

1989–1995: The final reports about the excavations of Masada are published.

1993: An exhibition about Masada, commemorating thirty years since the 1963 excavations, is initiated by the Institute of Archaeology of Hebrew University, Israel Antiquities Authority, and the Society for the Study of Eretz Israel and Its Antiquities.

1909–1996: Lifetime of Shmaria Guttman.

Summer 2001: A Masada exhibit focused only on the archaeological excavations on Masada is presented in the main hall of Hebrew University's Mount Scopus campus.

ONE
THE PUZZLE

How do we perceive our culture? How do we understand ourselves as beings in need of meaning? We are socialized into and live in complex cultures from which we extract the very essence of our identity, but at the same time we also construct these cultures. How is this process accomplished? What is the nature of those cultural processes which provide us with symbolic meaning and vitalize our perception of ourselves within our self-structured and regulated social orders? This book addresses these issues.

One interesting way of exploring cultures is to examine some of the myriad contrasts that characteristically make up cultures. These contrasts set boundaries, which in turn define the variety of the symbolic-moral universes of which complex cultures are made. In turn, these symbolic-moral universes give rise to and support both personal and collective identities. There are many such contrasts, some more profound than others. There are physical contrasts, such as black/white, day/night, sea/land, mountain/valley; and there are socially and morally constructed contrasts, such as good/bad, right/wrong, justice/injustice, trust/betrayal. The contrast we shall focus on in this book is a major and significant one: that between truth and falsehood. This contrast cuts across many symbolic-moral universes because it touches a quality to which we attach central importance—that between the genuine and the spurious. Profound feelings we all share resonate to this contrast, feelings which characterize entire cultures and organizations.

Robinson (1996) points out that the demarcating line between that which is truth and that which is not did not leap into existence overnight, but developed gradually in Western philosophical thought over many years. Issues of truth and falsehood have occupied the minds of such eminent scholars as John Dewey and William James, and indeed even phenomenologists such as Jack Douglas.

Until the tempestuous and confusing age of postmodernism was unleashed upon us, the demarcation between truth and falsehood could be established with little difficulty. Some postmodernistic analyses emphasize implosions, narrative analysis, and the concept that no boundaries exist between "real" and "unreal" because all narratives are different but equally "real" versions of reality, no one better than any other. In this situation demarcation lines have become blurred. Such a view makes many of the contrasts we mentioned earlier irrelevant. This most certainly is not my view. Indeed, I agree that a major characteristic of cultures is the existence of a great many versions of reality and numerous narratives. In fact, I believe that the more we have, the merrier, because then the professional challenge for sociologists examining these cultures is genuinely more demanding. However, I cannot possibly accept the claim that all these versions or narratives are equal; they are not, either morally or, much more importantly, empirically. Putting the Nazi version of reality on the same level with those of Mother Teresa, Albert Schweitzer, Martin Luther King Jr., or Mahatma Gandhi is to me empirically false and morally impossible, although I do concede that morality is a contestable and negotiable variable.

As scientists we must affirm that there are versions of reality which are inconsistent with, even contradictory to, "facts." The realities which these false versions create are synthetic and misleading. Browsing through Phillip Knightley's fascinating 1975 work on media deception and misinformation in times of war provides many illustrations of the apparent and actual gaps between "truth" and "falsehood." Taking different versions of reality as they are, without contrasting them and trying to find out which one is closer to the observable and known facts, will leave us in a haze of eternal uncertainties, a shadowy "reality" where nothing is true or false. Living in such a universe cannot be easy. Defining a reality where Earth is perceived to be the center of the universe had some very real and tangible consequences. However, it was based on falsehoods and on an incorrect empirical foundation. If a better and more empirically accurate understanding of the solar system and the universe was to be achieved, the Ptolemaic view of the universe had to be abandoned. Likewise, such empirically incorrect perceptions as the genetic theory promoted by Lysenko or the Phlogiston theory in chemistry had to be abandoned for more informed constructions of reality. Adhering to social realities which are based on incorrect empirical facts and false information is—evidently—possible, but carries a heavy price tag in terms of a genuine understanding of the world in which we live.

A major line of this book argues that the difference between truth and falsehood can, and indeed should, be stated as clearly as possible. True, as the

Japanese play *Rashomon*[1] so ably demonstrates, it is not always easy or even feasible to establish the distinction between truth and falsehood. However, the cases in this book do indeed lend themselves to just such a clear distinction.

There are several ways of exploring this fascinating contrast between true and false, between appearance and reality. One is to write a treatise on the social philosophy of this contrast. Another is to adapt a wide-angle view of all the possible situations where this contrast exists. I have chosen a third approach, focusing on one particular aspect of culture—science—and examining the true/false contradiction there. Science encompasses many areas and disciplines. I have already explored the issue of deception and deviance in science (1985, 1986), and examining one case in detail is a worthy addition. In the past, different scientific disciplines were examined for cases of deception and falsehood. However, archaeology was somehow left outside most of the literature dealing with that aspect of science. And yet, as we shall see later, the context of archaeological endeavor is such that the tendency to accusations of falsehood is almost built into it.

The method selected here to solve the puzzles raised above is the case study approach. Adhering to it, we shall focus on one specific aspect of our culture and see how it plays a role in constructing meaning. Specifically, we shall look at the scientific discipline of archaeology and examine how in one particular case—the 1963–65 excavations of Masada in the Judean Desert of Israel—it helped shape a central process of nation-building by helping forge a specific past and hence new national and personal identities. Forging that past required falsifying historical evidence and concealing facts, adapting deceptive techniques and inventing historical realities.

MY PREVIOUS WORK ON THE MYTH OF MASADA AND THIS BOOK

My 1995 book *The Masada Myth* focused on three issues. First, it charted the nature of the Masada myth. Second, it traced the beginning and evolution of the myth and the reasons for its creation and persistence. Finally, the book contextualized the historical development of the Masada myth within a conceptual framework of constructionism and collective memory.

Indeed, it had to be that way. As Kohl (1998, p. 223) points out, "nationalism requires the elaboration of a real or invented past" and thus his superb review focuses on "how archaeological data are manipulated for nationalist purposes" in a cross-cultural and historical perspective. In a very strong sense, nationalist archaeology has no choice but to be political. And in cases of disputed pasts it has to become manipulative as well. Manipulating archaeology to legitimize specific pasts—real or invented—is a potent concoction to use when one wants to forge a national identity and create cohesion by fostering a strong sense of a shared past (and hence future) among nations of immigrants. Using archaeology necessarily means invoking science and consequently ideas of objectivity and honesty.

One riddle which puzzled me at the time, but to which I paid little attention, centered on the main archaeological excavations of Masada in 1963–65. Masada was excavated by professional archaeologists who most certainly believed in the ethos and values of science. Nonetheless, the archaeologists involved in these excavations, most notably Prof. Yigael Yadin, who headed them, solidly supported the mythical version. It was that sponsorship that genuinely puzzled me. It was inconceivable that the archaeologists at the time did not know what they were doing. Why did they choose to ignore scientific and historical evidence in favor of a myth? Much more importantly, how were they able to harness science to support a myth? Were the factual findings subverted? Were the interpretations warped?

Furthermore, was contrasting archaeology as a "science" against the "myth" justified? In theory, archaeology could be used to substantiate a genuine past and not merely to show that some supposed past was nothing more than a fable. Thus it could be that a specific past and archaeology would be able to maintain a dialogue from which much could be learned.[2] As we shall see later in this book, this is not what happened in the case of the excavations of Masada.

That is what prompted me to write this book. Contrary to my study of the myth of Masada, the present one has an altogether different focus. It examines how and why archaeologists were willing to suspend skepticism and good science in favor of a myth. In this book I am thus interested in the creation of knowledge. The facts presented here will be contextualized within a specific point of view—that of deception in science, both specifically and generally. In this sense it is a continuation of my previous interest (1985, 1986) in deviance in science. But even more, it is a ramification of my previous interest in such contrasts as true/false, deviant/nondeviant, and the issue of symbolic moral boundaries. So this book is focused on science and deception, and not on myth or the issue of collective memory.

CHOICE OF CASE

It must be noted that the excavations at Masada were not merely some haphazard dig in a desolate site in the middle of nowhere, or a search for remnants of some culture about which few people know or care. Rather, like the attempts to find the city of Troy, the excavations at Masada stirred hearts in Israel and abroad. Yadin's excavations are also important because they supported in a most significant way the mythical Masada narrative,[3] and largely for that reason became world famous.

Indeed, the authors of the first volume of the final report of Masada's excavations state that "perhaps no other archaeological endeavor in Israel has attracted such widespread attention as the excavations of Masada."[4] To drive the point even further, the authors cite Feldman:

> No single event in the history of the second Jewish commonwealth has occasioned more discussion in recent years than the fall of Masada, the mausoleum of martyrs, as it has been called. . . . The spectacular discoveries in the excavations of Masada by Yadin in a nation where digging is a veritable form of prayer have made Masada a shrine for the Jewish people.[5]

Indeed, another facet of this book is focused on the quest into the nature of the interaction and mutual influence between Zionism and archaeology. I am also interested in examining the way in which a specific research site was selected, and how the interpretation of the archaeological discoveries was (or was not) made in accordance with social, historical, and political views.

METHODOLOGY

The methodology I used is novel. Studying the archaeological excavations of Masada provides us with a fascinating opportunity to examine and follow the development of the scientific interpretations attributed to the artifacts found on Masada.

The major archaeological excavations of Masada took place from 1963 to 1965. Yadin held daily evening meetings with his team of archaeologists which, to Yadin's credit, he recorded. Later these tape recordings were transcribed; and while no one seems certain who exactly did most of the transcriptions, almost all my interviewees seemed to agree that it was Yadin's wife at the time, Carmella. I was given full and free access to these original transcriptions at the Institute of Archaeology at the Hebrew University of Jerusalem. This indeed provides a unique opportunity to examine how the archaeologists reacted to their findings on an almost daily basis. Here are their debates, evaluations, impressions, disappointments, amazement, the manner in which they developed and applied interpretations to the artifacts and structures they were uncovering, and—yes—their jokes and moods as well. These transcripts provide us with an open portal to the daily archaeological work as it actually progressed. From here I followed the different publications of the findings on Masada from 1963 to 1965 and the evolving interpretations of the original findings. The search was stopped with the final publications of the Masada excavation reports in five large volumes between 1989 and 1995, almost thirty years after the excavations had begun. Yadin's main publication of his work on Masada appeared in 1966 with the publication of his Masada books (in both English and Hebrew). Other than these two books, he published very little on Masada. There was a very significant delay in publishing the final results of the excavations. While some early reports were made available,[6] the final reports began to be published only in the late 1980s and 1990s. For example, between 1989 and 1991 (almost twenty-six years after completion of the excavations) three volumes summarizing part of the final reports were published.[7] When all the final reports appeared between 1989 and 1995, Yadin was no longer alive, and the volumes were published by some of his students and other scholars. Yadin's 1966 books thus furnish a most important source for his thoughts on Masada. Moreover, Yadin gave many lectures and was regularly interviewed on the radio and by newspapers. I located and collected as many of these radio recordings and interviews as I could.

Consequently, the information we have about the evolution of the scientific interpretations of the Masada discoveries is based on a variety of sources: the transcripts of the daily meetings of the archaeologists which reflect their day-to-day work, other scientific and popular publications, and the media. Integrating all this information in a meaningful way enables us to examine how the archaeological interpretations were constructed.

In a very real sense, this book basically details the "excavation of the excavations of Masada."

STRUCTURE AND PLAN OF THE BOOK

Solving the puzzle of how archaeology supported the mythical account of Masada shapes the structure of this book. First we will acquaint ourselves with the historical tale of Masada as provided by Josephus Flavius, and with the Masada mythical narrative. It is necessary to know these two versions of the Masada tale fairly well before we continue our journey. Then I shall detail how and why archaeology was able to support a mythical narrative. Finally, the findings of this study will be conceptualized within the sociology of science, deception, and moral boundaries.

Examining both the Masada mythical narrative and the ways in which the archaeological discoveries were interpreted to support that myth raises some fascinating questions about fabrications, deceptions, and the slyness of different reality constructions. Indeed, the study presented in this book (as well as in my 1985 and 1995 books, which focused on the social construction of moral boundaries and the Masada myth, respectively) occasions—truly demands—a discussion of these issues. So the concluding chapters take the study presented here as a starting point to develop a discussion about deception, truth, and falsehood, all contextualized within a broader level of analysis.[8]

This book not only presents a discussion of a specific study of ideology, politics, and archaeology, but also utilizes that study to say something of a much more general nature about science, deception, and falsehood, and some of the ways we socially construct cultural meanings.

NOTES

1. See also Akira Kurosawa's 1950 (B/W, 83 minutes) cinematic version of the play.

2. See, for example, the fascinating works by Marcus 2001 and Finkelstein and Silberman 2001, as well as Niebuhr's 2000 report, covering such processes in the Middle East.

3. See, e.g., Shargel 1979; Ben-Yehuda 1995.

4. Aviram, Foerster, and Netzer 1989a, p. ix.

5. Louis M. Feldman, "Masada: A Critique of Recent Scholarship," in Jacob Neusner, ed., *Christianity, Judaism and Graeco-Roman Cults: Studies for Morton Smith at Sixty*, III (Leiden: 1975), p. 218. Quoted by Aviram, Foerster, and Netzer (1989), p. 1.

6. E.g., Yadin 1965; 1966e; 1966h; 1970. See also a progress report by Rabinowitz 1990.

7. Aviram, Foerster, and Netzer edited the first three volumes, two of which were published in 1989 and the third in 1991. The first volume focuses on the ostraca and inscriptions (written by Yigael Yadin and Joseph Naveh) and on the coins (written by Ya'acov Meshorer) found in the excavations. The second volume consists of an examination of the Latin and Greek documents found in Masada (written by Hannah M. Cotton and Joseph Geiger). The largest volume, volume 3 (written by Ehud Netzer), concentrates on the buildings, stratigraphy, and architecture of Masada. In the summer of 1994 the fourth volume (some 400 pages long) was published. It examined the oil lamps, fabrics, wood products, catapult stones, and the skeletons found in Masada. Volume 5e, which was prepared in 1994 (possibly the last), is focused on the architecture and art found in Masada. As is becoming increasingly clear, the scientific importance of Masada lies not so much with the Sicarii, but with important discoveries in other areas, such as coins, scriptures, fabric materials, Herodian architecture, and Roman army siege tactics.

8. In this case, the perspective of symbolic interaction generally, and contextual constructionism particularly.

TWO

JOSEPHUS FLAVIUS VERSUS THE MYTH

There are two basic versions of what took place at Masada in 73 C.E. The historical version is provided by first-century historian Josephus Flavius; the second version is a product of the early twentieth century and is essentially a myth. While there is some overlap between the two, and some elements of Josephus's original and historical version appear in the mythical version, they differ on almost all the important points. Understanding the political, social, and scientific context of the 1963–65 excavations of Masada, and hence how and why archaeology was used to support the mythical version, demands that we acquire a basic understanding of these two very different narratives.

MASADA—THE HISTORICAL NARRATIVE

Background

What has become known as the Great Revolt of the Jews against the Roman Empire, whose army occupied Judea at the time, took place between the years 66–73 C.E.[1] The Romans responded to the uprising with full force: they burned Jerusalem to the ground, destroyed the Jewish Second Temple (70 C.E.), and brutally reasserted their conquest of the land. The Great Revolt and the destruction it precipitated became one of the most traumatic events in the collective memory of the Jewish people. The period was portrayed as one in which brave and proud men and women tried to stand up for their national and religious rights, as well as their collective and individual identity, and sought to free themselves from the yoke of foreign Roman rule. The revolt, however, failed, and what has been seen by so many as a heroic effort ended in disastrous large-scale bloodshed, the agonized death of thousands of Jews at the hands of the Imperial Roman army, and the enslavement of thousands more. Masada probably fell in 73 C.E and was thus the last chapter in that doomed revolt. The Masada mythical narrative (Ben-Yehuda 1995; Paine 1994; Shargel 1979; Zerubavel 1995) is a direct remnant of that period. No real understanding of some of the basic elements of modern Jewish Israeli culture—certainly issues of national and personal identity—can be attained without understanding this tragic and heroic period.

There is only one major historical source available on Masada: the writings of Josephus Flavius (Josephus mentions that Justus from Tiberias also wrote a historical narrative of the Jewish war, a narrative with which Josephus disagreed. However, no copies of Justus's work have survived). Josephus thus becomes the baseline for Masada, and we must examine very carefully not only his account, but Josephus himself, who has become a controversial figure and whose writings are not free of bias.

JOSEPHUS FLAVIUS

Previous works about Josephus can easily fill a decent-sized bookshelf.[2] Across an enigmatic abyss of some two thousand years, his cryptic figure and monumental works glare at, ridicule, and challenge us.

Joseph Ben-Matityahu, later known as Josephus Flavius, was born in Jerusalem in 37 C.E. to a priestly family. He tells us that he was not an enthusiastic supporter of the Great Revolt; however, when it actually began, around 66, he became commander of the Galilee and was charged with the responsibility of defending it. In 67 Jotapata (Yodfat), the major fortress in the Galilee, fell. The last few survivors, including Josephus, hid in a cave. The desperate and hopeless situation appears to have led them to consider suicide, but Josephus managed to fool the others, and he and one other survivor remained alive. At that point Josephus persuaded the other man to surrender with him to the Romans instead of killing each other. The incident reveals Josephus as a skillfully persuasive man. According to his account, when he met with Vespasian, the commander of the Roman forces that had laid siege to and destroyed Jotapata, he impressed the Roman and struck up an interesting relationship with him. Among other things, Josephus supposedly prophesied to Vespasian that he would become emperor of Rome; and indeed, Titus Flavius Vespasianus did become emperor, ruling 69–79 C.E. as one of the better emperors Rome had known. The accuracy of Josephus's account notwithstanding, he did go to Rome, where he assumed a Roman name and where he became a Roman citizen and an official historian. He married four times and probably died sometime after 100 C.E. It seems likely that Josephus lived a Roman lifestyle in Rome and the question regarding the nature of his Jewish identity in Rome (or whatever was left of it, if any) remains open.

Josephus's history of the Jewish war lies at the heart of this book. One must remember that Josephus was a problematic figure, and the history he wrote was probably tinted by a complicated set of interests. For many Jews Josephus was a traitor and turncoat, and for this he was hated. As historian to the Romans, he had to write a history that would satisfy his masters. As a Jew, he had to cope with some uneasy issues of identity as well as the obvious necessity of justifying his own actions. Nothing is simple when it comes to Josephus.

According to Y. N. Simchoni, the first translator of Josephus into modern Hebrew,[3] the *Wars of the Jews* was written in Rome no earlier then 75 C.E. and no later than 79 C.E. (see also Mason 1997), i.e., five to nine years after conclusion of the Roman military campaign against the Jewish Great Revolt (1923, p. 11).

Most researchers agree that Josephus was not physically present during the Roman siege of Masada, and his account of the events there is thus based on secondary processing of primary sources. Josephus most probably used the reports (*commentarii*) and/or diaries written by the Roman military officers who had taken part in the siege of Masada. As Gill (1993) points out, Josephus's reliance on these sources may have caused him either to make some innocent mistakes or to be deliberately deceptive. Moreover, Josephus tells us explicitly that one of the two women survivors from the collective Masada suicide gave the Roman soldiers the details about the fateful last night of the Sicarii on Masada.

Of course, we should use Josephus cautiously, straying from his text only if we have some very compelling reasons to do so. For example, his recitation of Ben-Yair's two speeches is suspect, since he was not there. Moreover, these speeches had to make sense to the potential readership (which was not only Jewish), and thus it is possible that some parts of these speeches were written with a non-Jewish audience in mind, and consequently used language and images that made sense to that audience. Still, he knew the culture intimately and could have surmised the expressions such speeches could include. But we must regard these speeches with much caution.

Because the archaeological excavations in Masada could either support or refute Josephus's exclusive historical narrative of Masada, other accounts questioning the validity and accuracy of Josephus's narrative, which are not based on archaeological findings, become relevant for my work in only a very limited way.

Below I try to describe the events on Masada based primarily on Jose-

2. Aerial view of Masada, looking east. (Courtesy of the Government Press Office, State of Israel)

phus. In my narrative, I have tried to remain as close and as faithful as I can to the narrative Josephus provides, eschewing any reliance on other sources.[4]

Two points require emphasis at this stage. First, the events and processes which I describe took place more than 1,900 years ago, hence not all the details are completely clear. Second, some points are unclear in Josephus's account as well. In those few cases in which I was uncertain about the narrative, I tried to cross-check with later interpreters of Josephus. Whenever I used such later interpretations, full references are given and explained. However, I did make an effort to limit this mostly to clarification of what appear to be facts. For theoretical and historical reasons, I used the Wm. Whiston edition.[5]

Different interpretations of Josephus's writings obviously exist, and the question of which is the better one can easily keep a career flourishing for a lifetime. As we shall see later, the question of the different interpretations is of crucial theoretical and empirical importance. It was the systematic and deliberate choice of one interpretation over others that helped the Masada myth come into existence—which brings me to the next question.

Does Josephus Tell the Truth?

This is an important question if we are to establish the existence of a mythical narrative. How do we know whether any particular version is historically accurate?

The fact is that without Josephus we know very little. Virtually all our knowledge of the period and the relevant events is based on Josephus's writings. He is—fortunately or unfortunately—the main, and in most respects the only, historical source. If Josephus had not written a history, there would be no Masada, Sicarii, or revolt in our history books and encyclopedia. As Aberbach states, "Without him, the history of the last two centuries of the Second Commonwealth could be reduced to a few pages—and a good part of that would be legendary" (1985, p. 25).

Yadin, head of the most intensive archaeological excavations of Masada in the 1960s, states dryly, "The only source for the history of Masada is the writings of Joseph Ben-Matityahu" (1970, p. 374). Indeed, the interpretations of the archaeological findings in Masada make sense only if one knows Josephus's account. While several of these findings support some of Josephus's statements (e.g., the Roman siege and storming Masada, the architectural findings), they do not support all of them (e.g., the mass suicide, the riddle of the 960 missing skeletons, the burning of Masada). We are lucky in the sense that we have only one major source (or blueprint) for the events in question, making this research relatively easy. After all, it is easy to measure deviations from that one source. In this respect I find Ere'lli's 1983 account very relevant: "Either we disqualify Josephus's testimony altogether, regardless of whether or not it suits our national needs, or we accept it as it is" (p. 185).[6]

Hence, we simply must take Josephus's version as our baseline. When I refer to Josephus's historical narrative as truth this is exactly what I have in mind—a historical baseline. While it is possible that Josephus's version is a myth too, in my opinion that claim is quite fantastic. The chances that Josephus lied and cheated his own Roman masters as well as those who were actually involved in the events, and fabricated on a mass scale a siege that never was, people who never existed, an event that never took place, and the like, do not seem very high. And why would he have done that in the first place? Josephus's account was written very close to the events, it is the exclusive description of those fateful events, and all later interpreters, mythmakers, and other well-meaning researchers took Josephus's version as their starting point. As a historical source, Josephus unquestionably provides a problematic account, but it is the only historical account we have. Historically speaking, then, it is the closest thing to truth that we have about the Jewish Great Revolt and the Masada campaign.

It must therefore be reiterated that the accuracy or validity of Josephus's writings is *not* being judged, tested, or challenged here. Our puzzle is not whether Josephus's narrative is accurate (or to what degree),[7] but how some modern Israeli interpreters, specifically archaeologists, confronted and interpreted their own findings in relation to the way in which they interpreted the narrative provided by Josephus. Was their interpretation scientifically driven, or was it driven by nationalistic and political motivation?

This is an important point, because claims have been raised that perhaps Josephus himself was not telling the truth and that his own version may have been a mythical one, no better nor worse than that proposed by the twentieth-century mythologizers. Because of its importance, this specific issue requires further clarification. To begin with, Josephus provides the *only* available historical account about what happened on Masada. Without Josephus, all we have left are some physical remnants of a fortress in the Judean desert. Moreover, I must admit that I find incredible the claim that Josephus's narrative, written only a few years after the events by an important, involved, knowledgeable contemporary figure, as somehow equal to an imaginary mythical and fabricated narrative concocted by a variety of creative moral entrepreneurs some 1,800 years later quite incredible. It must be stated that no shred of evidence exists supporting the claim that—as some would have us believe—Josephus did create a myth, and that *all* of his account is false. As is the case with other historical accounts, one can find inaccuracies and mistakes by Josephus (e.g., see note 7), but that certainly does not discredit his entire text as myth. So in the absence of any other evidence, if we want to view the contrast between the original, first-century historical account and the twentieth-century mythical version, Josephus's baseline is either "take it or leave it." And, again, this has very little to do with whether what Josephus tells us is historically valid.

It is interesting to note that one of the most important mythologizers of Josephus, archaeologist Yigael Yadin, stated in a radio interview, "In Yoseph Ben-Matityahu [Josephus's Hebrew name], like in Masada and his statements about other places, there is a genuine accuracy that stuns us today, at least in terms of the facts" (September 13, 1966). Yadin's remarks are incredible, considering that he used Josephus as foundation for some rather free associations for his own interpretation of Masada. If anything, the scope of Yadin's misrepresentation of Masada is inconsistent with his public statements on Josephus's accuracy.

For example, it is one thing to know that Josephus refers to the rebels on Masada as Sicarii, and another thing to completely and deliberately ignore this and refer to the rebels as Zealots without bothering to tell us why. If one prefers Zealots over Sicarii, contrary to Josephus's text, some form of justification should be provided. Moreover, since Zealots are described as somewhat better than the Sicarii, such a justification is even more required. Another example is the disregard for the massacre and robbery that the Sicarii from Masada committed in Ein Gedi. Such acts unequivocally tell us something negative about the inhabitants of Masada. If, however, one wants to describe those inhabitants in a positive light, then the appalling escapade in Ein Gedi is conveniently made to disappear.

The point I am making is that if any particular interpreter examines Josephus's account and argues, either logically, historically, or with the support of archaeological tangible evidence, that some elements, or all, of the account is untrue, then we have a scientifically legitimate and acceptable debate about Josephus. Such a route constitutes a genuine attempt to discover the historical reality. One certainly can expect that changes made to our understanding of Josephus due to such a procedure may move in different directions. However, when changes to the original version of Josephus are made because of moralistic, national, and/or political reasons, all coming from and leading to a consistent type of change (e.g., depressing any negative connotation in the original account, emphasizing the positive and even adding positive, but imaginary, elements) then we are facing an entirely different situation. As we shall see, mythologizing Masada was based on such a process.

Masada—The Site

Masada is a mountain fortress nearly one hundred kilometers southeast of Jerusalem, about a ninety-minute drive from the capital via the Dead Sea road. The rocky outcropping is about two kilometers from the western shore of the Dead Sea, and about seventeen kilometers south of Ein Gedi, in one of the world's hottest regions (daily temperatures between the months of May and October typically average between 33 and 40 degrees Celsius). The mountain is about 320 meters high and is capped by a flat diamond-shaped plateau. Its long axis extends about 645 meters and its widest axis, some 315 meters (Livne 1986).

The mountain itself is very steep and accessible by foot either via the eastern "snake path" (the more difficult climb) or the Roman-built siege ramp built on a natural spur from the west (the easier climb). There is also a modern cable car which makes reaching the top of Masada from the east very easy.

The name of the mountain and fortress in Hebrew is *Metzada* (pronounced ME-TZA-DA), literally a fort, fortress or stronghold. The Greek transliteration of *Metzada* is "Masada" (Simchoni 1923, p. 513).

Josephus[8] states that Masada was originally built by "Jonathan the High priest" and was later rebuilt by King Herod. While researchers are uncertain who Jonathan was,[9] the identity of Herod is beyond doubt. It is evident from the majesty of the structures on Masada that they were indeed designed and constructed by Herod's engineers and builders. Situated where it is and being what it is, Masada could be used for a number of purposes: as a refuge from enemies (and Herod had quite a few); as a place to host special guests; as a prison; or as a stronghold in which to hide precious treasures or dear friends. Josephus himself states that Masada was built

> by our ancient kings, both as a repository for their effects in the hazards of war, and for the preservation of their bodies at the same time. . . .[10]
>
> Herod prepared this fortress on his own account, as a refuge against two kinds of danger; the one for fear of the multitude of the Jews, lest they should depose him and restore their former kings to the government; the other danger was greater and more terrible, which arose from Cleopatra, Queen of Egypt, who did not conceal her intentions, but spoke often to Anthony, and desired him to cut off Herod, and entreated him to bestow the kingdom of Judea upon her.[11]

Even today anyone visiting Masada can see the ruins of Herod's massive and awesome buildings. The stronghold was conquered by the Roman Tenth Legion in 73 (or 74), in the course of which considerable destruction was caused both by the Jewish rebels on top of Masada and by the Romans.

After the Roman conquest of the fortress, a Roman unit was left there for an uncertain period of time. Christian monks settled in Masada during the Byzantine period (fifth and sixth centuries). Masada appears in sixteenth-century maps of the area, and during the nineteenth century it was mentioned and correctly identified by several travelers, many of whose reports include paintings of the site as well as detailed descriptions and diaries of their visits.[12]

Masada is a spectacular site. The doomed fortress is located near the Dead Sea, in the middle of a harsh and desolate terrain, with difficult access. If one stands atop the big barren and serene yellowish plateau facing the silent, harsh, moonlike landscape, the cold desert breeze of early morning conjures up an eerie atmosphere, evoking the feeling that there is a mystical presence on the top of the mountain.

The extraordinary site and atmosphere conspire to provoke a powerfully suggestive state of mind. The narrative of the doomed Great Revolt and the tragic death of the rebels seems somehow to be in full harmony with the harsh and desolate terrain in the midst of which looms the bleak mountaintop fortress. The bleak physical environment of Masada seems to echo the historical narrative about the bloody revolt that ended in so much destruction. And as the ecology and geography of Masada have apparently not changed significantly since the days of the Great Revolt, the site and its landscape are today much the same as that seen by the rebels and the besieging Romans.[13]

The Historical Narrative

The Masada historical narrative is not a context-free event; it must be understood within the context of the Jewish Great Revolt, and specifically the place of the Sicarii in the uprising.

We can date the beginning of the Great Revolt to the year 6 C.E., when the Romans sought to conduct a census in the province of Judea. One of the main opponents of the census was Yehuda of Gamla (also identified as Yehuda of the Galilee) who, with Zadok Haprushi, kindled the fire of resistance. They developed and promulgated what Josephus called the "fourth philosophy." The first three philosophies were those espoused by the Essenes, the Sadducees, and the Pharisees. Little is known about it, but the fourth philosophy emphasized the value of freedom, and its adherents felt allegiance only to God. In all likelihood Yehuda was killed by the Romans, but the fourth philosophy did not die with him, continuing to spread throughout the land, apparently becoming the ideology of a group of Jewish fundamentalist rebels known as the Sicarii, who were totally opposed to, and identified with the aspiration to be free of, the rule of the Roman Empire.[14]

We first find the term *Sicarii* mentioned by Josephus in connection with events which took place between 52 and 62 C.E. The word *Sicarii* derives from *sica*, a small dagger which the Sicarii supposedly carried beneath their robes and which they used to attack and assassinate those whom they viewed as their opponents in Jerusalem, especially during holy days. Their tactics included intimidation and threats of violence against their political and ideological opponents. While the Sicarii were involved in indiscriminate terror activities, they did not shy away from purposeful political assassinations. Such was their killing of Yonatan Ben-Hanan, the former high priest of Jerusalem. They also kidnaped hostages whom they exchanged for their own people who had been caught by the Romans. Josephus describes the attitude of the Sicarii toward local inhabitants who were not overtly hostile to Roman rule:

> The Sicarii got together against those that were willing to submit to the Romans, and treated them in all respects as if they had been their enemies, both by plundering them of what they had, by driving away their cattle, and by setting fire to their houses: for they said, that they differed not at all from foreigners, by betraying, in so cowardly a manner, that freedom which Jews thought worthy to be contended for to the utmost, and by owning that they preferred slavery under the Romans before such a contention.[15]

In 66 the Sicarii, headed by Manahem, took Masada and captured armaments, taking them to Jerusalem, where they used them to capture the upper city.[16] They set fire to the house of Hanania the high priest and burned the central archives where legal and commercial documents, deeds, and notes were kept. Hanania and his brother Hizkiahu were killed, as well as a host of Roman soldiers who had surrendered. These acts not only marked the beginning of the Great Revolt, but also helped divide the Jewish population into zealots and moderates.

Manahem, the Sicarii leader in Jerusalem, was killed by followers of Elazar Ben-Hanania, who opposed the Sicarii. Under Elazar Ben-Yair (a relative of Manahem and a "descendant from that Judas who had persuaded abundance of the Jews . . . not to submit to the taxation when Cyrenius was sent to Judea"[17]) the Sicarii fled to Masada, where they remained. Josephus states that Ben-Yair "acted the part of a tyrant at Masada afterward,"[18] taking the role of "commander" of the "Sicarii" who "seized upon it."[19]

Josephus writes that the Sicarii on Masada attacked the settlement of Ein Gedi at the foot of the mountains near Masada, chased the men out and killed the women and children—about seven hundred people in all, and possibly more. They also pillaged and destroyed other nearby villages.[20]

According to Josephus, after the fall of Jerusalem Lucilius Bassus was sent to Judea as legate and continued to suppress the remnants of the Jewish Great Revolt, taking the fortress of Herodion and later laying siege to Macherus,[21] where fierce battles raged until that fortress surrendered as well. After these military successes, Bassus marched to the forest of Jarden, where refugees from Jerusalem and Macherus were hiding. In the ensuing battle all the Jews in the Jarden forest were killed. When Lucilius Bassus died,[22] Flavius Silva succeeded him as procurator of Judea. Upon assuming his duties, Flavius Silva sensibly decided to crush the last shred of the Jewish Great Revolt.[23] Realizing that

> all the rest of the country was subdued in this war, and that there was but one only stronghold that was still in rebellion, he got all his army together that lay in different places, and made an expedition against it. This fortress was called Masada.[24]

It is thus obvious that the siege of Masada was not laid immediately after the fall of Jerusalem in the summer of 70 C.E.

Most researchers assume that by the word "army" Josephus meant the Tenth Legion ("Fretensis"), which now moved on Masada under Flavius Silva. It is important to emphasize that although Josephus is at times vague in his identification of people in particular places, when he describes the siege on Masada his use of the word *Sicarii* is very consistent—perhaps the most consistent in his book.[25] For example,

> There was a fortress of very great strength not far from Jerusalem, which had been built by our ancient kings. . . . It is called Masada. Those that were called *Sicarii* had taken possession of it formerly.[26]

According to Josephus, the Roman army constructed a circumvallation wall around Masada to prevent the besieged from escaping, with a series of military camps for the Roman soldiers built around the mountain as well. The remnants of both the wall and the camps are still visible today. Flavius Silva then ordered the Tenth Legion to build a siege ramp up to Masada on the western side of the mountain. The remains of the ramp are also still evident. When the ramp was completed, the Roman soldiers effectively used their battering ram(s) on the ramp to pound at the wall around Masada, breaching it and destroying part of it. At that point the Sicarii in the stronghold hastily built another wall, this time a soft one made of wood and earth filling. It could absorb the ramming energy of the war machine(s) without yielding. But the Roman soldiers set fire to the second wall and destroyed it as well, undoubtedly signaling the end for the Sicarii in Masada.[27] Their choices were clear. They could (a) try to escape, (b) fight to the inevitable end, (c) surrender, or (d) commit collective suicide. By now, the first choice may have been hopeless. Alternative (c) meant slavery for the women and children and painful and humiliating deaths for the men. Of the 967 people on Masada probably only a few hundred were actually capable of fighting, most of the rest being women and children; that eliminated option (b). Elazar Ben-Yair made the extremely difficult choice for option (d), addressing the besieged population in two fiery speeches to convince them to accept the alternative. His words were ultimately persuasive, and the Sicarii killed one another.

The account provided by Josephus does not mention the role of the women and children in the decision. Were they even consulted or considered? As the hesitations after Elazar Ben-Yair's first speech are attributed to the "soldiers," it seems safe to assume that the decisions were probably made by men from the dominant social category on Masada (the Sicarii), and that everyone, including the women and the children, was killed by the men. The Sicarii left no choice for any would-be defaulters and the seven survivors—two women and five children—had to save themselves by hiding:

> Yet, was there an ancient woman, and another who was of kin to Elazar, and superior to most women in prudence and learning, with five children, who had concealed themselves in caverns under ground . . . and were hidden there when the rest were intent upon the slaughter of one another. These others were nine hundred and sixty in number.

Josephus's description of the hidden survivors hints at an element of coercion in the decision to commit collective suicide. When the Roman soldiers entered Masada,

> the women heard this noise and came out of their underground cavern, and informed the Romans what had been done, as it was done; and the second of them clearly described all both what was said and what was done, and the manner of it.[28]

The Roman breach of the wall and the collective suicide took place on the evening and night of the fifteenth of Nisan (March–April) 73.[29] When the Roman soldiers entered Masada the next day, they were met with utter silence. The suicide of the 960 men, women, and children who had occupied the fortress robbed the Romans of their final victory.

The Main Components of the Masada Historical Narrative

The Masada narrative, based on Josephus's account, includes the following components:

1. Masada was part and parcel of a much larger Jewish revolt against the Roman conquerors. The revolt ended in disaster and bitter defeat for the Jews. The fall of Masada was only the deathblow in the much larger suppression of that revolt.[30] It is interesting to note that Josephus implies that only a few minority groups of fanatics drew the Jews into the hopeless rebellion. Many modern researchers (see, e.g., Menachem Stern's works) tend to reject this implication, asserting that the revolt was both popular and widespread. Unfortunately for the Jews at the time, the military picture was bleak. Over two centuries earlier, the local Jewish population overthrew the weak Seleucid king who ruled the land and established an autonomous Jewish state under the House of the Hasmoneans. The Roman Empire of the first century C.E., however, was at the peak of its power, extending from Britain to Mesopotamia and controlling between twenty-five and twenty-nine well-armed, amply provisioned, battle-ready legions: awesome military might for those days. At the time of the Great Revolt, the Roman consular legate (perhaps equivalent to a "high commissioner") in Syria was considered the most important of all the legates, because of the threat of military challenge from the southeastern flank of the Roman Empire. He had four legions at his disposal, as well as the three legions stationed in Egypt and others that could be—and were—brought from elsewhere. The logic and justification of attempting to challenge that kind of military power are not easily discernible, especially without the benefit of having at least some political and military alliances.
2. During this period, the local Jewish population was divided among

several ideological groups, four of which can be singled out as important. For our purposes, the two most relevant groups are the Sicarii and the Zealots, who apparently may have carried the main burden of the revolt. Josephus makes a distinction between them, although he does not clarify the connection between the Zealots and the Sicarii. However, in his discussion of Masada Josephus consistently and repeatedly uses the term *Sicarii* to describe the Jewish rebels there.[31]

3. Sicarii forces under Manahem probably took control of Masada by force in 66, before the beginning of the Great Revolt. This very act may have marked the beginning of that Jewish rebellion.[32]

4. The Sicarii in Jerusalem were involved in so much terrorist activity against Jews and others that they were forced to leave the city long before the Roman siege began. Led by Elazar Ben-Yair (whom Josephus terms "tyrant"), they fled to Masada, where they remained (possibly with other non-Sicarii who may have joined them) until the bitter end, when most of them agreed to kill one another. While one cannot rule out completely the remote possibility that non-Sicarii were among those trapped on top of Masada, Josephus's historical narrative does not support this interpretation. Moreover, and even if one is willing to accept this unlikely possibility, his consistent use of the term *Sicarii* to describe the rebels on top of Masada must at least be taken to indicate that the Sicarii were the dominant group there. Furthermore, Josephus mentions that when Simon the son of Giora wanted to join the Sicarii rebels on top of Masada, the Sicarii were so untrusting of Simon that when he

> came to those robbers who had seized upon Masada . . . they suspected him, and only permitted him to come with the women he brought with him into the lower part of the fortress, while they dwelt in the upper part of it themselves. (4.9.3, p. 541)

It is thus evident that the Sicarii were not too hospitable to non-Sicarii.

5. It is clear that while they were in Masada the Sicarii raided nearby villages. One of the most brutal of these raids was on Ein Gedi, which Josephus describes:

> [T]hey came down by night, without being discovered . . . and overran a small city called Engaddi:—in which expedition they prevented those citizens that could have stopped them, before they could arm themselves and fight them. They also dispersed them, and cast them out of the city. As for such that could not run away, being women and children, they slew of them above seven hundred.

Afterward, the Sicarii raiders carried all the food supplies from Ein Gedi to Masada.[33]

6. Josephus does not say how long Masada was besieged; hence different time frames have been suggested. Evidently, the siege did *not* begin immediately after the destruction of Jerusalem in 70 C.E. First Herodion and Macherus were conquered, then Bassus died and was replaced by Flavius Silva, who had to gather his forces and only then launched the final attack on Masada. Researchers concur that the siege and fall of Masada only took a few months, probably from the winter of 72/73 until the following spring—a matter of some four to six (maybe eight) months (see note 29). This conclusion is supported by Gill's (1993) recent geological work, which suggests that the massive siege ramp on the western slope is based on a huge natural spur. If this is so, then the Roman army did not need to construct the ramp from the bottom of the mountain, but only had to add the actual ramp on top of that natural spur—a significantly less strenuous effort than previously assumed. In fact, Roth's most recent, and impressively meticulous, study (1995) on exactly this issue states that:

> All in all, a nine-week siege is the likely maximum, a four-week siege the likely minimum, and a siege of seven weeks the most probable length for the siege of Masada. Postulating a siege of some seven weeks fits in well with the date given by Josephus for the fall of the fortress, whatever calendar is being used. (p. 109)

7. Josephus's account of the siege of Jerusalem includes courageous raids by the Jewish defenders of the city against the Romans. His account of Masada includes no mention of defensive forays at all. After Jerusalem fell, the Roman army went on to conquer Herodion, which appears to have fallen quickly, and then Macherus, where the Jews put up a courageous fight, including raids against the Roman army, and finally Masada, in which no serious military activity seems to have occurred. Josephus had a clear interest in noting the Jews' heroism to demonstrate the even greater heroism of the Roman army that conquered them. His failure to mention any impressive action or resistance by Masada's defenders against the Romans is not insignificant. True, the topography of Masada would have made such assaults difficult, but certainly not impossible. Thus, while the impression is that there was a war around Jerusalem (and Yodfat, and Macherus), consisting of skirmishes, battles, raids, and forays, no such impression is projected about the Roman siege of Masada. In other words, there was no real battle over Masada; the military effort of the tenth legion in conquering the fortress was less pronounced than the engineering effort, but even that was not extraordinary by Roman standards.

The puzzling omission of any mention of a battle around Masada should be considered in conjunction with four additional pieces of information.

(a) Josephus describes the Roman siege and capture of another formidable contemporary fortress, Macherus, replete with fierce fighting and struggles.[34]

(b) Josephus states specifically[35] that the forces headed by Simon the son of Giora joined the "robbers who had seized upon Masada" and that both forces "ravaged and destroyed the country . . . about Masada." The people on Masada, however, would not join Simon's forces for "greater things," because they were used to living in Masada and "were afraid of going far from that which was their hiding place." Simon and his men were apparently not afraid and continued their battles, eventually ending their careers in the besieged city of Jerusalem, where they went to fight the Romans (as well as rival Jewish factions, including the Zealots). Simon was captured by the Romans, brought to Rome, and killed there.[36]

These two pieces of information strengthen the impression of the lack of a "fighting spirit" among the rebels on Masada, reinforced by what did *not* happen: the fighting forces on Masada *could* have killed the nonfighting personnel and then gone out to do battle against the Romans to the bitter end. But rather than choose this alternative, they killed one another. Interestingly, hundreds of years later, Joseippon (see Joseippon 1981) changed the Masada narrative to precisely this scenario. In his imaginary version, the warriors of Masada killed the civilian population and went on to fight the Romans until the last Jew was dead. Evidently, this is a more heroic ending than the one provided by Josephus. Both Zeitlin (1967, p. 262) and Hoenig (1970, p. 14; 1972, p. 112) point out that the Sicarii did not fight.

Certainly history provides many instances of such heroic fights "to the last":[37] the last stand of Leonidas and his three hundred Spartans at the pass of Thermopylae in 480 B.C.E.;[38] the Alamo in 1836;[39] the 101st American Airborne Division in Bastogne during the German counterattack in the Ardennes in 1944;[40] the U.S. Marines on Wake Island in 1941;[41] the Jewish revolt in the Warsaw Ghetto (April–May 1943). Even using a strictly Jewish analogy, when the Sicarii were faced with the choice, they selected suicide rather than follow the example of the biblical hero Samson, who took his enemies with him into death. It is imperative to note that the attribution of a "last stand" status to the rebels of Masada assumes a particular type of heroism, in which one *fights* to the end or, if death is inevitable, one tries to inflict as much damage on the enemy as possible. According to Perrett, "The concept of men selling their lives as dearly as possible forms an honorable part of most national histories and also the basis of much military tradition" (1991, p. 7). Accounts of genuine "last stands" are not too difficult to find. Josephus Flavius's Masada most certainly does not qualify as one of them, and indeed cannot be one.

(c) Josephus's discussion of the suicide is revealing. He notes that after the Romans entered Masada and discovered the dead bodies, the Romans "could [do no other] than wonder at the courage of their [the

Sicariis'] resolution, and at the immovable contempt of death which so great a number of them had shown, when they went through with such an action as that was."[42] The absolute resolution and courage of the Sicarii and their act of collective suicide in Masada apparently elicited much respect and wonder among the Romans and in Josephus. But the analytic leap from respect to heroism is *not* made by Josephus, but rather is socially constructed. Indeed, Josephus describes the Sicarii killing one another thus: "Miserable men indeed they were!" (7.9.1, p. 603).

(d) The implication of Magness's fascinating 1992 work is that if any "battles" were waged around Masada, they may have been confined to the last stage of the siege. Magness refers to "the mystery of the absence of projectile points at Masada remains" (p. 66) and, describing the possible late phase of the siege, states:

> Under covering artillery fire, the Roman forces dragged the battering ram up the ramp and broke through the wall that Herod had constructed around the top of the mountain. The Roman auxiliary archers added covering fire to that of the machines as the forces ascended the ramp. The Zealots certainly returned the fire with everything at their command, including bows and arrows manufactured during the last days of the siege of Masada. (1992, p. 67)

The major weight of the siege and battle for Masada may have been carried out not by the more prestigious units of the Tenth Legion, but by the much less prestigious auxiliares:

> The soft arrowheads from Masada indicate that there was a major contingent of auxiliari troops at Masada and/or that the Zealots had armed themselves in the manner of auxiliaries, with bows and arrows. . . .
>
> Strangely, the excavators seem to have found no projectile points of the kind that would have been shot by legionaries from torsion bows . . . [i]n contrast to the situation in Gamla . . . where numerous projectile points were uncovered. (p. 64)

One is left with the unavoidable conclusion that there simply is no evidence for significant resistance of the "last-stand" type around Masada.

The overall impression, then, is that the Sicarii on Masada, so adept at raiding nearby villages, were not particularly talented fighters and, in fact, avoided battle. Perhaps they never believed the Roman army could reach them and thus fought the attackers only halfheartedly during the siege. As it became clear that the end was approaching, they may have hastily put together some sort of defense, but if so, it was too little and too late. Eventually they did not "fight to the end," preferring suicide instead. If this deduction is valid, then the resulting conclusion is inevitable: the history of the Roman siege on Masada does not convey a particularly heroic picture.

8. Josephus specifically states that the 960 people on Masada committed suicide, swayed by the two addresses by Elazar Ben-Yair, which he supposedly quotes at length. The implication is that the Jewish rebels on Masada were at first reluctant to take their own lives.

Josephus states that although there were close to a thousand Sicarii on top of Masada, not all of them were warriors. There were women and children, and perhaps other noncombatants, and the number of actual fighters is unknown. Although Josephus does not tell us this, it is safe to assume that the Tenth Legion which carried out the siege on Masada was probably composed of a minimum of six thousand soldiers (the estimate found in the literature).[43]

9. Seven people survived the collective suicide. This is an important point, because the details of that last night on Masada were provided by one of the women survivors.

Thus, when we look at the main components of Josephus Flavius's narrative of the Great Revolt and of Masada, no portrait of heroism on Masada emerges. On the contrary, the narrative relates the story of a hopeless (and questionable) rebellion, of its majestic failure and the destruction of the Second Temple and of Jerusalem, of large-scale massacres of the Jews, of different factions of Jews fighting one another, of an act of collective suicide (hardly a positive act in Judaism) by a group of terrorists and assassins whose "fighting spirit" was suspect.

From the Roman military perspective, the Masada campaign must have been an insignificant action after a major war in Judea—a mopping-up operation, something which had to be done, but which did not involve anything special in terms of military strategy or effort.

Another item of information may add credibility to the above conjecture. Two almost identical ancient Roman inscriptions from 81 C.E. were found in Urbs Salvia in northern Italy, south of Ancona, in the late 1950s. The inscriptions describe the career of L. Flavius Silva Nonius Bassus. No mention of Masada can be found in the inscriptions (perhaps none should be expected).[44] It is stated that Flavius Silva was in charge of the "provinciae Iudaeae," and that during his career he commanded two Roman legions: the Twenty-first (Rapacis) and the Fourth (Scythicae). No mention is made of his commanding the Tenth Legion (Fretensis). Perhaps Flavius Silva gave orders to the Tenth Legion and intervened in strategic and tactical decisions, while the actual command was held by someone else during the siege and conquest of Masada.

The question that cannot be evaded is, how could the unsavory story that emerges from Josephus's narrative become such a positive symbol of heroism? Obviously, the mythical narrative which projects tremendous heroism had to be socially constructed and diffused, because it is totally absent from the original historical narrative.

THE MYTHICAL NARRATIVE

As I have pointed out elsewhere (1995), the mythical narrative about Masada began to develop among the Jewish population of British-mandate Palestine in the early decades of the last century, but accumulated momentum in the 1920s and had crystallized by the early 1940s. Although the entire Masada mythical narrative comprises a narrative with a trip to and climb up Masada—that is, a cognitive, physical, and emotional experience—we may easily delineate the cognitive aspect.

The Masada mythical narrative can be found in many textbooks, guidebooks, and pamphlets, and a large variety of other publications in Israel. It may be said to have evolved from a critical stance toward Josephus Flavius as historian. This critical view typically remolds such problematic issues as the identity of the Masada rebels, the massacre at Ein Gedi, the battle at Masada, the duration of the Roman siege, the suicide, and the survivors.

What Is the Masada Mythical Narrative?

If we summarize the many different versions of the Masada myth,[45] then the essence of the Masada mythical narrative may be sketched briefly as follows:

> The leaders of the popular Great Revolt were Zealots—adherents of one of the Jewish ideological trends of the period. The Imperial Roman army crushed the revolt, conquered and destroyed Jerusalem together with the Second Temple of the Jews. The Zealots who survived the siege and destruction of the city escaped to the fortress of Masada, a stronghold difficult to reach atop a mountain near the Dead Sea. From there the Zealots harassed the Romans and created such a threat that the Romans decided to make the tremendous military effort required to destroy Masada. Consequently the Romans gathered their army and made the long and arduous march through the Judean desert to Masada. There they surrounded the fortress and put it under siege. After three years of heroic resistance by the few Zealots against the huge Roman army, the Zealots on Masada realized that their situation was hopeless. They faced a grim future: either be killed by the Romans, or become slaves. Elazar Ben-Yair, the commander, addressed his followers and persuaded them all that they had to die as free men. They thus decided to kill themselves, a heroic and liberating death, rather than become wretched slaves. When the Roman soldiers entered Masada, they found only silence and dead bodies.

Masada has thus become a symbol for a heroic last stand. In the words of the famous Israeli chief-of-staff and politician Moshe Dayan (1983, p. 21):

> Today, we can point only to the fact that Masada has become a symbol of heroism and of liberty for the Jewish people to whom it says: Fight to death rather than surrender; prefer death to bondage and loss of freedom.

Clearly the popular, widespread Masada mythical narrative has some elements of truth in it, but in the main it is significantly different from what Josephus tells us. It takes a long, complex, and at some points unclear historical sequence and reduces it to a simple and straightforward heroic narrative characterized by a few clear themes. It emphasizes that a small group of heroes who had survived the battle of Jerusalem chose to continue the fight against the Romans to the bitter end rather than to surrender.

The Masada mythical narrative is thus constructed by transforming a tragic historical event into a heroic fable. The hapless revolt is transformed into a heroic war. The questionable collective suicide on Masada is transformed into a brave last stand of the heroic few against the oppresive many. The myth is thus based on the following points:

1. There were not many people on Masada.
2. They were soldiers who engaged in battle.
3. They were zealots or freedom fighters. The Sicarii are seldom mentioned. Yadin refers only to "zealots." Like Guttman and others, he probably preferred that term over the negative connotation of "Sicarii." Although Josephus does not refer to the Zealots in positive terms, the mythmakers managed to associate Zealots with such feelings as zeal for freedom, and thus to paint the Zealots in positive terms. No such exercise was (or could be) performed for the Sicarii. It is important to note that here again the mythologizers ignored Josephus, who in at least one place (7.8.1–4, pp. 598–99) included the Zealots among the brutal villains whose zeal for virtue was a sham. In any event, the mythmakers do not bother to explain why they chose the word *Zealots* over the word *Sicarii*.
4. The massacres in Ein Gedi (and elsewhere) disappear.
5. The people on Masada had come from Jerusalem, where they had been the last defenders of the city.
6. The siege of Masada was a protracted one (three years).
7. The suicide is repressed or explained away as a "no-choice" situation.
8. Masada is frequently portrayed as a rebel base for operations against the Romans.

9. Elazar Ben-Yair's two speeches are telescoped into one, eliminating the hesitancy of the Sicarii to take one another's lives.
10. The seven survivors of Masada typically disappear.

The result is the construction of a very powerful, persuasive, and consistently heroic tale.

Dating the Creation of the Myth

The return of Jews to Palestine with the explicit political goal of creating a Jewish state is typically dated to the 1880s. The secular Zionist Jews, both before and after the proclamation of statehood in 1948, doubtless craved tales of Jewish heroism, and creating the Masada mythical narrative played a crucial role in the crystallization of a new individual and collective identity for generations of Israeli Jews between the early 1940s and the late 1960s.

During the British Mandate period, the Zionist movement pushed hard for the return of the Jews to their ancient homeland. In British-controlled Palestine itself, it was clear that the Arabs did not welcome the returning Jews and that an Arab nationalist movement was developing. The local Yishuv (Jewish community in preindependence Palestine) and its leaders had to contend not only with this, but also with anti-Semitic stereotypes of Jews as noncombatants, passive, money changers, and so on. During those fateful years there was clearly an urgent need for new, nationalistic Jewish symbols of heroism, and the Masada mythical narrative came into being almost naturally.

The need for heroic Jewish symbols was magnified tremendously in the 1930s and 1940s, as the dangerous specter of fascism loomed over Europe and the Nazi threat became increasingly manifest. In the years 1940–42, the "Plan for the North" crystallized among the Jewish leadership. More popularly known as "The Masada Plan," it was a direct result of the fear instilled in the Hagana (the biggest and most significant preindependence Jewish underground organization in Palestine) by the successes of Rommel's Afrika Korps in North Africa in 1941. In early 1942 the danger of a Nazi German invasion of Palestine seemed a very real threat. The basic idea of the plan was to concentrate the Yishuv into a huge fortified locality around Mount Carmel and Haifa (the evacuation of women and children—perhaps to Cyprus—was considered). The plan assumed a perimeter covering an area of about 200 square kilometers, from where it was believed the fight against the Germans could be continued for a long time. Several scenarios of a German invasion and possible responses were envisioned, discussed, and debated.[46]

Those early years witnessed the activities of a few influential moral entrepreneurs who made it their goal to create the Masada mythical narrative, including Joseph Klosner and, perhaps the most dynamic of them all, Shmaria Guttman. Of course different moral entrepreneurs emphasized different aspects. For example, while Klosner did not hide the Sicarii—he portrayed them in heroic terms—Guttman did. By structuring the basic theme of the Masada mythical narrative, they provided an important building block of a new identity for secular Jews in Palestine. In the background was Simchoni's excellent translation of Josephus. The mythmakers could utilize this translation for their purposes by playing with the text.[47]

The story of Masada was embraced by youth movements, the preindependence Jewish underground organizations, and later by the Israeli army and the Israeli educational system as *the* symbol of Jewish heroism. The Masada mythical narrative was accepted as an authentic story of supreme heroism in the service of a genuine and justified cause. The narrative emphasized the pride and courage of Jews fighting for their liberty and their land. This heroic narrative not only created a two thousand-year-old link, but also kept it alive. The physical symbol of this connection was located in a harsh environment which had changed only slightly since 73 C.E., and which provided the narrative with a very powerful element of credibility. New Jewish settlers in Palestine (and later Israel) were encouraged to tour the country, and Masada became a preferred site.

Yadin's excavations of Masada in the years 1963–65 were actually the last chapter in the crystallization of the Masada mythical narrative. What these excavations provided was a scientific buttress for a national and popular myth, and it is for this reason that the excavations created so much political and social interest in Israel.

How Was the Masada Myth Disseminated?

Ben-Yehuda (1995) systematically charted the dissemination of the Masada mythical narrative by almost all available cultural means of expression imaginable. First, Masada was a major ingredient in the socialization processes of all five major secular Jewish youth movements in Palestine and Israel, and to a much lesser degree for the two religious movements. Second, the three major preindependence Jewish underground groups used Masada explicitly in their symbols and socialization processes. Third, the Israeli army likewise used Masada both as a symbol and as a site at which new soldiers were sworn in during boot camp. Fourth, elementary and high school texts, as well as general history texts and encyclopedias, propounded the myth. Fifth, the Masada mythical narrative appeared in travel guides and became part of the standard repertoire of local tour guides, eventually also encompassing the physical location as the site for ceremonies and cultural events. Sixth, both inside and outside Israel the myth figured in poetry and prose, plays and films, music, and the plastic arts. Finally, the printed and electronic media devoted space and time to transmit the myth.

Zionism and Masada

The Zionist movement helped develop and nourish the Masada mythical narrative as a central symbol of heroism. It began hesitantly in Europe, but picked up speed in the early decades of the twentieth century. The transformation of Josephus's original narrative into the national symbol of heroism was accomplished mostly thanks to two major moral entrepreneurs, Shmaria Guttman and Yigael Yadin.

Although Shmaria Guttman was certainly a key figure in the early years of the myth's development, the interest in Masada preceded him. This was expressed in at least three important developments. One was the debate between two very important Zionist intellectuals, Achad Ha'am and Berdyczewski, in which Berdyczewski used Masada as a symbol for Jewish heroism. Then in 1923 Y. N. Simchoni's excellent and very readable modern Hebrew translation of Josephus Flavius was published. Finally, in 1927 the poet Yitzhak Lamdan published his powerful and influential Masada poem. Moreover, parallel to Guttman, historian Joseph Klosner of the Hebrew University published studies that molded the Masada rebels as heroes. Shmaria Guttman was thus operating in a public atmosphere that offered little resistance and hungered for heroic Jewish tales. In the 1930s he crystallized the Masada mythical narrative as we know it, and created the notion that it was not enough to tell the tale. For him, the trek into the Judean desert and the final climb to Masada, where the tale was to be unfolded, epitomized the Masada experience: cognitive, physical, and emotional. But Guttman, however enthusiastic, was an amateur; it was archaeologist Yigael Yadin who accorded the myth its scientific credibility in the 1960s.

Simchoni's 1923 translation of Josephus and Lamdan's 1927 poem reflected the growing interest in Masada during the 1920s. Visits to Masada by individuals, groups, and organizations increased in frequency.

Two more important publications appeared later. One was a booklet published in 1937 by the Jewish National Fund containing an article by Bar Droma on the environment of the Dead Sea, and an essay by Yoseph Klosner. In his essay Klosner focused on what he referred to as the heroism of the Sicarii, whom he described as freedom fighters, and did his utmost to justify and glorify the suicide. Even earlier, in 1925, Klosner had written that Elazar Ben-Yair was a national hero, and that a nation capable of such a heroic act as Masada was invincible indeed.[48]

In 1941 a book edited by Israel Halperin appeared, *The Book of Heroism: A Literary-Historical Anthology*. It originally comprised two volumes (a third was added in 1980), and encompassed a survey of Jewish heroism. Anita Shapira (1992, p. 425) points out that this was the first book released by Am Oved, the publishing house of the Histadrut (the Israeli Workers' Union), whose chief editor at the time was Berl Katzenelson. According to Shapira, Berl's literary taste was usually better than this book reflected, but "this time his goal was didactic: he wanted to teach youth that Jews have already experienced in the past, dead-end situations, and knew how to die heroically." The Hagana (a preindependence Jewish underground) attributed much significance to this book and passages from it were read aloud during its meetings (Shapira 1992, p. 425). As Bitan (1990, p. 229) indicates, the main goal of the book was to demonstrate that Jewish heroism had existed throughout past generations. The book ends with the twentieth century; what is interesting is where it begins: the first incident of Jewish heroism described is the story of Masada (using Simchoni's translation).

Thus Guttman's initiative in the late 1930s and early 1940s did not develop in a vacuum. He acted as a much-needed moral entrepreneur, at the appropriate historical moment, when interest in heroic stories was at its peak. There was a genuine need for a positive symbol of Jewish heroism even before the fateful years of 1940–42. The idea of providing such a symbol would have fallen on receptive ears even without the threat of Rommel's invasion. Zionist ideology was ripe for symbols which could convey not only heroism, but also resolution, power, pride, and the will of determined Jews to live, fight, and even die for their homeland. As we have seen, the original narrative of Masada does not contain these elements. Although Shmaria Guttman did not invent the Masada mythical narrative from scratch or initiate the trips to the site, he definitely was the one who helped both to transform it into its complete mythical form and to institutionalize the treks to the site.

Guttman guided the Masada mythical narrative in several directions. To begin with, he understood the nature of this ecologically impressive site. Thus, the considerable physical effort involved in the trek to Masada and the climb to the top became a goal and symbol in themselves. The rigors of the Masada experience aptly suited a culture that encouraged hikes and trips to familiarize oneself with the country. The physical effort and challenge of reaching Masada to some extent illustrated and paralleled the difficulties of establishing a new Jewish homeland; both were not easily achieved, but both were feasible.

Efforts were therefore invested in the physical Masada—building new roads, excavations, museums, and so forth. As the Masada mythical narrative developed, Shmaria Guttman saw that there was a better, more powerful symbol than the actual site: the psychological Masada. For Guttman (and later Yadin), the more people came to Masada, the better. Hence he made a very serious effort not only to persuade the right individuals to excavate Masada, but also to enable as many people as possible to visit the ancient fortress.

In emphasizing both the mythical narrative and the visit to Masada, Shmaria Guttman was developing two major elements: the narrative itself and the powerful experiential ritual attached to it. In this way the Masada mythical narrative did not remain merely a tale to be told, but was also presented as a narrative embedded in an emotionally powerful site. The credibility of the Masada story was supported and magnified tremendously by the Masada experience. The power of the pilgrimage to Masada resides in the way that it combines both elements into one coherent, culturally integrated, personal experience.

It was not overly difficult to develop the Masada mythical narrative. The original historic version of the event already contained the major ingredients, some of which were laid out by Berdyczewski and expanded on by Klosner. Guttman did not publish many documents, but from the few he did, as well as from the reports by participants in his seminars, it is clear what he did to Josephus's original narrative. The main ingredients of the narrative remained, including the suicide. The siege and the fact that the rebels on Masada were part of the Great Revolt of the Jews were intact. But the massacre at Ein Gedi was omitted, and Guttman did not use the word Sicarii, referring instead to "the besieged of Masada" (e.g., 1964) and "Zealots." He asserted that there "must" have been battles around Masada, as well as Jewish raids against the Romans, going on to describe these battles and raids in detail. He also blurred the length of the Roman siege. His very carefully crafted narrative implies by its style and selection of words and images that the potent, efficient, and well-disciplined army of Imperial Rome was afraid of the fighters on Masada and was compelled to eliminate them, at great cost, by fighting a siege-war in a hostile environment. He also obfuscates the part of the original narrative which describes the origins of the rebels on Masada and their motivations for coming to the stronghold. Moreover, there is a marked difference between Guttman's lectures to unsuspecting audiences, which were characterized by a powerful and persuasive dramatic style liberally laced with pathos, and his writings, which are rare and do not reflect his evident rhetorical skills.

His 1964 Hebrew piece *With Masada* is an interesting illustration of his technique, and it is worthwhile to examine it in some detail. Guttman begins by citing some original descriptions from Josephus, selectively edited for brevity. Then, as if Josephus either said nothing, or said too much, Guttman moves on to *his* version. For example, he states that Josephus identified those on Masada as Sicarii; in the very next passage, however, without any explanation, he begins to use the terms "Zealots" and "the besieged of Masada" (e.g., 1964, pp. 144–45) interchangeably, totally ignoring Josephus's terminology. He admits that Josephus does not mention "battles" around Masada, but nonetheless avers that "it is certain that raids" took place and, even conjures them up for the reader (1964, pp. 144–45). Fabricating such important details enhanced the heroic tale in the process of being created. And when he spoke to audiences, Guttman allowed his creative imagination even greater freedom.

The presence of so committed and knowledgeable a moral entrepreneur at a period of cultural hunger for a heroic narrative such as the Masada mythical narrative, coupled with a truly threatening crisis such as that of 1940–42, made for a situation in which Shmaria Guttman simply could not fail. Exploiting the site itself to the limit, he transformed Masada into a place where amenable young minds were exposed to the mythical narrative. His seminar trips to Masada, in particular his 1942 seminar, represented turning points in the development of the mythical narrative. The influence he exerted must also be understood in terms of his audiences; he could not have succeeded without the receptive youngsters who were willing to embrace the Masada mythical narrative. These audiences were available for more or less the same reasons that led Shmaria Guttman to develop his moral initiative to begin with: a desperate cultural need for a genuine and tangible history of Jewish heroism. The newly emerging secular Zionist culture needed historical and symbolic heroism to give it substance. The Masada mythical narrative was one of the central tales and symbols of this new culture. Events both internal and external in the intense process of nation building going on in Jewish Palestine at the time were the necessary background factors against which the mythical narrative made sense. As this symbol made less and less sense in the 1970s, it declined in importance.

Shmaria Guttman constructed the quasi-historical sequence which we call the Masada mythical narrative, enhancing the powerful dramatic effect of the narrative by coupling it with actual site visits to Masada. His activities molded the pattern that was to be followed for years to come: the Masada experience. Once there, the visitors are exposed to an impressive and persuasive sight-and-sound show (see Donevitz 1976, 1984) retelling the heroic Masada tale. Participation in excavations, swearing-in ceremonies, concerts, operas, bar/bat-mitzvah celebrations—all these heighten the drama of the site itself. A powerful suspension of disbelief is achieved and the message of relentless determination and a gallant fight to the end against all odds unfolds before receptive minds.

With its popularity during the pre-1948 years among members of youth movements, including many of those who would later become the political, social, military, and educational elites of the country, an entire generation of Jewish Israelis were exposed to the Masada mythical narrative (including the present author). It became an integral part of the socialization process into the emerging Israeli secular Jewish culture in the formative years of the new state. This new generation was to carry the mythical narrative along with it as a basic component in its national and personal identity.

The early years of the State of Israel witnessed the continuation of the Masada ritual. The social activities surrounding the Masada mythical narrative reached a peak in the early 1940s, and lessened somewhat thereafter, but still continued well into the 1950s, in particular the military swearing-in ceremonies (mostly the Israeli armored units). A second peak was spurred by the archaeological excavations of Masada in the early 1960s, led by the second most important moral entrepreneur in the unfolding saga of the Masada story, Yigael Yadin. This will be dealt with later in the book.

SUMMARY

The two narratives which were presented in this chapter do not have the same moral stature. Josephus's version is far superior to the myth in terms of historical truth. Josephus provides us with the baseline of the Masada narrative; he was close in time to the events, took an active part in the Great Revolt, and was an official Roman historian. Had the mythologizers pointed out that the significant changes they introduced to Josephus were based on some persuasive evidence, it might have made sense; their primary motivation, however, was to create a heroic tale based only loosely on Josephus. None of Yadin's versions of Masada offer any explanation whatsoever for why he warped Josephus's version. His endorsement of a dubious narrative is surprising in light of his public statements that he considered Josephus to be both accurate and credible. We can only conclude that he actually wanted his audience to believe that the version he was promulgating was consistent with Josephus's. It was not, and Yadin (as well as other mythologizers) was clearly and intentionally engaging in deception.

We will treat Josephus as the historical truth (unless proved otherwise), and the myth as a falsification of his historical narrative. Moreover, the Masada mythical narrative was not merely an innocuous misrepresentation, but rather one of the most important national myths exploited by secular Zionism to create a new secular national and personal Jewish consciousness and identity. Thus we can see how a falsified narrative served an important need in helping to create a new social, moral, and political reality. The Masada mythical narrative was an important symbolic component in a process of social change, the result of which was the establishment of the State of Israel with a new type of a secular Jewish identity and consciousness.

NOTES

1. E.g., see Kasher 1983; Avi Yonah and Beres 1983; Stern 1984; Horsley and Hanson 1985, pp. 118–27, 190–243; Smallwood 1976.

2. For short biographical sketches of Josephus Flavius, his deeds, and his writings, consult *Encyclopaedia Judaica*, vol. 10 (1971), pp. 251–64; *The Jewish Encyclopedia*, vol. 7. For more detailed discussions see Aberbach 1985; Feldman 1984; Flusser 1985; Hadas-Lebel 1993; Horsley 1979a; Rajak 1983; Rapoport 1982; Stern 1987; Stone 1984; Thackeray 1968. Literally thousands of works have been written about Josephus Flavius, and it is impossible to delve here into all of them. The curious reader is referred to Feldman's monumental summarizing bibliographical works from 1984 (1000+ pages) and 1986 (some 700 pages).

3. The original modern Hebrew translation was published in 1923. I use the English title *Wars of the Jews*, which was used by translator William Whiston in *The Complete Works of Josephus*. Josephus wrote in Greek.

4. See, e.g., Aberbach 1985; Flusser 1985; Hangel 1983; Horsley 1979a; Rapoport 1982, 1984, 1988; Smith 1971, 1983; Stern 1973, 1983, 1984, 1987, 1989. See also Safrai 1970. For a more general perspective see Smallwood 1976 and Grant 1973.

5. Throughout the text, and unless stated otherwise, references to Josephus Flavius are to *The Complete Works of Josephus*, translated into English by William Whiston. I used the 1981 edition published by Kregel Publications (Grand Rapids, Mich.) for several reasons. First, I preferred to use a text that is easily available. Second, uncovering the deception in the archaeology of Masada requires that we attempt to know what the archaeologists at the time knew; hence which version of Josephus Yadin used is a crucial issue. Alas, Yadin does not tell us, but I checked Yadin's English quotations, and he appears to have used the Whiston edition word for word. (While I used the 1981 edition, the editions go back to 1960.) So if I want to examine in what way Yadin deviated from the only authoritative text he had, it is the Whiston edition that I must use. Citations to Josephus in this book follow the standard format, which is book.chapter.paragraph, except that for the convenience of my readers I also add the page in Whiston's translation. Thus the citation "7.8.3, p. 599" means book 7, chapter 8, paragraph 3, which is on page 599 of Whiston's translation. The book, chapter, and paragraph numbers are identical in all translations, and in the Greek text also, so it is not necessary to use Whiston's translation to locate the cited text. (Yadin, by the way, does not use the system which utilizes book, chapter, and paragraph numbers.)

6. See also Feldman's review on Josephus's reliability as a source for Masada (1984, pp. 772–89).

7. However, and for the sake of fairness, let me note briefly some of the possible inaccuracies in Josephus's account. There are six issues with which Josephus may have a credibility problem regarding Masada (see also Feldman 1984, pp.

772–89). It is important to note that none of these issues, to the best of my knowledge, in any meaningful way affected the development of the Masada mythical narrative.

The first issue concerns Elazar Ben-Yair's speeches, an issue which is commonly attacked. Josephus Flavius was probably not even near Masada when the fortress fell; How does he know what Elazar Ben-Yair said? There are two solutions to this puzzle: the first is that the only direct source for the speeches, the two women survivors, provided the details. Second, Josephus Flavius must have been an intimate acquaintance of the Jewish parties in the Great Revolt. He had been the commander of the Galilee and he must have known many (or all) of the leaders personally. He could easily have guessed what they *might* have said under such difficult circumstances. However, the issue of the speeches returns time and again to undermine his credibility.

The second issue is the color of Masada's casemate wall. Josephus states that the wall "was composed of white stone" (7.8.3, p. 599). In fact, Yadin's excavations revealed that it was made of nonwhite "hard dolomite stone which was quarried on Masada" (Yadin 1966, p. 141). To an outside observer the wall may have appeared white because it was covered with white plaster (ibid).

The third issue is the height of Masada's casemate wall. According to Josephus it was 6 meters high (7.8.3, p. 599; see also Yadin 1966, p. 141 and Livne 1986, p. 119). In fact, the height of the wall was not uniform, but never exceeding 5 meters. Again, the inaccuracy may be due to a mistake by an outside observer, possibly looking at Masada from the bottom up.

Fourth, Josephus states that the wall had thirty-eight towers (7.8.3, p. 599). According to Livne (1986, p. 119), not more than thirty towers were identified in the excavations. Either Josephus made a mistake here, or the archaeologists did.

Fifth, While Josephus implies that the Sicarii ignited one large fire on the last night, the excavations revealed many (see also S. Cohen 1988).

The first four problems, and possibly also the fifth, are not generally viewed as too serious. A more difficult problem is the sixth. The largest (and perhaps one of the oldest) building on Masada is the western palace built by Herod (Livne 1986, pp. 31, 36–37 and Netzer 1983 imply that the early construction may have been by the Hasmoneans. In an interview [November 4, 1993] Netzer stated that there is no evidence for this hypothesis. The problem is thus of dating the construction). The fact that Josephus does not mention this palace is puzzling (Yadin 1966, 42, p. 117; Livne 1986, p. 158), especially as the Romans breached Masada not far from that palace. The majestic palaces Josephus describes are those on the northern stairlike slope of Masada (Yadin [1966, p. 119] feels that Josephus's description simply concentrated on the "wondrous palace-villa at the northern point"). It is possible that this glaring ignorance on Josephus's part reflects the fact that he never was on Masada, or that part of his manuscript is missing. For more on this see Ben-Yehuda 1998.

For a more recent discussion on the credibility and reliability of Josephus see Mason 1997, and the debate which developed in *Biblical Archaeology Review* 24, no. 1 (January–February 1998): 13–16.

8. *Wars of the Jews*, 7.8.3, p. 599.
9. Possibly Alexander Jannaeus. See Cotton and Geiger 1989b, p. 4.
10. *Wars of the Jews*, 4.7.2, p. 537.
11. *Wars of the Jews*, 7.8.4, pp. 599–600.

12. For a short review see Livne 1986, pp. 123–28 and Yadin 1966e, pp. 231–46; 1970, 374–75).

13. Except, of course, for the modern roads, structures, cable car, and the receding Dead Sea.

14. See Feldman's 1984, pp. 655–67 review.

15. *Wars of the Jews*, 7.8.1, p. 598.

16. This is the standard version of the capture of Masada by the Sicarii. Josephus does not provide a very clear or consistent account of the events leading to the capture. For example, it is not clear from his description whether Manahem's forces were the ones who first took the fortress, or whether there were other forces (the implication is that around 66 C.E. Masada was captured twice). Also, it is not clear whether Manahem's men left a garrison there after they took the weapons from Masada, and it is entirely unclear whether upon their later return to Masada Elazar Ben-Yair and his men had to recapture it. Thus, Josephus states that "he [Elazar Ben-Yair] and his Sicarii got possession of the fortress [Masada] by treachery" (*Wars of the Jews*, 7.8.4, p. 599). For more details about this rather messy historical sequence of events, see Horsley and Hanson 1985, p. 212; Cotton and Geiger 1989b, pp. 1–24; and the last and meticulous paper by Cotton and Preiss 1990.

17. *Wars of the Jews*, 7.8.1., p. 598.

18. *Wars of the Jews*, 2.17.9, p. 492.

19. *Wars of the Jews*, 7.8.1, p. 598.

20. *Wars of the Jews*, 4.7.2, p. 537. On the fantastic possibility that skeletal remains of that massacre may have been found see Avichai Becker, "The Massacre in Ein Gedi," *Ha'aretz*, weekend supplement, March 30, 2001, pp. 88–90, 92 (Hebrew). The looting and robbery were also carried out by Simon the son of Giora. See *Wars of the Jews*, 4.9.3, p. 541. See also Hoenig 1970; Spero 1970; Zeitlin 1965, 1967.

21. *Wars of the Jews*, 7.6.4, p. 596.

22. Possibly at the end of 72 C.E. See Simchoni 1923, p. 512.

23. *Wars of the Jews*, 7.8.1, pp. 598–99.

24. *Wars of the Jews*, 7.8.1, p. 598.

25. See also Dvir 1966 (although he tries to blur this point somewhat).

26. *Wars of the Jews*, 4.7.2, p. 537.

27. For more on the end of Masada, from an archaeological and architectural point of view, see Netzer's fascinating 1991 work.

28. *Wars of the Jews*, 7.9.2, p. 603.

29. Josephus (7.9.1, p. 603) states that the collective suicide on top of Masada took place on the "fifteenth day of the month [Xanthicus] Nisan." Alas, he does not state in which year. Most researchers assume it was 73 C.E. However, in 1969, Eck suggested that 74 was probably more accurate. A controversy ensued around this issue. One problem with accepting Eck's new date of 74 is that it may create problems in dating other events. The debate ended with 73 still being considered the correct year (for a review of the debate see Jones 1974; Stern 1989, p. 370n.17; Cotton and Geiger 1989b, pp. 21–24; and Cotton's meticulous 1989 paper). The currently accepted traditional version is that the siege of Masada began in the winter of 72–73 C.E. and ended in the spring of 73, a matter of only a few months (see also

Feldman's review 1984, pp. 789–90). In fact, Roth's painstaking work makes a very persuasive and credible argument that the whole siege of Masada took between four to nine weeks, with seven weeks as the most probable length (1995). A prolonged battle is implied by Geva (1996), who speculates that the Romans may have built another siege ramp inside and on top of Masada, above the northern palace. This speculation—not mentioned by Josephus—was verified by Eshel (1999).

30. See also Avi Yonah and Beres 1983; Kasher 1983; Rapoport 1984; and Stern 1983, 1984.

31. See, e.g., Feldman 1984, pp. 655–67; Horsely and Hanson 1985; Stern 1973.

32. *Wars of the Jews*, 2.17.2 and 8, pp. 490, 491. See note no. 16 above.

33. *Wars of the Jews*, 4.7.2, p. 537.

34. *Wars of the Jews*, 7.6.4, p. 596.

35. See *Wars of the Jews*, 4.9.3, p. 541.

36. See also Horsley and Hanson 1985, p. 214 for a condensed description.

37. See, e.g., Philip 1994; Perrett 1991, 1995 for numerous historical accounts.

38. Military historians Dupuy and Dupuy (1970, p. 26) state: "To Thermopylae went Spartan King Leonidas, with about 7,000 hoplites and some archers. Save for Leonidas' bodyguard of 300 men, few of these were Spartans. In August (?) of 480 the battle began. Leonidas placed about 6,000 at the Middle Gate. Another force of about 1,000 was stationed on the mountains. The Persians tried to push their way through the pass, but were repulsed by the main force. These futile Persian attempts lasted for about three days. Then, a Greek traitor told Xerxes about a forest trail across the mountain behind Thermopylae. Xerxes did not fail to use this valuable information. He sent the 'Immortals' of his bodyguard. They quickly overwhelmed the Greek flank guard in a surprise attack. That was basically the end. Although desperate Leonidas sent there a reinforcement of 4,500, they arrived too late. While almost all of Leonidas' forces surrendered at this point, the King and his bodyguard fought till they were all killed."

Interestingly, the Thermopylae pass played an important part in World War II as well. The pass, which was only a few yards wide when Leonidas and his 300 Spartans tried to use it unsuccessfully to stop the invading Persian, has been widened to about three miles in modern times. In 1941 the British troops in Greece (about 60,000 men strong) were forced into retreat by the invading German Second and Twelfth armies. The British faced the danger of encirclement and capture. The pass of Thermopylae became the site of a very valuable defensive action by British army troops (mainly from Australia and New Zealand). That defense, which delayed the German advance until the night of April 24–25, 1941, enabled continued evacuation of British troops from southern Greek ports until April 27 and facilitated the escape of about 45,000 soldiers (alas, with very little equipment), mostly to Crete. The evacuation operation ended on April 28–29, and the total number of British soldier evacuees reached some 50,000 (see Parrish and Marshall 1978, p. 627; Wheal and Pope 1995, p. 462).

39. I refer here, of course, to the (mythical?) view of Davy Crockett choosing not to surrender to Mexican General Santa Anna at the Alamo (in San Antonio, Texas), and he and his men were killed in the final battle. I suggest that this is a "mythical" tale, because some of the authors in Lofaro and Cummings's 1989 volume imply that Davy Crockett did in fact surrender when the situation became hopeless,

but that the force in the Alamo was killed regardless. For some interesting notes on the comparison of Masada to the Alamo, see Bruner and Gorfain 1984, pp. 70–71.

40. The German offensive in the Ardennes (Battle of the Bulge) began on December 16, 1944. The French town of Bastogne was surrounded by German forces. On December 21, 1944, the commander of the Forty-seventh Panzer Division passed on an ultimatum to the American commander in Bastogne: surrender or die. The acting American commander of the 101st Airborne Division, Brig. Gen. Anthony C. McAuliffe, replied: "Nuts!" The American forces in Bastogne staged a stubborn defense that held the German Nazi forces for eight days. The forces of Gen. George S. Patton, commander of the Third Army, ended the German siege on Bastogne on December 26, 1944.

41. The American base on this Central Pacific island was defended by a marine force of about four hundred soldiers, commanded by Maj. James Devereux. The first Japanese attack on the island took place on December 7, 1941 (an air raid). The island fell to landing Japanese troops on December 23, 1941. Although there were survivors from that battle (who were sent to Japanese prisoner-of-war camps), there is no question that the U.S. Marines staged a heroic fight for as long as they possibly could. (See, e.g., Schultz 1978; Urwin 1997.)

42. *Wars of the Jews*, 7.9.2, p. 603.

43. Hawkes (1929, p. 204) estimates that 3,500 soldiers of the Tenth Legion, and 3,000 additional "auxiliari" soldiers, participated in the siege. Looking at the remnants of the Roman army camps around Masada, Yadin estimates that:

> the built camps alone could house almost 9,000 troops, including the legion. But there is no doubt that the entire besieging force was very much larger, probably reaching 15,000 men if we add to the fighting units the thousands of Jewish prisoners who, according to Josephus, were used to bring water and food and apparently also to work on construction. (1966, p. 218)

The size and structure of a Roman legion fluctuated. However, it seems safe to assume that the average size of a legion throughout this period was some six thousand soldiers. If this indeed was the size of the Tenth Legion, it seems safe to assume that the legion plus the auxiliary logistic forces (and the prisoners and slaves) may have numbered at least ten thousand (see also Magness 1992, p. 64; Richmond 1962; Shatzman 1993; and for a more general perspective, see Luttwak 1976). I am very grateful to the late Prof. Ernest David Coleman from the Department of Classical Studies, Tel Aviv University, who helped to guide me through this complex question.

44. See *Annee Epigraphique* (1969/70), sec. 183; Pauly-Wissowa, *Paulys Realincyclopödie Der Classischen Altertums-Wissenschaft*, Supplementband 14 (Munchen: 1974), pp. 121–22, entry 181. I am very grateful to Shmuel Sermoneta-Gertel from the Department of Classical Studies at the Hebrew University who helped me with this issue.

45. See my 1995 book for the different presentations.

46. For a brief summary see Ben-Yehuda 1995, pp. 131–38.

47. For a more thorough and detailed analysis, see my 1995 book.

48. Klosner 1925, pp. 115–18, 240–41; Blaushild 1985, p. 21.

THREE
EXCAVATING MASADA

Many consider the first modern identification of Masada as the one made in 1838 by Robinson and Smith during their travels in the area,[1] although they did not actually climb the mountain. In March 1842 the American missionary S. W. Wolcott and his English painter W. Tipping climbed Masada via the Roman siege ramp. From then on Masada enjoyed a continuous stream of visitors, who made significant discoveries concerning different aspects of the fortress, its water supply system, and so on. It is commonly agreed that the most important study of Masada was written by German scholar Adolf Schulten, who spent an entire month on Masada in 1932. As Yadin states, "it is his plans that laid the foundation for the future study of the ruins" (1966e, p. 243).

With the increased interest of Palestinian Jews in Masada during the 1920s, and with the impetus of Shmaria Guttman's enthusiasm in the following decades, the desire to excavate Masada began to crystallize. The magnificent ruins seemed to be hiding some fascinating and vital secrets from times past. This interest received a boost in 1944 when Joseph Breslavski published a booklet which summarized the work accomplished by Masada researchers up to that point. The booklet served as a guide for the many travelers to Masada in the decade following its publication (Livne 1986, p. 128).

From the 1940s, Jewish secular interest in excavating Masada was focused within groups of enthusiastic amateurs and, only later, among some professional archaeologists. That amateurs should be interested in, and contribute to, archaeology is not an isolated case in science.[2] Indeed, as Yadin (1970, p. 374) points out, the most important contribution in creating the motivation to excavate Masada was made by an obviously amateur archaeologist who turned the Masada mythical narrative into his central life interest, Shmaria Guttman.[3] As Guttman relates, during his many different climbs to Masada he made several small discoveries that whetted his appetite for more work. He reported his trips to different archaeologists, trying to interest them in excavating Masada. Together with Azaria Alon he made an examination of the water supply system to Masada built by King Herod.[4] In 1953 Ze'ev Meshel (still a zealous advocate of the myth in the 1990s) and Micha Livne were the first to publish more or less accurate plans of the structures found in the northern slope-stairs of the mountain, making the correct identification of Herod's palace as described by Josephus Flavius (Yadin 1970, p. 375; Livne 1986, p. 128). A summary of all the known and available research on Masada was published in 1953–54 (in Hebrew) by the Israeli Society for the Exploration of Eretz Israel and Its Antiquities (Livne 1986, p. 128). These efforts, made mostly by enthusiastic and interested individuals, culminated in some major discoveries, and form the beginnings of the efforts to unravel some of the mystery that shrouded Masada.

This sporadic research helped create impetus among the Israeli Society for the Exploration of Eretz Israel and Its Antiquities, the Hebrew University, and the Israeli government antiquities department to initiate a survey and excavation of Masada. Thus the work done by the first few local Jewish amateurs and professionals served as a catalyst to raise and focus interest in Masada as a legitimate site for continued professional archaeological research,[5] much along the lines of the British and German tradition of gentlemen archaeologists particularly interested in biblical, Egyptian, and classical Greek sites.

SHMARIA GUTTMAN

Two moral entrepreneurs (Becker 1963) had a decisive influence on the excavations of Masada—Shmaria Guttman and Yigael Yadin. Guttman's impact on the youth movements was decisive, especially in the formative years of the 1930s. More than anything else, it was his personal motivation, conviction, and zeal which helped bring the Masada mythical narrative into being at that early stage. Yigael Yadin was the one who gave the myth a scientific cloak of reliability and veracity many years after the mythical narrative had already been well established.

Shmaria Guttman was born in 1909 in Glasgow, Scotland, into a Jewish family that had immigrated from Russia. He was one of five brothers and sisters. In 1912 the family immigrated to Palestine and settled in Merchavia, a settlement in northern Israel. Guttman's father, a baker, was a member of the group that organized *Poalei Zion* ("Workers of Zion"), together with such prominent political and ideological leaders as David Ben-Gurion, Berl Katznelson, Yitzhak Tabenkin, and others who later became the leadership of the Jewish community in Mandate Palestine. Thus Shmaria Guttman grew up in an ideological and political ambience that was very sympathetic to socialist ideas and to secular Zionism. He remained in Merchavia until the age of seventeen and was among the activists and organizers of new branches of the *Noar Oved* ("Working Youth") socialist youth movement in the Jezreel Valley. His involvement with the *Noar Oved* was to have a profound influence on the development of the Masada mythical narrative. Thus at seventeen, Guttman went to study in the agricultural school Mikve Israel near Tel Aviv, where he spent two years before returning to his parents' farm. Deeply involved in his youth movement, he soon left the farm and became a youth counselor in the movement, working in different cities in Palestine. In 1934 he came to Kibbutz Na'an, where he was to spend the rest of his life (he died in 1996).

Guttman has told Michael Shashar (1987) that the atmosphere in his home emphasized not only socialist Zionism, but also Judaism, as symbolic Jewish traditions were followed (e.g., lighting Sabbath candles). Guttman's teachers included Breslavski, who wrote some of the most influential popular books and papers about Masada, and Yael Gordon, daughter of A. D. Gordon, one of the most potent ideologists of the Jewish community in Palestine in the early years of the twentieth century.

Guttman and two friends had hiked around the Dead Sea and reached Masada in 1933. He took with him a copy of a summary of Josephus Flavius's book.[6] The three hikers were not aware of the "snake path" and took another, extremely difficult way to the top. As a site, Masada left a tremendous impression on young Shmaria Guttman, and there can hardly be any question that this trip convinced him that Masada deserved special attention.

Before embarking on the 1933 trip, Guttman had asked Yitzhak Ben-Tzvi, then the head of the Jewish national committee, for advice and help in regard to the trip. Upon returning from the trek, he requested a meeting with Ben-Tzvi in order to share his experiences. According to Guttman, Ben-Tzvi asked him, "Tell me, Shmaria, why are you so excited? Masada? Nine hundred Jewish robbers ran from Jerusalem to Masada and committed suicide. So what? What is this excitement all about?"[7] At that time Shmaria told Ben-Tzvi that he was an emotional young Jew and that Masada as a site was exciting. Guttman was not deterred by Ben-Tzvi's response and continued to develop his interest in Masada. In Shmaria's own words,

> As an educator I realized that there was an interest in bringing the story of Masada to the attention of the youth. These were difficult years (1941–1943). There were fears that Rommel would arrive [in Palestine] through Egypt. I was in the Hagana and I [knew] what was planned. . . . [W]hat

> would the young adolescents do? I thought that they had to be socialized into being prepared for anything, [particularly so] for freedom and liberty. Then I said, there is nothing like Masada for this purpose. So, I prepared the seminar. . . . [T]he guides will take the young adolescents there. . . . Since then I saw myself committed to study the war of the Jews against the Romans. (Shashar 1987, p. 22)

Guttman was apparently puzzled by the Roman Imperial army's interest in a remote and desolate fortress with some 960 "robbers" on its top. He concluded that these "robbers" were in fact genuine and fierce freedom fighters and rebels who somehow posed a threat to the Roman Empire. But 960 rebels in a single isolated stronghold could not possibly pose a grave threat unless there was something more behind their presence. And thus the way was paved for the unsubstantiated construction of Masada as a base for raiding operations against the Romans and the possible resistance of an imaginary Judean state in the Judean desert. These fantastic claims most certainly magnified the importance of Masada well beyond its historically minor significance. According to Guttman's imaginative narrative, Rome perceived the desert stronghold as a threat to continued Roman hegemony in the area and to ultimate military victory. Masada could well have served as the locus for a new revolt against the Romans. Consequently, according to Shmaria Guttman, the military effort of the Roman Imperial army against Masada was unprecedented. Interesting as this conjecture may be, one important question is, why did not Josephus tell us all this? After all, it was in his interest to demonstrate how the mighty Roman Imperial army could cope with, and neutralize, serious threats. He probably would not have missed a tale where a mighty fortress in a threatening and powerful Judean state was crushed by the mighty Roman army. My guess is that there probably never was a Judean state. Moreover, the Roman decision to crush Masada was probably part of a mopping up operation, and the military move against Masada did not involve a very strenuous or exceptional effort for the Romans.

For Shmaria, as well as for so many other secular Zionists, familiarity with and knowledge of the land were coupled with a willingness to fight for and defend it as basic components of Zionist consciousness. For these secular Zionists it was essential to forgo the comfortable surrender of Jews outside Palestine and Israel to the pleasures and comforts of European and American material existence, and instead to create a new type of hardworking and determined Jews. These new Jews had to seek personal freedom and national liberty, and above all had to be connected to their land, ready to fight for it and, if necessary, to die for it. For Shmaria Guttman constructing Masada as a national symbol for this type of socialization was both imperative and natural.

Thus the myth was born. As I have shown elsewhere (1995), it was Shmaria Guttman who created much of the mythical narrative. How? Simply by emphasizing some aspects of the original Masada narrative, repressing others, inventing new elements, and giving the whole new mythical construction an interpretation of heroism. Guttman helped develop the belief that the few remaining Jewish fighters of the Great Revolt actually fought the last battle on Masada. In his view these were proud Jewish Zealots who hoped to rekindle the fire of resistance. Rebellion, taking a proud stand, fighting to the end for one's country—these are the main messages of Guttman's interpretation. Retelling the mythical narrative during an arduous desert trek and climb to the top of Masada before sunrise helped to suspend disbelief and transform the fantastic and grossly inaccurate narrative into a credible and powerfully persuasive experience.

Guttman was searching for a genuine Jewish heroic narrative to use in socializing young adolescents, and Masada offered him a golden opportunity. The greatest advantage of the Masada story was the site itself; the narrative was problematic. So it was reconstructed to suit a heroic narrative. The technique was simple: emphasize and magnify the heroic elements, adding and fabricating if necessary; ignore or discount the more problematic aspects. For example, disguise the Sicarii as Zealots; do not mention the Ein Gedi massacre, or revise its context. This technique was precedent-setting because the creation of the Masada myth was based on effective manipulation. Let us look at one illustrative example: the suicide.

Of all the problematic aspects of the historical narrative, the suicide was perhaps the most problematic. First, Josephus's description leaves very little, if any, room for manipulations or blurring. Second, Judaism does not worship death; it is a life-loving religion devoid of any cultural phenomena extolling suicidal bravery such as Kamikaze and Kaitans,[8] Fedayeens (Moslem suicidal assassins) or Hamas suicide bombers. Jewish religious law, in fact, stipulates that suicides be buried outside the consecrated cemetery. Only under very specific and rare circumstances are Jews required to even consider taking their own lives, for example, "Kiddush Hashem" (sanctification of G-d) when threatened with forced religious conversion. Thus the suicide on Masada had to be either deemphasized, ignored, or explained away as a matter of no choice, a heroic and liberating death, or even a bona fide case of "Kiddush Hashem" (which is a very problematic claim in this case).

Early Excavations

Professional archaeological interest in excavating Masada, certainly propelled by the myth, was expressed in two efforts at two different periods, both of which owe much to Shmaria Guttman's initiative and drive. Guttman of course realized that an added bonus to the mythical narrative which he helped into being would be archaeological verification of the version he was so energetically and successfully disseminating. He had not only a heroic tale, but also an actual site which could be constructed to give tangible physical testimony to that tale. One must add that although Guttman's interest in Masada was the most spectacular, it was embedded within a more general concern for the land and its archaeology. Years later, he was the living spirit and drive behind the archaeological excavations of ancient Gamla, also mentioned by Josephus Flavius, in the Golan Heights. Josephus's narrative of the siege and fall of Gamla is indeed one of heroism and undaunted sacrifice; unfortunately, when the Masada mythical narrative was crystallizing, no one knew where Gamla was.

The first Jewish archaeological excavation of Masada was headed by Michael Avi-Yona, Nachman Avigad, Yochanan Aharony, Immanuel Dunayevski (an architect), Joseph Aviram (an administrator), and, of course, Shmaria Guttman, who was an amateur archaeologist. They worked on Masada for about ten days in March 1955. The major goals of this expedition were to make a thorough survey of all the visible remnants on Masada and to excavate the northern Herodian palace. Exactly one year later Yochanan Aharony and Shmaria Guttman returned for an additional ten days to continue excavating the palace and carry out a small but important excavation in one of the storage areas. These two early expeditions made several discoveries and enabled the accumulation of important field experience.[9]

In the early 1960s Guttman made a few more interesting discoveries at Masada. He was involved in the excavation and reconstruction of one of the Roman siege camps,[10] located the "snake path" and discovered, excavated, and reconstructed the "snake path" gate to Masada (Guttman 1964).[11] All these excavations obviously helped prepare the groundwork for the intensive archaeological excavations of the 1960s.

Guttman realized the limits of his influence and power.[12] He knew that only someone with the power and prestige of Yigael Yadin could turn the fantasy of excavating Masada into reality. At first Yadin was not particularly interested in excavating Masada, which he thought was a Herodian fortress where criminals were sent. Guttman was not the person to let such statements pass unchallenged. He knew that if he could persuade Yadin to invest an effort in Masada, major excavations could follow. Yadin himself acknowledged Guttman's key role, describing him as having "greatly advanced the study of Herod's water system: and finally, it was he who spurred the scientific institutions in Israel to undertake the excavations at Masada" (1966e, p. 245). Netzer also notes that Shmaria Guttman was "the first and the head of the research about Masada" (1990, p. 185).

Together with similar pressure on the part of archaeologists and nonarchaeologists alike (e.g., Joseph Aviram), Guttman's continued appeals to Yadin coalesced with the exciting and successful results of the previous expeditions. It is possible that Yadin also believed that he could find new scrolls on Masada, and that could have been a significant factor in his motivation to excavate Masada. Yadin reconsidered and took the next step: intensive excavation of Masada in the early 1960s (Netzer 1990, p. 187). While Guttman's initiatives in the 1930s and 1940s had achieved spectacular results in terms of creating social and moral commitment to Masada by important groups and individuals, Yadin's excavations of Masada in the early 1960s had an even more spectacular impact, this time worldwide (see also Feldman 1984, pp. 763–65).

YADIN'S EXCAVATIONS—AN OVERVIEW

Background

While Yadin's major excavations of Masada are the focal point of this book, it needs to be added that, archaeologically speaking (at least according to many of our interviewees), Masada was not an important site, unless one is interested in that distinctive phase of the last days of the Jewish Second Temple. Even then this interest must be translated specifically to accommodate Masada, which is neither simple nor self-evident. Indeed, we have already seen that one of the main motivations of a significant driving force behind the excavations of Masada, Shmaria Guttman, was national zeal. For him, one of the main reasons to excavate Masada was patriotic, not scientific; he was secondarily interested in the architectural value of the Herodian structures, in the coins, the written materials, the fabrics, and so on. His primary interest was the scientific validation of his imaginary version of Josephus's Masada tale as one of heroic proportions. Indeed, he participated in early expeditions to Masada and did his utmost to bring about the excavations by talking to various people and trying to persuade whoever he could that Masada had to be excavated. Here is one illustration of his attempts.

Shmaria states that about four years before Yadin's excavations (around 1959) light diggings were carried out at Masada. The goal of these diggings was to examine the feasibility of a full-scale excavation. Shortly thereafter, Shmaria had a discussion with Nachman Avigad, Yochanan Aharoni, and Avi-Yona, all famous archaeologists, in Avigad's home. Shalit, an expert on the Herodian period, was also invited to this gathering. Shmaria talked about his interpretation of the Jewish war against the

Romans, elaborating on Masada. Shalit disagreed with him. He felt that Herod built the fortress as a refuge for himself in time of need. Shmaria, on the other hand, believed that Masada was one of the most important fortresses in the land at the time, a place that was strategically located to enable forces from it to threaten a hostile enemy. So, as you can imagine, the debate became quite heated. Shmaria realized after a while that Shalit simply had never visited Masada. So, in response to Shalit's question of how he could calculate Masada's strategic superiority over the fortresses at Macherus and Herodium, Shmaria's answer was, "You see, I *was* there." Shalit, however, was not persuaded (Ben-Yehuda, 1995, pp. 81–82).

The archaeologist who excavated Masada had to be a professional with impeccable credentials. Hebrew University professor of archaeology Yigael Yadin was just the person for the job. Yadin carried on Guttman's dissemination of the Masada mythical narrative, exploiting his powerful credibility as former Israeli Defense Forces Chief of Staff and senior professor of archaeology at Hebrew University to promote his overhauled version of Josephus Flavius on the events in Masada. Moreover, and unlike Shmaria Guttman, Yadin was a natural for the media. Listening to recordings of his many radio interviews on Masada (and I listened to quite a few of them) gives a vivid impression of a man comfortable and persuasive in both broadcast and print media, who presents himself well as an articulate, poised, self-assured, eloquent, and authoritative professional, someone who knows what he is talking about. His projection of the fabricated version of Josephus helped tremendously to sell the myth. Indeed, Silberman points out that "Yadin's genius was his ability to draw people into a web of mythmaking, into a deeply felt communal consciousness" (1993, p. 284). "The drama of the Masada excavations and the virtuoso brilliance with which Yadin conveyed the discoveries to the public made the project as much an exercise in patriotic inspiration as in scientific research" (1993, p. 288). Unfortunately, what emerged from Yadin's desk about Masada was clearly more of an exercise in "patriotic inspiration" than "scientific research." The full scientific results of the excavations of Masada were published only after Yadin's death (in 1984), in the late 1980s and early 1990s.

Yigael Yadin

Yigael Yadin had moved from one career role to another and achieved prominence in at least three areas: the military, the scientific, and the political.[13] He was born on March 21, 1917, in Jerusalem, the son of well-known archaeologist Eliezer L. Sukenik. Yadin joined the Hagana underground in 1933 and quickly assumed commanding posts. In 1947 he was appointed the officer in charge of operations and planning, a key position as the 1948 War of Independence was about to break out. Following the establishment of Israel in 1948, Yadin was appointed chief of staff of the newly created Israel Defense Forces in 1949, a position he held until 1952, after which he devoted his professional life to archaeology at the Hebrew University. He received his Ph.D. from that university in 1955 for his work on the scroll of the War of the Sons of Light against the Sons of Darkness, one of the Dead Sea Scrolls unearthed in Qumran, not too far from Ein Gedi in the Judean Desert. After that he taught at the university, and was made professor in 1963. After the 1973 Yom Kippur War Yadin was appointed member of the National Committee of Inquiry investigating the preparations that culminated in that war. Prior to the 1977 national elections Yadin formed and assumed leadership of a new political party, Dash, which made an impressive showing in those elections and secured a large number of seats in the Knesset, the Israeli parliament (15 out of 120 seats). The party joined the coalition government headed by Menachem Begin, and Yadin became deputy prime minister. But lacking any genuine social or political integration and agenda, and torn by inner feuds, conflicting personalities, and the absence of effective leadership, Dash eventually disintegrated. Yadin died June 28, 1984, at the age of sixty-seven.[14]

Thus Yigael Yadin was many things. Before becoming a professor and archaeologist, Yadin had held formative roles in the creation of Israel, and was fully committed to secular Zionism. Once he had been persuaded to undertake the excavation of Masada, he viewed these excavations as a national and patriotic issue. As such, he wanted to confirm the mythical and heroic narrative of the Masada tale.

The Excavations

The archaeological excavations of Masada under Yadin took place in two consecutive periods, from October 1963 to May 1964, and from November 1964 to April 1965—in all, about eleven months of excavations.

> Due to their efforts and their discoveries, Masada became the most famous project in the history of Israeli archaeology, and—perhaps second only to the clearance of the tomb of Tutankhamen—the most publicized excavation in the twentieth century. (Silberman 1989, p. 89)

The excavations heaped additional fuel on the bonfire of the myth. The topic was discussed intensely on Israeli radio, in schools, in the army, in the newspapers, and among the public. For an entire generation of Israeli Jews, the experience of participating in the excavations, and of digesting the spurious myth, became a fixated and permanent ingredient of their identity as Israelis. The excavations drew a large number of volunteers from outside Israel as well, and hence considerable foreign press coverage. The publication of Yadin's books on Masada in 1966 kindled the flame of debate once again, eliciting interest among intellectuals and lay persons alike.

Ultimately, Yadin wrote, "we excavated 97 percent of the built-on area of Masada" (Yadin 1966e, p. 203). Many of the excavated structures and artifacts were also reconstructed. The architectural findings revealed the majesty and beauty of the Herodian buildings, but the excavations neither confirmed nor refuted important elements in Josephus's narrative, only that there was a fortress called Masada, that the Romans had laid siege to it, that the Romans built a siege ramp, and that they conquered the stronghold. Questions regarding the Sicarii, the suicide, Elazar Ben-Yair's speeches, the massacre at Ein Gedi, the duration of the siege remain unanswered to this day. The reliability of Josephus's general description was proven (Netzer 1990, pp. 193, 195)—at least, nothing of significance was found in the excavations to contradict his historical narrative.

A detailed archaeological survey of the ruins of Masada was already planned in 1955. Dr. Shmuel Yeivin, director of the Israeli Department of Antiquities, told reporters that the survey would serve as basis for decisions on a possible excavation of Masada, which would "expose the important fortress in the history of the destruction of the Temple. . . . This will be one of the important archaeological enterprises in the country."[15] Although the main excavations of Masada took place only in 1963–65, the 1955 preparations indicated that serious intentions and planning in the highest echelons of government agencies had begun many years earlier.

Ze'ev Meshel, a well-known figure in the context of Masada, felt that there were two reasons for excavating Masada. First, it was a worthwhile archaeological site. He pointed out that archaeologists may tend to choose places for excavations that suit their personal interests, and added that there was no question that Yadin was personally interested in excavating Masada. Second,

> Masada is not just one more site among many. It is a site with a fascinating history. It has what every archaeologist searches for: a connection between the site and historical sources. . . . Masada is connected to an extraordinary and important chapter in the history of the Jewish people during the days of the Second Temple. . . . This makes Masada a site of the utmost national significance. . . . It is the spirit of Masada which is so important. In terms of national relevance and in terms of archaeology, the important factor is a shared common past and pivotal events, all of which constitute part of the past of a group referred to as a "nation." In Masada, one such event of extreme importance, took place.[16]

Meshel's perception is that a common past is crucial for the crystallization of a national identity. He does not realize that the important past which he attributes to Masada did not exist in Josephus Flavius, but was invented. When, in my interview, I tried to suggest or hint at that, Meshel's reaction tended to be angry and emotional.

In a Hebrew-language interview on the Israeli radio on September 9, 1963, Yadin emphasized the "national historical importance of Masada in our history. . . . [F]rom an educational and pedagogic point of view . . . it was like a lighted beacon." In an English-language transmission in October 1963, Yadin stated that one of the main reasons for excavating Masada was that "[i]t was the last stand . . . against the Romans, and . . . served as a symbol for us." Yadin also mentioned "archaeological reasons" in both these interviews, but only vaguely and without any specific reference or explanation; e.g., Masada was located in a dry place (which could easily apply to any number of other sites) and that Masada could help further our understanding of Second Temple times (without specifying how). However, it is noteworthy that the term "dry place" could be interpreted as a sort of a code. One of the reasons Yadin was interested in Masada was his hope to find scrolls there. The chances of finding such scrolls in an intact condition, in an area characterized by a dry climate, were considered pretty good. Still, Yadin was more focused on April 26, 1964, when he told a radio audience that the value of Masada lay in its nationalistic aspect, and thus in its ability to unite and integrate into a common morality different Jewish Israelis. For an emerging nation of immigrants, Masada could serve as an important integrative narrative, linking past, present, and future into one culturally unifying patriotic and national tale.

Some clear conclusions can be drawn from the nineteen interviews with those who were involved in excavating Masada which were conducted for this study:[17] (a) While there was indeed scientific value for the excavations, the most important motivation was national, and in that respect Yadin played a major part. (b) While no one seemed to doubt Shmaria Guttman's important role before 1963 in bringing Masada into public consciousness, only one archaeologist—Kampinski—felt that organizing the excavations was not beyond Guttman's capabilities (a view not expressed by Guttman himself). Yadin had the necessary background and connections (to the Israeli army, to Israeli academic circles, to overseas [mainly British] philanthropists, and to newspapers). His personal and professional prestige, drive, and personality made him ideal for the media. Yadin was extremely charming and a spell-binding lecturer whose organizational talents were unmatched. (c) Several interviewees pointed out that Yadin's original interest in Masada was lukewarm and he required considerable persuasion before embarking on the excavation. His main interest in Masada was undoubtedly patriotic, and his professional interest only secondary. His professional interest focused on the prospect of discovering some new and important scrolls. (d) Until his death, Yadin was effective in blocking any major scientific publication about findings from the excavations. He may have wanted to control all scientific publications concerning Masada, and simply may not have had the time to organize and publish the findings. (e) Yadin may have wanted his popular 1966 books to remain the definitive works on Masada. In fact, only many years after Yadin's death was a series of impressive scientific books on Masada published summarizing the main empirical findings of the excavation. (f) A sixth conclusion touches on careers. Livne (1986, p. 130) implies that taking part in the excavation of Masada constituted a turning point in the careers of the participating archaeologists. Without exception, *all* interviewees denied this, claiming that the most important element in the excavation was the experience of sharing in these dramatic excavations. Almost all of them pointed out that, professionally speaking, the excavations at Hatzor in the north of Israel far surpassed Masada. (g) The scientific merit of Masada resides in the architecture (both Herodian and that of the rebels), the coins, fabrics, and pottery discovered, and the fact that it is a complete site.

Unique to the excavations at Masada were that it was reconstructed as it was excavated, and that so many volunteers were employed in the excavation. There can hardly be any doubt that from the very beginning Yadin wanted to excavate as much of the site as he could,[18] reconstruct the ancient ruins, and make Masada accessible to as many people as possible.

That the nationalistic reasons to excavate Masada in 1963 diluted the scientific reasons is clear. Of all the possible excavation sites in Israel, Masada was not the most important. The main impetus for the excavations was patriotic. Consequently, interesting questions emerge on the financing of the excavations. How much did they cost? Who paid for them and why? In an important sense, answering these questions can provide us with another clue as to the nature of the relationship between archaeology and politics.

As it turns out, it is very difficult now, in the early twenty-first century, to estimate the costs involved in excavating and restoring Masada. We do, however, have access to a few vignettes that reveal the nature of the funding.

Yadin became deeply involved in obtaining the necessary funding. In a 1965 report, he thanks a group of people in England who had become very involved in Masada, the London weekly *Observer*, and especially expresses gratitude to David Astor, then editor of the newspaper. Yadin states that this group of supporters financed the excavations, encouraged him, visited the site, and contributed about half a million Israeli pounds—in 2002 values, about 1.5–2 million U.S. dollars.[19] Thus, much of the money needed came from outside Israel thanks to Yadin's connections and the *Observer*'s support. A few families also provided funding: Miriam and Harry Sacher, Mathilda and Terence Kennedy, and Leonard Wolfson and the Wolfson Foundation.[20] Direct monetary support from within Israel was minimal, but different organizations in Israel contributed either manpower or equipment.

Here is what Yadin (1966) has to say about this:

> The operation of excavating Masada is the result of combined help and cooperation on the part of many thousands, and of many bodies and organizations. First and foremost I would like to mention the decisive contribution of the Israeli army, which built the expedition camp, the stairs going up and down Masada, and the freight elevator. Without this help, it is difficult to imagine that the excavations could be carried out. . . .
>
> The excavation was implemented under the supervision of the Hebrew University of Jerusalem, the Society for the Exploration of Eretz Israel and Its Antiquities, and the Israeli government Department of Antiquities. The means required for this excavation—nearly one million Israeli Lira, were contributed by Miriam and Harry Sacher, the late Matilda and Terrence Kennedy, the Wolfson Foundation, and the Londonian *Observer*. The money for reconstructing Masada was contributed by many citizens of Israel, by the government of Israel, and by the Rothschild family. The work is not completed, and much more money will be required to finish the job. (p. 2)

There were also individual contributions: composer Igor Stravinsky, for example, donated the U.S. $15,000 he received for drafting his *Abraham and Yitzhak* and all the income derived from the premiere performance of that work in Caesaria went toward the restoration of Masada —the hefty sum of a quarter million Israeli lira.[21]

The British *Observer* was instrumental in the Masada excavations both by encouraging volunteers to join and by providing financial assistance. Here is what Yadin told the Israeli radio in October 1963:

> Most of the money for this expedition, for the six months work, was contributed by contributors from Great Britain. A third or actually 40 percent of the money was given by the Wolfson foundation, another 40 percent was given together by Mrs. Harry Sacher and Mrs. Tilly Kennedy, who are sisters, and quite a considerable part was given also by the *Observer*.

In response to my query regarding why the London *Observer* would take any interest in excavating Masada, David Astor, who had been editor of the *Observer* at the time of the excavations, wrote to me on May 31, 1995:

> In my time, "The Observer" was a paper that took a close interest in Middle Eastern affairs, including the fate of Israel. A member of our staff introduced the late Professor Yadin to us. He had already obtained a large part of the finance required for his excavations of Masada from a well-

> known Zionist. His proposal to us was that we should have the exclusive rights of publishing news of the excavations, giving regular news of how they were proceeding. In this way it was hoped that young volunteers from amongst our readers would be found who were willing to take part in the excavations: this proved to be successful. There was no request for more than a token financial contribution from us: I cannot remember how much this was, but it was small.
>
> The reason for "The Observer" accepting this invitation was that the prospect of this excavation finding interesting material was good and the reporting of this story would be an attraction to our readers in general.
>
> The only other excavation that "The Observer" has undertaken in my time was of a site in this country where it was thought possible that remains of a wooden palace belonging to King Arthur might be found.

Interestingly, the Israeli Government Press Office photo archive contains photo no. #32550, showing a man and a child tellingly subtitled in English: "Mr. David Astor, sponsor of the excavations, at Masada and his son visiting the lower part of Herod's summer palace on Masada."

Moreover, the *Observer* also helped sponsor a Masada exhibition in London's Royal Festival Hall in 1967.[22]

In December 1964, a large-scale fund-raising campaign called *Sela Metzada* ("the rock of Masada") was launched. Thousands of youngsters in grades 8 to 10 were recruited from schools and youth movements to visit hundreds of thousands homes in Israel to ask for money to reconstruct Masada.[23] One donation unit of *Sela Metzada* cost 5 Israeli liras, and the goal was to collect a total of 1.5 million Israeli liras.

The campaign received official backing. The president of Israel called on Israelis to donate to *Sela Metzada*, and the call was reinforced by Yadin, who claimed that Masada would become a national pilgrimage site (*Ha'aretz*). The campaign was launched on November 27, 1964, on Masada. Teddy Kolek, then general director of the prime minister's office and later mayor of Jerusalem, sold one *Sela Metzada* unit to each participant in the ceremony (*Ha'aretz*). Throughout December 1964, thousands of Israeli teens collected donations from thousands more Israeli residents. The campaign is instructive not only because it must have helped raise money, but also because it involved the entire nation in a large-scale effort in support of Masada.

The Israeli army provided the manpower for the dig. Israeli army headquarters viewed the Masada excavation as an "educational enterprise" (Yadin 1965, p. 5). Senior government ministers viewed the excavations in much the same manner. Yadin's impeccable reputation and his infectious zeal and conviction most certainly were crucial factors. Almost all the archaeologists we interviewed pointed out that it is doubtful whether Masada could have been excavated if Yadin had not headed the effort.

3. David Astor and his son visit Masada. Picture taken on the lower level of the northern palace on April 1, 1965. (Courtesy of the Government Press Office, State of Israel)

The Israeli army, which had a permanent representative in the excavators' camp, built and maintained the camp, the stairs to the mountain and to the northern palace, the freight elevator, and more.

Yadin's archaeological expedition initially encountered severe problems with the water supply to Masada, which consisted of truckloads of water that was pumped to the top of the mountain, so Yadin approached Minister of Agriculture Moshe Dayan, an enthusiastic amateur archaeologist himself, and also a former IDF chief of staff, and asked him to intervene and help solve the water problem. Yadin reportedly threatened to abandon the excavations unless a regular and plentiful supply of water was made available. Dayan used his position to persuade Israel's water corporation, Mekorot, to install a special pipe line 7.5 kilometers long to Masada to establish a reliable and continuous supply of water.[24]

The Solel Boneh construction company donated the huts in the camp. The Dead Sea company and the Kaiser Illin car factory contributed mechanical equipment. The Jewish Agency, Youth Aliyah, and the Ministry of Health supplied blankets. Other firms contributed paper, a radio, and other items.

Another major effort (managed by Yadin's wife, Carmella) was the continuous influx of volunteers from abroad. The *Observer* was certainly effective in spreading the word about the excavations and encouraging volunteers, who came from thirty-three different countries. An average of two hundred people were on Masada at any given time. Of those, fifty to eighty were volunteers from Israel and abroad, thirty were military personnel, forty to fifty were Israeli youngsters, and the rest were staff.

The volunteers kept changing every two weeks or so, a rate of turnover that meant that eventually thousands of Israelis and non-Israelis alike participated in the experience of the excavations and exposure to the Masada tale in the most intimate and direct way.[25] Indeed, many fifty-five- to sixty-five-year-olds in Israel and abroad today can lay claim to having had a share in the excavations as volunteers. The importance Yadin attributed to the volunteers' contribution was so great that he devoted a whole chapter in his book to these volunteers (1966e, pp. 247–52).

NOTES

1. For a review see Livne 1986, pp. 123–28; Yadin 1966e, pp. 231–46; 1970, pp. 374-75.

2. For example, Lankford (1981) documented the major (albeit usually neglected) advances that amateurs have made in astronomy and astrophysics. As I have pointed out, it was the amateurs who were willing to take risks in the early days of the discipline, and to invest their time and resources into something they

believed in. I have shown that a similar process took place in the early days of radio-astronomy (1990, pp. 181–219).

3. See my 1995 book, pp. 71–82.

4. See Yadin 1966e, p. 245; Livne 1986, p. 128. The discoveries and excavations of Shmaria Guttman and Azaria Alon appeared between 1952–54 in a series of papers called "Mefarkei Masada" (literally, "the dismantlers of Masada") which were published in *Mebifnim*, the quarterly journal of the Kibbutz Hameuchad movement (vols. 16 and 17).

5. Yadin 1970, p. 375; see also previous note.

6. My first interview with him, January 1987.

7. Shashar 1987, p. 24; and my January 1987 interview with him.

8. World War II Japanese Human guided suicidal airplane and torpedoes respectively.

9. See Livne 1986, p. 129; Yadin 1970, p. 129; Netzer 1990, pp. 185–86. A report about these excavations was published (in Hebrew) in a 1956 special issue of the quarterly journal *News of the [Israeli] Society for the Exploration of Eretz Israel and Its Antiquities*.

10. Camp A. See Guttman 1964.

11. For more on the paths to and around Masada, see Livne 1990.

12. The following is based on my interview with Guttman in 1987.

13. For a recent, noncritical biography, see Silberman 1993.

14. See *Encyclopaedia Judaica*, vol. 16, pp. 694–96; and Silberman 1993.

15. *Ha'aretz*, March 2, 1955, p. 6.

16. Interview with the author, January 11, 1994.

17. Conducted personally by me and/or by my research assistants, particularly Ms. Iris Wolf.

18. A fact that one interviewee presented as "nonprofessional," pointing out that by excavating almost all of the site, and reconstructing it, little was left for future archaeologists with better and more sophisticated means at their disposal.

19. I am grateful to Mr. Avi Shoshana for providing this formula.

20. See Yadin 1966e, 1970; Yadin and Gottlieb 1969.

21. *Ha'aretz*, August 14, 1964.

22. Personal communication with Prof. Gideon Foerster, March 16, 2001.

23. See, *Ha'aretz*, December 7, 1964, p. 13, and December 16, 1964, p. 11.

24. *Ma'ariv*, November 3, 1963; see also *Hatzofe*, October 22, 1963, p. 3.

25. For a report in English, see Kossoff 1973.

FOUR

THE SOCIAL CONSTRUCTION OF KNOWLEDGE 1

Different Cases

The text of Josephus Flavius provided both a historical narrative of what happened on Masada and a physical description of the site. Thus Yigael Yadin and his staff had a relatively potent and detailed historical base to serve as the interpretative backbone for the findings. They could have made Josephus's historical text interact and converse with their findings and thus give rise to fascinating (and sometimes competing) explanations and interpretations. Such a dialogue could have influenced both the historical narrative and the interpretations of the findings. However, this road was not taken. Instead, they used their findings to buttress the Masada mythical narrative, which was based on a biased and distorted interpretation of Josephus. Clearly, the excavators set out to find archaeological evidence to support the myth, not Josephus's historical narrative. Let there be no doubt, the two most influential persons on the site were Yigael Yadin and Shmaria Guttman, and for both of them the major motivation was national ideology. It was crucially important for them that archaeology corroborate the heroism of the Masada rebels.

Providing scientific credibility for a myth is not an act, it is a process in which myth-favoring interpretations are given to physical evidence by the social construction of scientific knowledge. Unveiling the process of the social construction of scientific knowledge requires that we look at how scientific knowledge is constructed: the actual way scientists work, formulate hypotheses, conduct experiments, justify failures, plan success, and so forth. Fortunately, we have an interesting (albeit incomplete) way of seeing how scientific knowledge was manufactured during the Masada excavations. During the two periods of excavation, the staff held almost daily meetings, usually at 7:15 P.M., in which all the professional staff exchanged views, discussed findings, made plans, and reported on the events of the day. Probably because of Yadin's keen sense of history, most of the daily sessions were taped and later transcribed by his wife, Carmella.[1]

While these transcripts open for us an enchanted portal to a fascinating enterprise, they need to be treated with caution. These daily sessions were not for publication, participants were probably not careful about what they said, they probably never thought that some forty years later their conversations would be used and analyzed for a book like this one; and more than anything else, these transcripts should be thought of as daily diaries. And yet, the enthusiasm, interest, excitement, first hypotheses, debates, on-the-spot reflections, and impressions of the archaeologists are all to be found in them.

The transcripts cover the two periods of the excavations: October 17, 1963, to April 29, 1964—125 sessions, and November 24, 1964, to April 7, 1965—80 sessions, altogether 205 taped sessions. The transcripts are available for reading in the Institute of Archaeology at the Hebrew University, and they provide an unprecedented opportunity to look at archaeologists creating and processing knowledge on a daily basis. Reading these transcripts gives us a very strong sense of observing the dramatic excavations at Masada as they unfolded in 1963–65.

The session transcripts range from three to fifteen typed pages, with significant differences between sessions when Yadin was present and when he was not. Sessions with Yadin are longer and tend to include debates about interpreting the findings. What do these transcripts reveal?

Throughout the transcripts, it is evident that there is continuous interest in coins, naturally enough because coins can be dated and thus provide tangible evidence of time frame, and possibly about the people who were on Masada. For example, in the transcript of October 29, 1963, Yadin frames his references to coins that were found in relation to the Great Revolt as the point of structuring and uses the terms "before" and "after" the Great Revolt.

The transcripts reveal the fondness that so many of the archaeologists have for their work, for example in the use of superlatives regarding the finds. A draining channel for water, for instance, is referred to as "simply a wonder";[2] a bathing house "is wonderful," or "beautifully primitive";[3] a stone is "cute"; a piece of a knife, or of a sword is "a beautiful thing";[4] and a glass bottle is "magnificent."[5] Such terms as *great, awesome, tremendous,* and *beautiful* can be found frequently in the transcripts. True, Shmaria Guttman and Dan Bahat tended to use such superlatives more than others, but it was a question of degree, not principle. It is fit, perhaps, to note also Shmaria Guttman's reaction to a Byzantine artifact: "very miserable."[6] On one occasion discontent was expressed on a Jewish find; on January 8, 1964 (p. 4), the archaeologists found evidence of construction which they felt was clearly made by the Zealots. "A room was found, with a *Tabun* [cooking/baking stove] built by the Zealots in the corner. . . . [Building this *Tabun*] disregarded the wall painting and makes everything in that corner dirty" (p. 7). Undoubtedly, contempt is expressed because smoke from the *Tabun* ruined the wall painting. Another issue which emerges from the transcripts is the archaeologists' amazement at the evident remnants of the fires, quite enormous at some places, which were found almost everywhere on Masada.

The transcripts also reveal humor. The transcript from November 28, 1963 (p. 1), for instance, reveals that while volunteers from the Israeli navy were excavating they found some grape pips and, surprisingly, fish bones as well. This prompted Yadin to remark, "I have already said that when the navy digs, it finds fish." No solution is offered to the riddle of how fish bones found their way to desert-bound Masada. Another transcript from December 1964 reveals that some members of the expedition hoaxed the press by leaking a story that hundreds of cats had been brought to Masada to kill snakes. Yadin asked that such fabrications not be repeated.[7]

Josephus does not describe any battles around Masada, but the mythical version emphasizes a battle as an essential component of the heroic "last stand" narrative. On November 5, 1963, a puzzling find of "sand stones" was reported. Yadin notes that Shmaria Guttman found many such stones, cautioning against making too early an interpretation. However, Yadin does mention one possible interpretation. He states that during the battles parts of the Masada walls were destroyed, and that the rebels took materials from nearby buildings to make repairs, thereby creating the "sand stones." This preliminary interpretation *assumes* that battles indeed took place.

WHO WAS ON MASADA?

Josephus consistently claims that the Masada rebels were Sicarii. With one exception, he does not refer to anyone else on Masada, the one exception being Simon (son of Giora) and his forces. Simon escaped to Masada but the Masada rebels ". . . suspected him, and only permitted him to come with the women he brought with him to the lower part of the fortress, while they dwelt in the upper part of it themselves."[8] The mistrust eventually dissipated and Simon and his forces joined the Sicarii of Masada in raiding the countryside.

As noted, Yadin deliberately and systematically avoided using the term *Sicarii* to describe the rebels on Masada, preferring the term *Zealots* instead. This is completely at odds with Josephus Flavius, who distinguishes between the two groups. Although Yadin does not explain why he preferred *Zealots* over *Sicarii*, it is obvious that *Sicarii* conjures up images of a nasty group of marauders, while *Zealots* is more positively associated with such terms as *freedom fighters* and the more neutral term *rebels*. Yadin's preference is in keeping with his political and ideological views, but scientifically misleading. How did Yadin use the evidence he had to support his assertion that there were *Zealots* on Masada? This exercise is worth following.

One of Yadin's early tactics was to argue that there were *many* groups on Masada; if he could establish this line of argumentation, there would be no need to say that Sicarii were present. Here is Yadin's statement at the daily meeting of November 25, 1963 (p. 2):

> It seems to me that the most natural interpretation is that some of the Qumran people, factions of them—in fact escaped to Masada. . . . We know that different and new groups were always convening in Masada. Once it was Bar-Giora [Simon—N.B.Y.], once it was [someone else] with his group, and another one with his group.

To begin with, Josephus does not mention any type of "different and new groups" meeting in Masada. On what, then, does Yadin base his argument?[9] Lacking any textual evidence, such an argument needs to be grounded in some physical archaeological findings. Were there such findings?

Yadin here may be referring to a small scroll fragment found in one of the casemates in Masada which he identified as being of Essene origin. The scroll fragment was actually found in one of the rooms in the northwestern side of the casemate wall (locus 1039, just south of the synagogue structure), in the southeastern corner of the room. The transcript of December 2, 1963 (p. 1), identifies the text as similar to the texts of the Essenes in Qumran.[10] Yadin realized that the line of writing on the scroll was identical to the text of one of the scrolls which were discovered in Qumran and which detail "songs of the Sabbath sacrifices." The text was no doubt attributed to the Qumran sect, identified by many scholars as the Essenes (Yadin 1966e, pp. 172–73). Indeed, there were Essenes in Qumran (not too far from Masada), and Yadin may have been tempted to conclude that the presence of this scroll on Masada may be taken as an indication that there were Essenes on Masada as well. In fact Yadin wrote that a "minority of scholars have long suggested that the Qumran sect should be identified with the Sicarii Zealots, the very Zealots that occupied Masada" (1966e, p. 173); and

> It seems to me that the discovery of this scroll serves as proof indeed that the Essenes also participated in the great revolt against the Romans. . . . It is . . . likely that a considerable number of Essenes also joined the rebellion. And after the country had been destroyed and Masada remained the sole stronghold and outpost in the war against the Romans, it is likely that all who had fought together and survived found shelter there, among them

> also the Essene participants. This, it seems to me explains the presence of the Qumranic sectarian scroll in Masada. (1966e, p. 174)

By making this proposal, Yadin achieves two important goals. First, he supports the claim that the Great Revolt was not the act of a small, fanatic and irresponsible group of Jews, but that active participants in the Great Revolt came from all walks of life and that the revolt reflected popular feeling. This interpretation contradicts Josephus's version that the revolt was led by a small group of fanatics.[11] Moreover, scholars concur that the Essenes were a small sect of pacifists. To claim that these peace-lovers took to arms against the Romans is no easy statement.

Second, Yadin systematically tries to avoid Josephus's claim that the rebels on Masada were the infamous Sicarii. "Proof" that pacifist Essenes were also to be found on Masada, possibly in large numbers, helps discredit the idea that the morally questionable Sicarii were there. However, although suggesting that there were Essenes in large numbers on Masada is an interesting and important speculation, this strange hypothesis receives absolutely no substantiation from Josephus.

Of course, there is another, more plausible explanation for the presence of the Essene scrolls on Masada, but one that Yadin prefers to conceal. We know that the rebels of Masada raided nearby Jewish settlements, the best-documented raid being that on Ein Gedi. Josephus states that in that raid, just prior to the Jewish holiday of Passover, the Sicarii from Masada murdered some seven hundred women and children in Ein Gedi and took the food supplies of the settlement to Masada. If the Sicarii also raided an Essene settlement, or if there was an Essene settlement in or near Ein Gedi, it is possible that the marauding Sicarii took some scrolls with them. The presence on Masada of a scroll with an Essene text can thus be attributed not to the questionable presence of Essenes on Masada, but to the pillaging of the Sicarii. This interpretation, however, is not conducive to the general line of argument Yadin wanted to develop—that there were many different groups on Masada, thereby neutralizing Josephus's assertion.

Indeed, in 1998 a Hebrew University archaeologist, Yizhar Hirschfeld, who headed the archaeological excavations of Ein Gedi, reported that his team had found remnants of a simple village near Ein Gedi which they felt was an Essene settlement. They found the village on the upper part of a cliff, 200 meters above the Dead Sea level, about 500 meters from the site of the ancient Jewish settlement of Ein Gedi, which dates to the period of the Second Temple (Sheri 1998c; Kav Pnim 1998).[12] Moreover, Josephus knew the Essenes fairly well, and probably spent some time among them (see Hadas-Lebel 1993, pp. 27–33). Had there been a major element of Essenes on Masada, Josephus's failure to even mention them would require some explanation.

FIRE IN THE STORES

Josephus "quotes" Elazar Ben-Yair's entreaties to suicide, including an admonition that before they kill one another, they

> destroy our money and the fortress by fire; for I am well assured that this will be a great grief to the Romans, that they shall not be able to seize upon our bodies, and shall fail of our wealth too: and let us spare nothing but our provisions; for they will be a testimonial when we are dead that we were not subdued for want of necessaries; but that, according to our original resolution, we have preferred death before slavery.[13]

The implication is that the food stores are not to be destroyed, but when the archaeologists excavated the stores on Masada, they found clear evidence of a great fire there. In fact, the transcript of the session of January 6, 1965, reveals that ashes 40 centimeters deep were found in the stores. This obvious contradiction did not evoke any discussion during the meeting in which it was first mentioned.[14] But while the transcripts of the daily sessions reveal nothing, Yadin had developed a neat interpretation for this puzzling physical evidence already in 1965, and repeated it in a way which may be viewed as keeping Josephus's version intact:

> The fact that we found storerooms . . . which were broken and burned suggests a contradiction to the words of Josephus. But our discovery of empty and unfired storerooms perhaps explains his report, or the report that was transmitted to him, in this way: in order to achieve their purpose, the Zealots did not need to leave *all* their stores of food to the Romans. It was enough for them to leave one or two rooms with untouched victuals to show that they had not died through lack of food. (1966e, p. 95)

This sophistry can, indeed, explain why some stores were destroyed and others not. True, this is not what Josephus writes, but it is an elegant explanation nevertheless. Indeed, this text gives evidence that when Yadin wanted to, he could be very sensitive to the variety of possible explanations for any particular discovery. Let one add that it is puzzling why Ben-Yair felt that he had to persuade the Romans that his people did not die of starvation in the first place.

According to Josephus in the passage quoted above,[15] when Elazar Ben-Yair addressed his people, he instructed them to destroy their money and the fortress by fire. Josephus added (7.9.1, p. 603) that after Ben-Yair's speeches, the rebels "made haste to do the work," and that when the last man alive "perceived that they were all slain, he set fire to the palace" and then killed himself. Indeed, Josephus writes that before killing one another "they . . . laid all they had in a heap, and set fire to it." This description implies that the rebels collected all their material belongings, except the food, and destroyed them, as suggested by Ben-Yair's speech. Then, Josephus states, the last man alive set the "palace" on fire.

Masada has at least two structures which qualify for the term "palace"—the western palace (not mentioned by Josephus) and the northern palace. It is entirely unclear which is the palace that was set on fire.[16] This description also implies that one could expect to find signs of one large fire on Masada where all the belongings of all the families had been placed. However, different interpretations, including Yadin's, raised the possibility of more than one fire, in fact many, as each family set its own possessions ablaze. Thus, the issues of one big fire versus many small ones, the burnt "palace," possible collections of material goods in one (or many) heap(s) can all help decipher and clarify these inconclusive points in Josephus's description.

It is interesting to see how these problematic issues were dealt with by Yadin. The transcripts of the daily activities do not reveal puzzlement. On November 6, 1963, the discussion focuses on the findings in the rooms. Yadin states that "items" were found in the rooms in either one corner or in an area comprising one-third of the room. This could be the subject of several interpretations (considering the time that had passed and the fact that, after the conquest of Masada, others lived there as well), but Yadin insisted that: "It seems that at a certain stage, it is as if all this [the "items"] was concentrated, at the stage of life [that is, when the people were still living]. I hope that in the other casemates . . ." (p. 4). Yadin is evidently structuring an expectation that those "items" in the casemate wall rooms (where the rebels lived) will be found to be concentrated in one location. Add fire to this, and a particular interpretation of Josephus is both structured and empirically supported. Thus on December 11, 1963, Yadin discusses a fire stratum found in Masada as if it were "the final fire." On December 17, 1963 (p. 5), he tried to explain the existence of two heaps of the remains of goods by stating that "I have now a certain feeling that these two heaps can only be explained in one way: that here, deliberately, [things] were collected, and of course wooden tools etc. in two heaps in the backyard—and were set on fire." On March 9, 1965, he said about a heap of ashes,[17] "Maybe this is an illustration of a pile of burnt belongings, which the Zealots burnt in their last night" (p. 6). These statements obviously contradict what could be interpreted as Josephus's description of one concentrated heap of belongings which was set on fire, but are evidently supportive of Yadin's interpretation.

Yadin notes (1966e, p. 144) that the unique casemate wall surrounding Masada had 110 rooms inside the wall and towers. Based on the physical evidence, the archaeologists concluded that the rebels lived in those rooms. Yadin then states,

> There were rooms... which at first glance had not been burnt, but we would find in a corner a heap of spent embers containing the remains of clothing, sandals, domestic utensils and cosmetic items, which told the poignant story of how, perhaps only minutes before the end, each family had collected together its humble belongings and set them on fire. This also is how Josephus describes what happened. These small heaps of embers were perhaps the sights that moved us most during our excavations. (p. 154)

Yadin's statement that there were rooms that had not been burned (with heaps of "items" in them) is not particularly congruent with the general fire theory (unless they were unoccupied, which would then require an explanation for the heaps). Moreover, Yadin explicitly states, "[T]he dwelling rooms of the Zealots within the casemate wall had for the most part not been fired.... We found many of their domestic vessels strewn about the floors" (1966e, p. 146), obviously contradicting the previous statement cited above. Yet Yadin finds it difficult to distance himself from the theory that each rebel family burned its belongings in its own dwelling place. Thus the transcript of the January 5, 1965, session reflects a discussion about findings in locus 185 and bears witness to Yadin's statement that "the fire which exists on the floor, so it seems, is the usual fire of a Zealot locus" (p. 1). Again, please note his use of "usual fire" supporting his interpretation, and the 1966e (p. 146) statement that most Zealot dwellings were *not* burned. Also, it is not at all clear in how many rooms these heaps were found or in what arrangement. Most important, what Yadin describes is most certainly not what Josephus describes, as Yadin claims above, but rather Yadin's *interpretation* of Josephus. His assertion is fascinating. Here we have Yadin saying that something is "as Josephus says," while in fact this is most definitely *not* what Josephus says. This type of blatant falsification of Josephus appears more than once in Yadin's work.

Finally, while finding those heaps must have excited the archaeologists, the transcripts and interviews certainly do not support Yadin's dramatic claim that the heaps they found were "perhaps the sights that moved us most during our excavations" (p. 154).

Establishing and substantiating the Jewish identity of the rebels on Masada was an important issue, one which recurred in different sessions. It was raised as early as November 17 and 21, 1963 (in the first month of the excavations). Moreover, especially at the beginning of the dig, Yadin tended to get into discussions on the Jewish issues. For example, the transcript of October 30, 1963 (p. 2), reveals that remnants of cloth had been found. The tendency was to conclude that these were remnants of a *tallith*, a Jewish ritual prayer dress. Yadin used the opportunity to deliver a speech in which he compared this cloth—supposedly a *tallith*—to others found earlier in the Nachal Chever caves.

There were, however, some obvious Jewish artifacts whose presence on Masada could help settle this issue, specifically, animal horns, a *mikve* (ritual bath) and, of course, a synagogue. On February 6, 1964 (and again on February 10), the discovery of deer horns on Masada attracted much attention in the daily sessions. Yadin's interpretation for what was, prima facie, a strange discovery was that they might have been there to make *shofarot*, that is, ritual horns blown on certain Jewish holidays or occasions.

THE SOUTHERN *MIKVE*

On February 10, 1964, Yadin discussed a strange structure in the southeastern part of Masada's casemate wall (locus 1197). The odd structure had pools and conduits and generally gave the appearance of being intended for bathing. But the structure of this bathing room did not quite fit what the archaeologists knew about baths. Yadin suggested that it might have been "a Jewish version of a *mikve*." Jewish law specifies how such a structure should be constructed and when and who should immerse in it. On February 11, 1964, a group of Orthodox rabbis visited Masada; the transcripts do not reveal how they got there, but Yadin's 1966e account (p. 166) states that, after the press reported that a *mikve* had been found on Masada, the rabbis expressed their desire to visit. Rabbi Muntzberg was presented as the Israeli expert on the Jewish ritual laws concerning the *mikve*. Yadin showed them what looked like the southern *mikve*. Now, according to Jewish law, a ritual bath must be at least partially filled with rain water (and not only with water brought in jugs). The structure of a genuine *mikve* would have to reflect some sort of way to lead rain water into the *mikve*. Yadin indeed commented that "There is a conduit which goes through the entry . . . and it is obvious that its function was to lead rain water from the outside" (February 11, 1964, p. 1). Apparently, the structure was measured and its general dimensions supported the hypothesis that the structure was a *mikve*. Together with Yadin's persuasiveness, the visitors concluded that the structure in the south was indeed a *mikve*. However, it seemed too low in height, but it did not take Yadin long to suggest a solution for this problem too, and that was that the person coming to be immersed had to do it "like a fish," i.e., lying down.

The religious-political implication of this discovery did not escape the sharp eye of *Yediot Aharonot*'s reporter Menachem Barash. His February 17, 1964, article began by stating that:

> The fighters and heroes of Masada were observant Jews, keepers of the TORAH and the religious commandments, careful to fulfill the lightest and severest of these commandments. They made sure that even during

4. Remains of the Mikve found in the southern wall. (From: Joseph Aviram, Gideon Foerster, and Ehud Netzer, eds., *MASADA III: The Yigael Yadin Excavations 1963–1965*. Final Report, volume written by Ehud Netzer [Jerusalem: Israel Exploration Society and the Hebrew University of Jerusalem, 1991], p. 508)

> the days of stress and siege, they would have a purifying *mikve* in which they could immerse when necessary and observe the religious commandments of purity in all their detail. (p. 5)

The cultural meaning of this statement cannot, and should not, be overlooked. Yadin and the other archaeologists were secular Jewish Zionists, at odds with Orthodox Judaism. Adopting the Masada rebels as symbolic heroic figures for secular Judaism, and discovering that these rebels may have been observant Jews, certainly creates a strong sense of sardonic historical irony.

Once it was decided that the structure in question was a *mikve*, the "strangeness" of the structure disappeared. The system of getting water into that structure became "meaningful" and was then described as "interesting" and "deciphered." The next question was whether the Masada rebels had built it. Yadin does not hesitate to state (February 11, 1964, p. 2) that if "this is not a *mikve* of the Zealots—then it is Herodian." The problem is that it is difficult to conceptualize Herod as an observant Jew, and Yadin indeed adds that this *mikve* was not planned together with the rest of the palace but was added later, proposing that the *mikve* was built for Herod's Jewish guests. A difficulty arose when the rest of the archaeologists present during the discussion did not accept this interpretation, and a harsh and protracted debate ensued. Yadin was obviously not very successful in persuading the other archaeologists that what they had found was a bona fide *mikve*. He was eventually exasperated and tried to stop the argument, but to no avail. Only after two attempts did the debate subside. Yadin summarized this debate by admitting that there were severe difficulties in accepting the interpretation that the structure in the south was a bona fide *mikve*: "it is not entirely clear that this is a *mikve*, and who says that then they bathed like [we do] today?" (p. 5).

The structure of this argument is fascinating. It is worth analyzing Yadin's attempts to develop an explanation that would "make" that structure a "Jewish ritual bath." First, the archaeologists found a strange structure in the southern part of Masada. How could it be explained? Yadin thought it was a Jewish *mikve*. How does one support this hypothesis? There were a few obstacles along the way. First, the size was not quite right. Solution: the bather immersed himself "like fish." Second, a team of Jewish religious experts was brought to Masada. After persuasion, their verdict was secured that the structure was a *mikve*. Third, it did not make much sense that King Herod used a *mikve*. Solution: he built it for his guests. Finally, when the argument became too tough, a hard-pressed Yadin suggested that bathing customs in 70 C.E. were different from those in 1964, meaning that the strange structure could reflect different customs (not realizing, of course, that this argument invalidates the verdict of the religious experts).

On February 16, 1964, a pool for the collection of rain water was found. This, Yadin insisted, solidified the interpretation of the structure as a *mikve*. One should note that the visit of the rabbis preceded this find.

How was this problematic find reflected in the publications? Yadin's first report was in 1965, and in it (pp. 102–103) he stated that the structure found in the southeast part of the casemate wall was indeed a *mikve*. He added that the structure had been examined by Rabbi David Muntzberg and IDF Chief Rabbi Shlomo Goren and that their examination proved that the *mikve* had been built in accordance with Jewish law. Not a word was said about the debate or the doubts and speculations. Yadin's 1966 book (1966e, pp. 164–67) goes even further, totally ignoring the questions of who built the *mikve* and why, as well as the problem of its size. Moreover, in complete contradiction to the daily transcripts and the 1965 report, Yadin's 1966e book reports that the rabbis were tremendously enthusiastic and that they "had been deeply stirred by what apparently was a very humble structure, though, admittedly, dramatically sited within a wall at the edge of a steep escarpment. This *mikve* meant more to them than anything else on Masada" (1966e, p. 166). Absolutely nothing of this sort is mentioned in any of the previous reports. And was the *mikve* structure really more important to the rabbis than the synagogue found on Masada? In any event, all the hesitations and questions raised in the transcripts disappear from Yadin's later reports. Stranger yet is the fact that while Yadin's 1965 report quotes Rabbi Goren as supporting the idea that the structure was a *mikve*, this piece of information does not appear in the transcripts. The missing evidence of Goren's visit to Masada, and his opinion regarding the *mikve*, are in the daily *Ma'ariv* of February 16, 1964.

Yadin's 1970 account (p. 384) repeats his conviction that the structure identified as locus 1197 in the southern part of the casemate was used as a *mikve* (another *mikve*-like structure was uncovered in the northern part of Masada).

Finally, Netzer's summary of the findings on Masada discusses locus 1197 under the heading of "southern *mikve*" (1991, pp. 507–10). Although he uses the term *mikve*, he is less certain than Yadin and concludes that the structure was "most probably used as a *mikve*" (p. 507).

THE SYNAGOGUE

The transcripts of the November 6, 1963, session (p. 6) reveal that the archaeologists raised the possibility that a structure in the casemate's western part (locus 1042) could have been a synagogue. This is important because a synagogue on Masada could have significant implications for the identity of the inhabitants, their lifestyle, and the type of Judaism they practiced. However, the transcripts reveal that while the possibility was discussed, Yadin expressed extreme caution and wanted solid and definite evidence. His caution virtually evaporated, however, when it came to the media. On November 10, 1963, the front page of *Yediot Aharonot* read, "An ancient synagogue found in Masada," adding that "it seems that the high point . . . is the discovery that excited even the most reserved of archaeologists, although it has not yet won official approval because the excavations are not completed. Even if we use Yadin's careful language, we can already establish that the most ancient synagogue in Israel, a remnant from the Second Temple period and which was used by the warriors, was discovered on Masada." On the same date, *Hamodia*, an Ultra-Orthodox Jewish newspaper, also reported on the possible discovery of a synagogue on Masada. The other major newspaper at the time was *Ma'ariv*, which had an agreement with Yadin for publishing discoveries from Masada. *Ma'ariv*'s report on the same date does not hide the fact that "the most significant" discovery in Masada was that of a structure that may have been a synagogue. How-

5. Remains of the synagogue on Masada's west side. (From: Joseph Aviram, Gideon Foerster, and Ehud Netzer, eds., *MASADA III: The Yigael Yadin Excavations 1963-1965. Final Report*, volume written by Ehud Netzer [Jerusalem: Israel Exploration Society and the Hebrew University of Jerusalem, 1991], p. 404)

ever, one cannot fail to notice that the report is phrased in much more cautious language than the one which appeared in *Yediot Aharonot*.

The issue of the synagogue came up again on November 11, 1963, when Shmaria Guttman was willing to risk a stronger statement. Yadin refused to cave in, again demanding more caution. But a month later, on December 11, 1963, Guttman felt comfortable talking openly about the synagogue, as if it were obvious that that was indeed what the structure was. But the discussion heated up again about a year later, and a great deal of time and energy was devoted to the synagogue issue in the daily sessions of November 29 and December 1, 4, 6, 7, and 9, 1964.

December 22, 1964, witnessed a dramatic find. In locus 1043 (adjacent to locus 1042, which is the synagogue) underneath the floor, Shmaria Guttman and Ehud Netzer found a scroll containing passages from Deuteronomy.[18] At the daily meeting this discovery was hailed as "the most important from the point of view of scrolls" (other portions of scrolls were found in Masada). Much discussion was devoted to this discovery and its possible meaning. The last meeting at which the synagogue was discussed was January 3, 1965, when the synagogue was compared to other synagogues in Capernaum Korazim in northern Israel, at the time when the archaeologists were excavating locus 113, where many ostraca were found, including one on which the name Ben-Yair was inscribed.

Thus the synagogue constituted an important issue. How was it reflected in later publications?

Yadin's 1965 preliminary report headlines the word "synagogue" with a question mark (pp. 87–89), a clear indication of Yadin's uncertainty about the identity of this structure as a synagogue. Support for the idea that it was a synagogue was based on the following considerations: the place was evidently constructed to house an assembly of people; parts of scrolls were discovered in its vicinity, as were silver coins; and its rear is directed toward Jerusalem. But Yadin did not have any plans of synagogues during the first century. He was careful in stating that if locus 1042 was indeed a synagogue, it was the oldest known synagogue, and the only one known from Second Temple times.[19]

By 1966 all uncertainty had vanished (Yadin 1966e, pp. 181–91). What helped Yadin reach his conclusions were the facts that the entrance to the locus faced east, and the discovery of ostraca,[20] one with the inscription "Priestly tithe" and another one with the name "Hezekiah." The most decisive fact, however, was the discovery of scrolls with texts from the Ezekiel and Deuteronomy in a pit which seemed to serve as a *geniza*—a burial chamber customarily used by Orthodox Jews for no-longer-usable documents written in the holy language, Hebrew. Thus Yadin became convinced that they had indeed found a synagogue. In 1970 (pp. 384–86) he repeated this conviction.

Finally, Netzer (1991, pp. 402–403) seems to have no doubt that the structure was a synagogue. His conclusion is based on the internal structure of the building, the scroll fragments found beneath the floor of room (locus) 1043 (the *geniza*), and the discoveries around the building. He points out that the rebels introduced substantial structural changes into the original structure.

The synagogue certainly starred both in contemporary reports to the media and in visitors' comments about Masada. For example, Eliezer Livne, who was a major commentator for *Yediot Aharonot*, visited Masada with his family, and his report dated January 3, 1964, focused on the synagogue.

Focus of the Excavation

The major interest of the archaeologists concerned Jewish relics, and especially relics from the period of the Great Revolt of the Jews. The excavators were keen to verify their interpretation of Josephus's narrative. Indeed, Yadin wrote that "the discovery of the remains of the Masada defenders proved to be one of the most impressive experiences of the expedition" (1966e, p. 16). Consequently the transcripts of the daily sessions contain many discussions about the rebels whom Yadin referred to as Zealots, who lived in the casemate wall rooms and introduced architectural changes in these rooms (and others) to suit their needs.

As noted, and contrary to Josephus, Yadin refers to the Masada rebels as Zealots and not as Sicarii. It is fascinating to read in the transcripts how his staff developed a vocabulary which associated the word Zealot with a variety of artifacts and issues; for example, Zealot ceramics, Zealot floor, Zealot wall, Zealot room, Zealot level, Zealot oven, and so forth. The consistent use of these expressions most certainly reinforced the atmosphere, in which it became understood and unquestionable that there had indeed been Zealots and not Sicarii on Masada. By socially constructing such ambience, emphasis was placed on those Jewish rebels. No such expressions were used or developed regarding the Byzantine, Nabatean, or Roman artifacts found on Masada, which brings me to the next issue, that of exclusion.

The flip side of focusing so much archaeological attention on Jewish-related topics was that non-Jewish items were either disregarded or downplayed. The digs on Masada revealed many artifacts from other cultures, most notably the Nabatean and the Byzantine. True, the volume of physical findings there was not overwhelming, but still, the relative disregard of these non-Jewish items in the interpretations was pronounced. Similarly, the Roman army, certainly a major factor in the conquest of Masada, was of little interest to them. This lack of interest is even more salient considering the relatively well-preserved siege system and the Roman military camps.

The Byzantine presence on Masada (hypothesized to be in the fifth and sixth centuries) manifests itself in several areas: the church, the caves which the monks occupied, their coins, and the alterations they made to previously built structures. Concerning the church, in the transcript of the daily session of October 20, 1963 (p. 8), Shmaria Guttman suggests: "About the church . . . the English fellow who worked with me can possibly take care of it—do an accurate plan and cuts." No similar suggestion to farm out any of the work was made regarding any other site on Masada, and it is not difficult to suspect a subtext here: "Let the non-Jew among us excavate the Christian structure." Byzantines are mentioned on only a few other occassions, all of which can be listed here:

- November 7, 1963 (p. 7): Yadin complains about not finding "any Byzantine ceramics."
- November 12, 1963: Transcripts note possible Byzantine changes introduced.
- January 2, 1964: Yadin was puzzled at the discovery of a destroyed mosaic floor in one of Masada's palaces. He felt that the damage had been incurred many years after the fall of Masada and attributed it to some unspecified Byzantine inhabitants, perhaps the monks who lived in Masada, who were looking for "things" on the site. At first Yadin rejected the suggestion that the Roman soldiers might have been to blame (like the Byzantines, they were probably looking for hidden treasure), but after some arguments he abandoned the issue. Yadin's main claim was that this

6. The Byzantine church, looking east. (Photographed by author)

treasure hunt had taken place *after* the building was destroyed, hence initially it seemed reasonable that the Byzantines had caused the damage. This is so interesting because it illustrates how, when Yadin was not too immersed in trying to find supporting evidence for his interpretation of Josephus, he became a more effective scientist and took both evidence and context into account. He was willing to weigh alternative explanations, and to leave the relevant question with more than one answer when the evidence was not conclusive. In this case the archaeologists disclosed evidence of an apparent search that destroyed a mosaic floor. What was the purpose of the search? To find treasure. Who did the searching? Either Roman soldiers or inhabitants from the Byzantine era.

- January 8, 1964: A Byzantine coin is found.
- January 27, 1964, p. 4: Mention is made of Byzantines, but Yadin was preoccupied with trying to find verification for the Jewish "Zealot" presence on Masada.
- February 11, 1964, p. 12: A Byzantine vessel is found.
- February 19, 20, and 24, 1964: The last item in the daily discussions is the church. For the first time, on the twenty-fourth, there is some substantial discussion about the remnants of the church structure.
- March 3, 4, 5, 1964: Very short reports about the church, again, the last item in the daily meetings.
- April 9, 1964: Some discussion of Byzantine pottery and a Byzantine structure built on top of a "Zealot" structure.

• April 4, 1964: The excavation at locus 111, which is identified as a Byzantine remnant, is completed.

• December 15, 1964: The report of the discovery of a large number of Byzantine pottery shards elicited no remarks; a "Zealot" find, however, spurred a prolonged discussion.

• December 16, 1964: Gideon Foerster reports substantial amounts of Byzantine ceramics, but elicits no discussion about interpretation of the discovery. Another report by Foerster (December 28, 1964) on more Byzantine ceramics proves similarly unproductive.

• January 20, 1965: Mention of the discovery of a Byzantine structure and pottery evokes only sparse comment.

• March 21, 1965: Report of the discovery of "beautiful" Byzantine pottery.

Over all, the obvious conclusion is that the archaeologists were not particularly interested in (or, perhaps, knowledgeable about) either the structure of the Byzantine church on Masada, or the Byzantine coins and ceramics, and this in almost stark contrast to the animated discussions and debates that followed the discovery of coins, ceramics, or structures which were identified with the Zealots.

How were these findings reflected in Yadin's reports? The chapter on Byzantine structures in the 1965 interim report numbered four pages (pp. 111–14) out of a total 133 pages. Some mention of the impact of the Byzantine period on other locations on Masada can be found here and there, and when deemed relevant (e.g., p. 30). In general the Byzantine remains are discussed only in relation to other findings. Questions about who those Christian monks were, when they lived on Masada, and why, remain unanswered. This effect is even more dramatic in Yadin's 1966e book. Out of 256 pages of text, only five are devoted to the Byzantine chapel, and two of those are pictures of the mosaic floor (1966e).

Netzer's (1991) final survey of the structures on Masada devotes some space to an in-depth analysis of the Byzantine church (pp. 361–69). The latest addition to the riddle of the Byzantine period on Masada is Meshorer's (1993, p. 137). He points out that of the coins found on Masada, only five can be attributed to the period during which the Christian monks lived there. He attributes the meager find to the small number of monks.

THE NABATEANS

The Nabatean culture and kingdom seems to date from the sixth–fourth century B.C.E. Originally nomads, the Nabateans occupied mainly the southeastern part of the Jordan river valley (today, the Hashemite Kingdom of Jordan), and effectively disappeared by the seventh century

C.E. At different periods, the kingdom may have expanded to encompass an area extending between Syria and Arabia, from the Euphrates to the Red Sea. The high point of Nabatean prosperity probably occurred between the second century B.C.E. and the second century C.E. The Nabateans established an empire whose expansion and influence was apparently considerable. Eventually they established permanent settlements, became involved in commerce, and developed very impressive methods of desert agriculture (mostly focusing on sophisticated use of flood waters). They left behind virtually no written sources describing their culture, and thus much of their history is shrouded in mystery. Most information regarding them comes from Greek and Roman sources, as well as from inscriptions they left and from the remains of their cities (e.g., Shivta and Avedat in the Israeli Negev, Petra in Jordan). Nabatean skill in architecture and constructions were evidently impressive. Looking at the magnificent rock-cut structures in Petra gives an idea of the grandeur. In the first century B.C.E. and the first century C.E., the Nabatean kings fought the Romans but also helped the Roman army put down the Jewish Great Revolt, assisting Vespasian in the siege of Jerusalem. But Roman gratitude was short-lived, and in 106 the Roman emperor put an end to Nabatean independence and made their southern country a Roman province. Despite this conquest, the Nabateans continued to practice their beliefs until the fourth century, when Byzantine agents began to spread Christianity throughout their culture. After the Arab conquest of the region in the seventh century, Nabatean culture disappeared.[21]

Nabatean artifacts were found in Masada, and quite a few of them. Much like the Byzantine artifacts, they elicited little discussion during the daily sessions, beyond mention of their discovery. The first appearance in the transcripts is January 14, 1964 (p. 7), when notice is given that Nabatean findings were discovered, but with no account of the nature of these findings, the context, or any discussion on the meaning of their discovery. Similarly, subsequent finds of Nabatean coins and ceramics on Masada were reported, but provoked no discussion or debate.

The Nabatean remains on Masada include pottery,[22] inscriptions,[23] unspecified remains,[24] more pottery (bowls),[25] and an ostracon.[26] According to Ya'acov Meshorer (1993, p. 136), fifty-nine Nabatean coins were found on Masada according to the following temporal dispersion:

Number of Coins	Time Period
22	9 B.C.E. to 40 C.E.
35	40 to 70
2	70 to 106

7. Nabatean bowls. (From: Gila Hurvitz, ed., *The Story of Masada: Discoveries from the Excavations*, English edition [Provo, Utah: BYU Studies, 1997], p. 95)

The only discussion about Nabatean coins in the transcripts is on January 29, 1964, when the discovery of a coin led Guttman and Yadin into dialogue about the coin and its possible meaning. Yadin concluded the discussion by stating, "It does not mean a thing" (p. 5).

Indeed, Yadin's 1966e book barely mentions the Nabateans. Page 219 is an illustration of a fragment of a Nabatean bowl and on p. 178 Yadin states that they found "beautiful Nabatean vessels which enabled us to determine their exact date," but no explanation is provided of how. His 1965 interim report contains even less on the Nabatean findings.

The discovery of Nabatean artifacts on Masada is fascinating, and could be very significant too. What were they doing there? Since the Nabateans were avid traders, can't we at least make some inferences about some ancient commerce in the region from what we know of the Nabateans and of Masada? More intriguing, was the Nabatean role in Masada confined to commerce only? According to Yadin, it most certainly was not.

Yadin's 1966e book suggests that the large quantity of Nabatean pottery discovered in the Roman camps and some buildings on Masada suggests that the Nabateans "constituted part of the auxiliary" Roman forces that took part in the siege and were later left there as a garrison force (p. 220). In 1970 (p. 386) Yadin added that Nabateans may have also been present on Masada during the period of the Great Revolt.

A much more enticing suggestion was made by Avraham Negev, an expert on Nabatean history and culture. In a 1978 public lecture he stated that the Nabateans' rare construction skills and architectural knowledge were in high demand. His hypothesis was that they "built Masada" (i.e., either helped Herod plan and even build it, or were involved in the pre-Herodian construction of the fortress).[27] If so, this has fascinating implications for the type and quality of contacts among Nabateans, Jews, and Herod.[28]

THE ROMAN MILITARY CAMPAIGN

Part of Yadin's mythical interpretation of Josephus emphasized that the Roman military move against Masada and the siege around the fortress were uniquely difficult and protracted. Yadin's version constructs a huge Roman army against a few defenders. The Roman army is portrayed as being engaged in an arduous military, logistical, and engineering effort aimed at quashing those few heroic defenders of Masada. Here is how Yadin describes it:

> In 72 A.D. Flavius Silva, the Roman governor, resolved to crush this outpost of resistance [Masada]. He marched on Masada with his Tenth Legion, its auxiliary troops and thousands of prisoners of war carrying water, timber and provisions across the stretch of barren plateau. . . .
>
> Silva's men prepared for a long siege (1966e, pp. 11–12)

and:

> The powerful effort put into the construction of the siege wall (circumvallation) round Masada . . . arouses our wonder to this day.(1966e, p. 212)

adding that:

> the built camps alone could house almost 9,000 troops, including the legion. But there is no doubt that the entire besieging force was very much larger, probably reaching 15,000 men if we add to the fighting units the thousands of Jewish prisoners who, according to Josephus, were used to bring water and food and apparently also to work on construction. (1966e, p. 218)

Let us examine some of the main elements which Yadin used to construct his version of the unparalleled Roman military campaign against the heroes of Masada.

Josephus does not tell us exactly when the siege on Masada began or how long it lasted. It did *not* begin immediately after the destruction of Jerusalem in 70 C.E. According to Josephus, Herodium and Macherus were first subdued. Then the chief Roman official in the region, Bassus, died and was replaced by Flavius Silva, who decided to crush Masada too, gathered his forces, and only then marched to Masada, where he launched his siege and final attack on the fortress. These processes took time, and consequently most researchers assume that Silva's war against Masada probably began in the middle or end of winter 72–73 C.E. How long was the siege? Josephus[29] says that the collective suicide on Masada took place on the "fifteenth day of the month Xanthicus [Nisan]." Alas, he does not state which year. Most researchers assume that this was 73. Thus, the currently accepted version is that the siege of Masada began in the winter of 72–73 C.E. and ended in the spring of 73, a matter of a few months. Roth's (1995) meticulous and persuasive contribution to this debate is that the siege of Masada probably lasted only about seven weeks.

Yadin's mythical interpretation of Masada could not countenance a short siege. In his book (1966e, p. 11) he states that Jerusalem fell in 70 C.E. and that Masada "held out" as a base for raiding operations for three years. But on the same page he states that Silva's military move against Masada began in 72, implying a one-year siege. Undoubtedly, constructing a prolonged siege magnifies the effort of the Roman army as well as the heroism of the defenders.

The assertion made by Yadin and others would have us believe that the campaign against Masada was unique in terms of military effort, an indication not only of the genuine heroic quality of the rebels, but also of their military and political importance as a threat to Rome. How else are we to explain the tremendous Roman effort? Insignificant rebels could not possibly merit such pointedly intense attention from the mightiest military machine of the time. Remove the "uniqueness" of the Roman military campaign and the purported duration of the siege, and the logic of this argument collapses. Roth's meticulous examination of the duration of the siege (1995) undermines the mythical argument about a protracted one; what about the "uniqueness" of the Roman military effort?

Adolf Schulten, the German scholar who spent an entire month on Masada in 1932, wrote a report which conveys his deep impression from the siege system. However, more modern versions downplay that impression. Roth's work (1995) is one. Another is Shatzman. In a careful and well-argued paper (1993), Israel Shatzman, a historian of the classical period and an expert on the Roman army, examines not only the Roman military campaign against Masada, but also the general military strategies of the Roman military campaign against the Jewish Great Revolt. His conclusions are clear. The logistics of managing a siege in harsh terrain, in terms of supplying food and especially water, were indeed difficult. The size of the Roman army that laid siege to Masada was probably 7,000–8,000 soldiers—about 11 to 22 percent smaller than Yadin's estimate.[30] One reason for the difference is that Yadin must have assumed that units of the Roman army were fully manned; Shatzman knows that this was not the case.

Shatzman estimates that building the circumvallation wall and the eight Roman military camps around Masada took two weeks at the most (p. 117). He points out that the only unique thing about the Roman siege of Masada is that only here are the structures that the Roman army built for the siege so well preserved. Shatzman's main conclusion is that there was nothing unique about the Roman siege of Masada. The Roman army applied well-tested, efficient, standard Roman siege techniques and nothing more. Undoubtedly Shatzman's meticulous work undermines the logic of "uniqueness" attributed by Guttman, Yadin, and others. The interesting fact is that Shatzman did not hide his views. In the early 1980s "I brought different data and explained why this siege—in terms of the Roman effort—was not anything unusual, but could be understood within a routine series of actions taken by the Roman army. Later on, many asked me why I talk like this" (1995, p. 41). One should not ignore Shatzman's note about the criticism he received for stating a view which contradicted the mythical construction of Masada.

Another item which is relevant to this argument concerns the siege ramp which the Romans built. Masada's tactical Achilles' heel appears to be its western side, where a huge natural spur leads from the bottom of the mountain to its top. It was probably used by the builders of Masada as the main entrance to Masada, and it was this natural spur on which the Roman army built its siege ramp. Even today, climbing Masada from the west along this spur takes only a few minutes and involves only a moderate effort.

The Romans focused their main military effort on penetrating and conquering Masada from the west precisely because of that natural spur. Here is what Josephus tells us about it:

> [T]he Roman commander Silva . . . undertook the siege itself, though he found but one single place that would admit of the banks he was to raise; for behind that tower which secured the road that led to the palace, and to the top of the hill from the west, there was a certain eminency of the rock, very broad and very prominent, but three hundred cubits beneath the highest part of Masada; it was called the White Promontory. Accordingly, he got upon that part of the rock, and ordered the army to bring earth; and when they fell to that work with alacrity, an abundance of them together, the bank was raised, and became solid for two hundred cubits in height. Yet was not this bank thought sufficiently high for the use of the engines that were to be set upon it; but still another elevated work of great stones compacted together was raised upon that bank.[31]

Josephus is very clear: the Romans chose the western ascent via the natural geological spur to Masada. But even the natural spur was not high enough for their war machines (e.g., battering rams), so the Romans had to add a top structure. Unquestionably, building that additional structure could not have been either easy or quick even under normal circumstances, and must have been even more difficult under siege conditions. In any event, what is important is that the Roman army did not build the western ascent to Masada from the bottom of the mountain; most of that massive ascent was there before the siege began and probably served as the main road into Masada, and the Romans only added to it. This means that the Roman army's effort in building an elevated platform to be used for its attack on Masada was not a particularly striking one.

Unfortunately, almost all the texts on Masada fail to make this point clear or explicit. The impression one gets from sources[32] is that the Roman army built the entire western ascent to Masada, implying a grueling engineering effort. Indeed, Ben-Dov (1993), quoting other anonymous archaeologists, claims that the entire siege ramp is an artificial structure.

This issue came into focus in 1993, when Israeli geologist Dan Gill published a paper in the prestigious journal *Nature*. The main point of that paper was that "[c]ontrary to the prevailing opinion that the Roman assault ramp at Masada in Israel was entirely man-made, geological observations reveal that it consists mostly of natural bedrock" (p. 569). Based on his geological observations, Gill added that: "These geological observations . . . reveal that the bulk of the ramp consists of natural bedrock which was adapted by the Romans . . . The triangular prism probably represents the remnants of an artificially raised earthwork. Thus, some earthwork was piled up on top of the spur, but based on a reasonable reconstruction of the slope required to haul up the wall-battering siege machines, they would have had no need to raise the spur much higher along most of its length" (p. 570). Gill went on to argue that in the relevant passage of Josephus, his "description is highly exaggerated" because he was not near Masada during the siege and his measurements are grossly inaccurate. Basically, Gill argues that the effort invested by the Roman army in building the siege ramp was minimal and by no means as difficult or impressive as the myth would have it, and that building the siege ramp could be accomplished in a relatively short period of time.

Josephus does mention a natural spur, but he does not refer to any major engineering effort. While our archaeologists were aware of this, Yadin preferred to paraphrase Josephus thus:

> The ramp built as an assault embankment by the Romans on the western slope of Masada, rising towards the Casemate wall just north of its west gate, is undoubtedly one of the most remarkable siege structures of the Roman army which exists in the world today. (1966e, p. 220)

Yadin would have us believe that the structure on the western side of Masada, leading so comfortably (as compared to the eastern "snake path") to the top, was built by the Romans; this is simply incorrect. Moreover, Yadin had no physical evidence available either way regarding the ramp, simply because this issue was never seriously explored by his archaeological expedition. The siege ramp built by the Romans, most of which has since eroded, was *added* on top of the natural geological spur. And contrary to Yadin's carefully constructed and misleading text, Livneh's 1986 book on Masada states plainly and explicitly that the Roman siege ramp "was built on a natural spur that rose . . . to Masada" (p. 82). Even Yadin's book (1966e) directly quotes (p. 220) the passage from Josephus indicating a natural spur, but Yadin's rhetoric in describing the siege ramp could easily lead a naive reader to remain unaware of the spur's significance. Since Yadin never explicitly mentions the spur, our naive reader will almost certainly get the impression that the Roman effort in taking Masada was considerable—which was precisely Yadin's intention. Of course, constructing the siege ramp on top of the spur was no easy feat, but hardly as impressive as building the whole structure on the western side of Masada as Yadin and others would lead us to believe. Here is what Yadin says about the siege ramp itself: "The ramp . . . is undoubtedly one of the most remarkable siege structures of the Roman army which exists in the world today. It is in a good state of preservation" (p. 220). But in fact almost all of the constructed ramp has been eroded, and what a visitor to the site actually sees is mainly the natural spur. By presenting the effort of building that siege ramp as unprecedented, and by not telling the unsuspecting reader explicitly that the Romans did *not* build the entire structure on the western side, the implication Yadin creates is that the Roman effort was indeed enormous. Visiting Masada and looking at the structure certainly magnifies this impression. And why bother fabricating so massive a Roman effort? Because this implies that there must have been something very important on Masada to justify such a titanic effort. If we keep this in mind, the next conundrum becomes more easily resolved.

Gill's paper is puzzling; we can read Josephus Flavius's statement about the existence of a spur on the western side of Masada, on which the Roman Tenth Legion built the siege ramp, so why does Gill seem to assume that it is not mentioned there? My guess is that Gill was influenced by Yadin's book. As we saw earlier, while not explicit, Yadin's books (1966e, pp. 220–21; 1966h, pp. 226–30) suggest strongly that the Romans built the entire structure on the western side of Masada.

In 1994 the siege ramp received more publicity when archaeologist Ehud Netzer published a long piece in *Ha'aretz* about it. In response to a letter by one of the volunteers who had participated in the dig at Masada, Netzer states very clearly: "No one has claimed that the entire ramp was man-made. . . . It is also clear that the engineers of the Roman army, in seeking to erect the siege ramp under particularly difficult circumstances, chose the place where it would be easiest" (1994, p. 7). Netzer declares

8. Aerial picture of the spatial arrangement of the western natural spur on which the "siege ramp" was built. (Courtesy of the Government Press Office, State of Israel)

that he does not disagree with Gill "in principle," but that they do seem to have different opinions about the degree of effort expended by the Roman army. Netzer feels that Gill's conclusions about the size of the natural spur are mistaken and that "it is thus possible that the bedrock is smaller than Gill imagines it to be."

Josephus, Gill, and Netzer seem to concur in principle; that is, they all agree that there was a natural spur leading to Masada on its western side. They differ on the size of the spur and the implications of that size. A small prominence means that the Romans had to make a supreme effort; a large spur means that they didn't.[33]

The mythical tale most certainly conveys the impression that *all* of the slope leading to Masada from the western side was constructed by the Roman army, reinforcing the magnitude of that army's efforts to conquer Masada. Virtually no texts (nor explanations by tour guides) explicitly mention the natural spur or the fact that the Roman army built its siege ramp on top of it (Livneh's 1986 book being a glaring exception). Because the actual size of the original spur (and whether it had been heightened before the Roman siege) is unknown, it is difficult to accurately assess the effort expended by the Roman army in constructing its siege ramp. What is very clear is that the Romans did not build the entire slope on the western side of the mountain.

THE COLUMBARIA

A genuine enigma which aroused much curiosity and speculation, indeed one of the most puzzling structures found on Masada, was the so-called *columbarium*. The evening meetings on January 20 and 24, 1965, were devoted to discussing the discovery of a *columbarium*-like structure on Masada.[34] The main question was whether the small niches in the structure were for pigeons, or were burial sites for ashes or bones. When a small pigeon was brought to Masada, the cells in the *columbarium* proved to be too small, and thus Yadin concluded that the structure was designed to hold the remains of cremations (p. 139). Since this was not a Jewish burial practice, Yadin postulated that this was Herod's arrangement for his own people.[35] In 1995, however, Gideon Foerster meticulously examined the evidence and the possible purposes of the structure, concluding that the weight of evidence indicated that the *columbaria* were indeed dovecots (p. 220).

In this case Yadin was simply mistaken; but in the other cases we have looked at the presentation of findings was warped to accommodate the concept held by Yadin and others of what happened on Masada. We examined the "battle" of Masada, the fire in the stores, the burning of the possessions, the Jewish presence on Masada (horns, *Mikve*, synagogue), the focus on the Jewish remains on Masada and exclusion of non-Jewish elements such as Byzantine remnants and the Nabateans, the Roman military campaign and the duration of the siege, its nature, and the siege ramp. As a neutral comparison, we examined last the columbaria. In all this, it is easy to see a fascinating process in action. The process consisted of emphasizing Jewish artifacts and presence on Masada, downplaying the significance of artifacts which did not fit the archaeologists' mythical concept of Masada. Moreover, so skewed was the interest in these Jewish related artifacts that even such things as the Roman siege system and the Roman military camps (with the potential of yielding some valuable and insightful findings about the Roman army in the first century) were simply ignored.

9. Remnants of the circular structure identified as a columbaria, looking east. (Courtesy of the Government Press Office, State of Israel)

NOTES

1. Personal conversation with Gideon Foerster (and others), December 27, 1994.
2. January 28, 1964.
3. February 24, 1964.
4. February 25, 1964.
5. December 15, 1964.
6. January 28, 1964, p. 3.
7. January 1, 1965, p 1.
8. *Wars of the Jews*, 4.9.3, p. 541.
9. While Josephus does mention that the forces headed by Simon the son of Giora joined the "robbers who had seized upon Masada," he states explicitly that these forces lived in the lower city on Masada. Unfortunately, no one seems to be able to define precisely what that means. The easiest interpretation is that they did not live in the fortress atop Masada, but somewhere down below.
10. See also Yadin 1966e, p. 174.
11. A counterclaim is that it is not always easy to distinguish between the Zealots and the Sicarii and that, for reasons of convenience, both can (and perhaps should) be referred to as Zealots (personal communication, Prof. Gideon Foerster, March 16, 2001). Obviously, and for reasons explained earlier, I disagree with this interpretation.
12. Some archaeologists maintain that Hirschfeld's findings are insufficiently substantiated and hence unacceptable (personal communication, Prof. Gideon Foerster, March 16, 2001).

13. *Wars of the Jews*, 7.8.6, p. 601.

14. Transcripts of the session of December 30, 1964.

15. *War of the Jews*, 7.8.6, p. 601.

16. For more on this issue see Ben-Yehuda 1998.

17. Found in a passage near locus 1137, located in the southeastern part of the casemate wall.

18. See Yadin 1966e, p. 186.

19. This statement was valid in 1965.

20. A piece of pottery which was used as a base for inking short texts.

21. See *Encyclopedia Judaica*, vol. 12, pp. 739–44; and *Encyclopaedia Britannica* for short descriptions. Negev (1965) provides a more comprehensive description.

22. January 16 and December 22, 1964. One was found in a Roman camp on April 1, 1965.

23. February 16 and March 30, 1965.

24. December 4, 1964.

25. December 9 and 23, 1964. One was found in a Roman camp on March 24, 1965.

26. March 22, 1965.

27. See "The Nabateans Were the Builders of Masada" in *Ha'aretz*, March 13, 1978, p. 5 (in Hebrew).

28. Unfortunately, Dr. Negev's severe illness prevented us from conducting an interview with him.

29. *The Wars of the Jews*, 7.9.1, p. 603.

30. Pp. 109, 116. For Yadin's inflated estimate see his 1966e, p. 218.

31. *The Wars of the Jews*, 7.8.5, p. 600.

32. And from the explanations given by most tour guides.

33. Prof. Gideon Foerster informed me that in 1996 Prof. Ehud Netzer and associates excavated two meters deep into the siege ramp somewhere in its midst. They could not find the bedrock, but did find evidence for the ancient beams supporting the ramp. While this find tends not to support Gill's approach, its tentative nature does not warrant a decisive conclusion yet (personal communication, March 16, 2001). It is also possible that an artificially heightened Western ascent to Masada preceded the Roman siege. For a new report about some excavations in the siege ramp, see Doug Nelson, Sara Karz, and Aaron Black, "Excavation of the Roman Siege Ramp at Masada, June–July 1995," The Bible and Interpretation [online], www.bibleinterp.com/articles/Masada_RampExcavation.htm [March 28, 2002]. Some of Gill's recent thoughts can be found in Dan Gill, "It's a Natural: Masada Ramp Was Not a Roman Engineering Miracle," *Biblical Archaeology Review* 27, no. 4 (September/October 2001): 22–31, 56–57.

34. See also Yadin 1966e, pp. 138–39.

35. Yadin 1970, p. 382.

FIVE

THE SOCIAL CONSTRUCTION OF KNOWLEDGE 2

Two In-Depth Case Studies

We have examined several cases illustrating how different professional archaeological findings were molded and understood according to Yadin's interpretation of the events at Masada. Now we shall examine in depth two specific discoveries and their interpretations: the "lots" found in locus 113, and the riddle of the "missing bodies," emphasizing the discovery of different skeletal remains in two distinct locations: locus 8 and loci 2001–2002.

THE FINDINGS AT LOCUS 113—THE "LOTS"

Among the discoveries on Masada, one of the most curious was of ostraca inscribed with names, including "Ben-Yair." Ben-Yair, we should recall, was the name of the last Sicarii commander of Masada. The most tempting explanation is that the ostraca were the lots by which the Sicarii decided who would die first and who would be last. This explanation hinges on Josephus's account of that fateful last night on Masada, in which he states that the Sicarii rebels on Masada

> chose ten men by lot out of them, to slay all the rest; every one of whom laid himself down by his wife and children on the ground, and threw his arms about them, and they offered their necks to the stroke of those who by lot executed that melancholy office; and when these ten had, without fear, slain them all, they made the same rule for casting lots for themselves, that he whose lot it was should first kill the other nine, and after all, should kill himself. Accordingly, all those had courage sufficient to be no way behind one another, in doing or suffering; so, for a conclusion, the nine offered their necks to the executioner, and he who was the last of all, took a view of all the other bodies, lest perchance some or other

> among so many that were slain should want his assistance to be quite dispatched; and when he perceived that they were all slain, he set fire to the palace, and with the great force of his hand ran his sword entirely through himself, and fell down dead near to his own relations.[1]

Relevant in this passage is the account that those last ten rebels on Masada drew lots to decide who would die first and who would be the last to die by killing himself.

Can you imagine the sensation if the archaeologists had found those "lots"? Well, they did—sort of. Or did they? Here is Yadin's version:

> At every archaeological excavation, there is always at least one visitor who, after being shown all the digging sites and the finds, asks: "Well, what was your most important discovery?" This, for me, is a difficult question to answer. The structures, the wall-paintings, the mosaics—all are of great value for a study of Herodian period architecture, the nature of Masada, and the character of King Herod. The coins and the ostraca are of considerable importance for certain paleographic and historical studies. The thousands of pottery sherds and stone vessels, articles of leather and straw, cosmetic vials, jewelry, the ovens and cooking stoves, the ritual baths (*Mikves*), the synagogue, and especially the scrolls—these are invaluable for research into the Jewish archaeology of the Second Temple Period.
>
> If, however, I were pressed to single out one discovery more spectacular than any other, I would point to a find which may not be of the greatest importance from the point of view of pure archaeology, but which certainly, when we came upon it, electrified everyone in Masada who was engaged in the dig, professional archaeologist and lay volunteer alike. This find was in one of the most strategic spots on Masada, close to the gate which leads to the "water path" and near the square between the storehouses and the administration building where all the northern tracks on the summit meet. The debris on this site was being cleared by a group of volunteers—one of whom, incidentally, is an elephant-tamer in civilian life—when they came across eleven, small, strange ostraca, different from any other which had come to light on Masada. Upon each was inscribed a single name, each different from its fellow, though all appeared to have been written by the same hand. The names themselves were also odd, rather like nicknames, as for example "Man from the valley" or *Yoav* ("Joab"). ("Joab" may seem perfectly ordinary, but it was extremely rare during the period of the Second Temple, and it was almost certainly applied to a man who was particularly brave.)
>
> As we examined these ostraca, we were struck by the extraordinary thought: "could it be that we had discovered evidence associated with the death of the very last group of Masada's defenders?" Josephus writes [Yadin quotes Josephus here]. . . . Had we indeed found the very ostraca which had been used in the casting of the lots? We shall never know for

> certain. But the probability is strengthened by the fact that among these eleven inscribed pieces of pottery was one bearing the name "Ben Ya'ir." The inscription of plain "Ben Ya'ir" on Masada at that particular time could have referred to no other than Elazar Ben-Ya'ir. And it also seems possible that this final group were his ten commanders who had been left to the last, after the decision had been wholly carried out, and who had then cast lots amongst themselves. (Yadin 1966e, pp. 195, 197)

The discovery of those ostraca is hailed by Yadin as the single most significant find in Masada, "more spectacular than any other . . . of the greatest importance." If these ostraca were indeed the "lots" used by the last ten rebels, then Yadin's statement is valid. But are they? Probing the details leaves one unsure; Yadin himself admits that "We shall never know for certain." However, one must admit that an ostracon with the name "Ben-Yair" on it, found on Masada, is very suggestive. It is not too difficult to understand why Yadin became so excited. Let us, however, examine the discovery and the history of its presentation more skeptically.

The first thing which we notice is that more than ten ostraca were found—that is, too many. Now let's look at what some experts have to say about the discovery.

Yadin states that the eleven ostraca he refers to as the "lots" were found in a very strategic place in Masada. Not quite; they were found in locus 113, which, from the outline chart of Masada, is revealed to be an elongated room, adjacent to the west side of the large bath house on the northern part of the plateau, close to the storerooms and similar in structure to those storerooms. It is very difficult to imagine 960 people crowding into that elongated room. Moreover, Netzer describes locus 113 (1991, pp. 63–65) as a complicated area to analyze. It was where the archaeologists discovered a large amount of refuse, violent conflagration, some coins, and "236 ostraca bearing letters, sixteen ostraca inscribed *Yehohanan*, five inscribed *Judah*, seven inscribed *Shimeon*, one with a list of names, and a group of twelve bearing names (including "Ben Ya'ir")—the supposed 'lots'" (Netzer, 1991, p. 65—note Netzer's qualification—"the supposed 'lots' "). It is clear from Netzer's detailed and thorough analysis of the debris found in locus 113 that the ostraca were dumped into the room from another location. They were found above the conflagration layer, and by Netzer's count, we have two ostraca too many for the "lots."

Yadin and Naveh (1989, pp. 30–31) and Naveh (1993) also point out that the group of ostraca Yadin refers to numbered twelve, not ten as Josephus stated, or eleven, as Yadin said. The nicknames inscribed on these ostraca were in identical handwriting. Why then, asks Naveh, does the discovery consist of twelve "lots" and not ten? "Yadin solved the problem by not counting in this group one ostracon the inscription on which was

10. The ostracon with the inscription "Ben-Yair" on it (magnified). (From: Gila Hurvitz, ed., *The Story of Masada: Discoveries from the Excavations*. English edition [Provo, Utah: BYU Studies, 1997], p. 106)

'Beni' (because he assumed that it was a failed attempt to inscribe 'Ben Ya'ir'); and the eleventh ostraca Yadin attributed to Elazar Ben-Yair and his ten friends" (1993, p. 89). Naveh goes on to ask whether this particular group of ostraca is different from other ostraca found in Masada. The answer to this question is not clear-cut. Thus while Yadin's interpretation of this particular group of ostraca as the "lots" is interesting, it is an inaccurate interpretation on the basis of Josephus, and technically problematic. Yet Yadin's interpretation, one must hastily add, is nevertheless very neat. Neither Naveh nor Netzer projects the same level of assurance as

Yadin regarding these ostraca and their possible identification as the fateful "lots." On the contrary, Naveh expresses doubts and a very high level of uncertainty whether these twelve ostraca were indeed the "lots."

The excavations in locus 113 were discussed at several meetings. The excavations began on December 28, 1964 (p. 6 of transcript), and the first two days were uneventful. On December 30, reports of the discovery of some ostraca began to appear.[2] On December 31 it was obvious that locus 113 had a rich lode of ostraca. Already then, Danny (probably Bahat)—who was in charge of excavating the locus—pointed out that locus 113 was probably not the origin of the ostraca, but that they had been poured into it from elsewhere.[3] This possibility became a certainty between January 1 and 5, 1965. Reports on locus 113 appear daily in the transcripts, within a very technical context. Then on January 6, 1965, an ostracon with the inscription "Ben Ya'ir" is reported:[4]

> Danny: . . . locus 113—the locus of the ostraca—today 11 ostraca came out, of which 7 are "Yochanan," one ostracon on which "Ben-Ya'ir" is inscribed, on one "Talta," on one "Yoav" and one "sh-k." In fact, we are finished there too. There is nothing more to do there.

Danny continues his very dry and factual report. Not even one of those present at the meeting, including Yadin, reacted to this extraordinary discovery. Only on January 10 did Yadin refer again to this startling discovery (pp. 2–3 of the transcript), commenting that one ostracon was probably a failed attempt to write "Ben" and that "Ben-Ya'ir" was exactly that—"Ben-Ya'ir," plain and simple. In Yadin's terminology, "bli chochmot," meaning in Hebrew "without any tricks." The transcripts of the daily meetings at the time that the discovery of these ostraca was made do not reflect Yadin's 1966e avowal that discovery of these particular ostraca was the single most important and spectacular find in Masada. On the contrary, other discoveries which clearly much less spectacular received decidedly more attention. Moreover, his 1965 interim report (in English and Hebrew) simply ignores the discovery altogether. How are we to explain this? Perhaps simply because it did not seem so spectacular at the time. Perhaps it was discussed extensively, but outside the daily meetings. In any event the transcripts very clearly reveal that when the ostraca were found, no excitement was generated—puzzling indeed, considering Yadin's later assessment.

Yadin mentioned the "lots" again in two other important publications. The *Encyclopedia Judaica*'s entry on Masada[5] was written by him, and on page 1090 he writes, "Eleven small ostraca each inscribed with a single name and all written by the same person may be the lots described by Josephus which the last ten survivors at Masada drew to choose who would kill the other nine and then himself." Yadin also wrote the "Masada" entry for the *Encyclopaedia Hebraica*,[6] where he stated that some ostraca were found on Masada "and the 'lots'—ostraca, on which were inscribed names or nicknames. Maybe these were the lots that the defenders used, at the last stage of the battle, in order to choose 'ten that will slay everyone.' " In 1970 Yadin wrote again that the ostraca were "perhaps the lots of which Yoseph Ben-Matityahu[7] tells . . . and, if so, it turns out that the last defenders of Masada were its commanders, headed by Ben-Yair" (p. 387). In all these statements Yadin was clearly careful in what he wrote. However, this carefulness seems to have evaporated in his most popular and impressive 1966 books. As a comparison, it is interesting to note that when Gideon Foerster (who participated in the 1963–1965 excavations of Masada) wrote the entry for "Masada" in the *Encyclopedia of Zionism and Israel*,[8] he stated that several hundred ostraca were found, but did not even mention the "lots." That was no coincidence.

The Masada excavations were covered fairly extensively in the media, and appropriate mention of this "single most important and spectacular discovery in Masada" could have been made. But if the find was so spectacular, that was certainly not reflected in the media. It did not even merit mention in the *Observer*—and we must recall that this newspaper partly sponsored the excavations and gave other discoveries (scrolls, coins, the synagogue) wide coverage.

On January 31, 1965 (p. 8), *Ha'aretz* reported the discovery of the ostraca very hesitantly, referring to it as "most interesting":

> Professor Yigael Yadin . . . stated in the press conference that the name Ben Ya'ir was found among the names. It had to be assumed that this referred to Elazar Ben-Yair, commander of Masada. Having said that, it was speculated that it was difficult, perhaps impossible to prove that these ten ostraca were used in the final drawing of lots. . . . This particular group of ostraca was found in the most essential place on the mountain—near the northern inner gate leading to the storage area and to the northern palace.

The excavations were to end in April 1965, and as that date approached some summaries appeared in the daily newspapers. On January 31, 1965, Yadin published a partial summary of his findings in *Ma'ariv* (p. 3). He wrote that the excavators found a strange group of ten ostraca inscribed with names:

> But the biggest surprise came from the ostracon on which the name "Ben Yair" was written. This, most probably, refers to the well-known Elazar Ben Yair, commander of the Zealots on Masada. In any event, it appears that all this group consisted of commanders or other dignitaries, maybe . . . the last ten who remained alive and who, according to Yoseph Ben

11. Location of the lots—locus 113 (spot where the "lots" were found). (Photographed by the author)

> Matityahu, used lots to [decide on the] slaughter the rest of the 967 men women and children so that the Romans would not capture them, and then used lots among themselves to decide who will kill the rest of the nine. In any event, this is an appealing interpretation.

Ma'ariv's report dated March 29, 1965, was more definite (p. 8), declaring that Yadin had told reporters that "[e]verything that could be discovered—was discovered, including the ten lots of the last defenders who committed suicide by using lots" (p. 8).

The next public occasion in which Yadin mentioned the "lots" was April 11, 1973, in a speech made atop Masada at a meeting of the members of the Society for the Exploration of Eretz Israel and Its Antiquities, and of the Society for the Protection of Nature:

> From all the findings, the most exciting—even though not necessarily the most important one from the scientific point of view—was the discovery of eleven ostraca . . . on each one of them was an ink written name. . . . Can it be that we have discovered the lots of the last ones on Masada? . . . This question was answered when we read on one of the ostraca the almost legendary name: 'Ben-Yair'! Perhaps we can hypothesize—and this is a logical conclusion—that the last warriors . . . were the commanders of Masada, headed by Ben-Yair. (Yadin 1973, p. 33)

In all the issues of the Ultra-Orthodox *Hamodia* newspaper, only one brief mention is made of this discovery, in its February 1, 1965, issue (p. 3). In a long report focusing on the discovery of two scrolls on Masada, it notes that during the excavations in the northern palace, a group of ostraca were found and that the name "Ben Yair" was inscribed on one of them, the conclusion being that this must be the name of the commander of Masada, Elazar Ben-Yair. The *Hamodia* report goes on to state that these ostraca could be those of the last ten defenders of Masada, and possibly from the high command of Masada, who used lots to decide who would be the last person alive to kill himself. The news of the ostraca take only twenty-five out of a total 145 lines of text. The potential significance of this discovery is not even hinted at.

Like *Hamodia*, all the issues of *Hatzofe*, a National Religious Party newspaper, mention news of the ostraca and the supposed "lots" only once. The January 31, 1965, issue (p. 4) includes a long report on discoveries at Masada, focusing on the synagogue and the scrolls. There, in a paragraph entitled "Regards from Elazar Ben-Yair," mention is made of ten small ostraca, one of which was inscribed with the name Ben Ya'ir. The report states that these ostraca were written in a similar handwriting and that they were probably the lots used by the last commanders of Masada to verify that the decision on the collective suicide would be carried out.

Again, no one reading this report could be impressed with any special importance attributed to the discovery.

So the find in locus 113 was indeed intriguing. Its presentation, however, went through some transformations. Clearly, Yadin was initially puzzled by this highly suggestive discovery, and the interpretation he developed is fascinating. If he could substantiate his theory that these were the lots used by the last rebels on Masada, then he could provide powerful empirical support to the historical narrative of Josephus Flavius. However, there were evident problems with Yadin's interpretation. While careful not to present too assured a version, Yadin explained away the fact that more than ten ostraca were found, that they were not found in a particularly central (or in any way "strategic") location, or one which could possibly hold 960 people for a final collective act of suicide, that they were probably thrown into locus 113 as refuse, and that, at the time it was made, the discovery was not considered the most important find (as he later implied). Moreover, because some skeletal remains were found elsewhere (locus 8), Yadin did not shy away from suggesting that the collective suicide may have actually occurred in a different locality. He never made up his mind which place was the suicide scene. The way in which Yadin represents the discovery in locus 113, especially in his 1966 books, leaves very little doubt about his opinion that these ostraca were indeed the lots, and particularly that the name "Ben Ya'ir" must have referred to Elazar Ben-Yair, the last Sicarii commander of Masada. Hence the archaeological interpretation provided for this discovery by the most authoritative contemporary voice—that of Yadin—helped bring into being a construction which appeared to give unequivocal support to Josephus's narrative. That interpretation, one must hastily add, did not have, and still does not have, strong empirical support. That an ostracon inscribed with a text which suggests the name "Ben-Yair" was found on Masada is exciting and indeed suggestive. But, factually speaking, that is all it is. The precise usage of that ostracon is entirely unclear. In fact, Netzer's latest presentation of locus 113 (1991, p. 65) indeed creates a healthy distance from what he refers to carefully as the "supposed 'lots.' "

THE RIDDLE OF THE MISSING BODIES

One of the unresolved riddles of the excavations of Masada is that of the missing bodies. According to Josephus, 960 people committed collective suicide on top of Masada on that fateful night of "the fifteenth day of the month Xanthicus [Nisan]."[9] Indeed, Yadin retained the hope of finding the remains of the 960 rebels, or at least some of them (1966e, p. 193). Obviously, discovering 960 skeletal remains on Masada would have provided major empirical support for the historical account provided by Josephus.

There are a few plausible answers to what happened to those 960 bodies and why they have not been found. One simple answer is that the Romans threw the bodies over the Masada cliff. Indeed, A. Y. Bror[10] makes a strong argument for this possibility, suggesting that the Romans discarded them by throwing them into the desert. If so, then the possibility of finding anything significant after almost two thousand years is virtually nil. My guess, however, is that this is not what happened. Throwing 960 bodies off the cliff to be eaten by animals and rot in the desert sun is unlikely; the smell and the daily sight of the bodies would not be something desirable. Moreover, Josephus tells us specifically that the Roman soldiers who found the bodies

> wonder[ed] at the courage of their resolution, and at the immovable contempt of death which so great a number of them had shown, when they went through with such an action as that was.[11]

This attitude of respect by the Roman soldiers does not support the hypothesis that the bodies of the rebels were simply, and disrespectfully, thrown over the cliff. Yadin also discarded this possibility for the same reason.[12] The next possibility is that the bodies were burned. In a report by Mordechai Arzielli[13] Yadin is quoted as assuming that the soldiers of the Roman garrison who were left on Masada for more than twenty years burned the skeletons and dispersed the ashes—a possibility indeed, but burning 960 bodies is a major undertaking, requiring burning materials that may have not been available in the desert. However, as the archaeological excavations revealed, there were many strong and intense fires on Masada at the time it was conquered, and the Romans could have—had they acted quickly enough—burned the bodies by throwing them into those high-temperature flames. If they were indeed burned, any hope of finding the remains of those 960 rebels is lost.

The third possibility is that the Romans buried the bodies. The respect shown by the Romans to the rebels and the need to discard them as quickly as possible for sanitary reasons gives some support for the burial hypothesis. Moreover, the large element of Jewish slaves accompanying the Roman army lends support to the idea that there may have been those who wanted to give the rebels a Jewish burial. This third possibility nourishes the expectation of finding remnants of the bodies.

Yadin confirms that they were looking for those "missing skeletons" and writes that

> In our search, we made several exploratory sectional-cuts in places where such finds seemed likely, but without success. It is possible that we may have missed some pit where bodies might have been cast. (1966e, pp. 194–95)

Although finding the skeletal remains is an important issue, the transcripts of the daily meetings reveal no discussions about this topic. It is unclear where those sectional-cuts were made, or why particular places were selected to make them. Yadin states his view that

> on the whole our excavations confirmed our earlier view that the Roman garrison which occupied Masada for several decades after the dramatic event cleared the area of all such human remains. Thus, apart from the twenty-five skeletons found in the cave and possibly[14] the three found in the palace-villa, no physical remains of the last defenders of Masada were left. (1966e, p. 197)

The archaeologists were thus explicitly hoping to find the remains of the 960 suicides. Unfortunately for the archaeologists, and to this day, their hopes were never realized. Some might interpret this as implying that Josephus's account is not valid; but this argument rests on a dangerous assumption: that "no find" means that there was nothing to find.

Nevertheless, the interesting fact is that some skeletal remains were found. Yadin (1966e, p. 193) reports three skeletons found in the lower terrace of the northern palace-villa (in locus 8), and about twenty-five skeletons found in one of the caves at the southern end of the Masada cliff (in loci 2001–2002). A few other skeletons and burial places were also found.[15] These few skeletons most certainly do not resolve the question of what happened to the 960 bodies.

Ironically, not solving the riddle of the missing bodies gave rise to some fascinating processes as the interpretations of these discoveries underwent a major transformation within a period of ten years in a fashion that clearly supported the Masada mythical narrative.

The discovery of skeletons was first mentioned in the transcripts of November 14, 1963 (p. 3), when Amnon (probably Ben-Tor) reported that the bones of a child or infant and those of an adult have been discovered in locus 8, which is in the northeastern part of the lower terrace of the northern palace. This locus is part of a small structural complex to the east of that level of the villa-palace identified by Netzer (1991, p. 167) as "Frigidarium 8." The report adds that a large number of armor scales and arrows, all in good condition, were also found in the locus. The transcripts indicate that the discovery did not generate any debate or significant discussion. The next time this discovery was discussed was November 26, 1963, when the archaeologists considered the remains of the three skeletons. The relevant section of the transcript is:

> Dr. [Nicu] Haas: Three skeletons were found in locus 8. . . . One of a female . . . aged 17–18, and one of a child aged 11–12 . . . the third skeleton . . . is that of a man and his age is between 20–22, also quite young.

> Yadin: It is obvious that the child and woman cannot be mother and son because of the age difference, so if there really was a family here, the man might be the father of the child. . . . In those periods *Ya Habibi*! there is a plus-minus of a year . . . here you make it 23 and there 10 and everything is OK. . . .
>
> The man and the woman can certainly be a couple! But the son is not this woman's. . . . Maybe it is her brother or his.

We next encounter this discovery two months later, on January 17, 1964. Amnon reported that he was continuing to excavate locus 9, but added that while excavating locus 8, he discovered an almost complete skeleton as well as hair, armor scales, a sandal, and an adult skull. Altogether three skeletons were found in locus 8. No discussion followed the dry report. It is important to add that no further discussion of the discovery in locus 8 can be found anywhere in the transcripts.

Nothing in the November 26 discussion could prepare us for what would take place the next ten years. Like others, Yadin was looking for empirical support for the Masada mythical narrative, some tangible proof that would end all doubts about the supposedly heroic acts that took place on Masada. As we move forward in time from 1963, we shall need to remember the discussion which took place on November 26.

Our next stop is 1965, the year Yadin published the interim summary for the first season of excavations of Masada. The document was published in Hebrew by the Israeli Exploration Society. On page 22 Yadin wrote:

> It cannot be stated with certainty that these skeletons are those of the family of that last warrior who . . . took the lives of his family and set the palace on fire . . . but there seems to be no doubt that these skeletons are those of the people of the Great Revolt.

In the English version of the report, the section which includes the information about the discovery in locus 8 does not even mention the skeletons, but in the Hebrew version he seems to be absolutely certain that the skeletons are those of rebels of the Great Revolt. No justification for so strong a statement is offered. But Yadin states that the remains *may* be those of the last rebel left alive (he prefers the word "warrior"), who killed his family, set the palace on fire, and then killed himself. Yadin is very careful in phrasing this statement, but the factual basis for this wild speculation (which is exactly what it is) is simply not there. Yadin also assumes that the palace which Josephus mentions in the context of the collective suicide is the northern palace. What if it occurred elsewhere (e.g., in the western palace not mentioned by Josephus)? If so, then Yadin's claim has no support. By the time the uninformed reader finishes reading this, the careful phrasing which precedes this speculation—"It cannot be stated with certainty"—has evaporated as this incredible speculation is laid out by the man who became *the* authority on Masada. Since Yadin is going to expand this particular speculation to its astonishing climax in 1973, let us go back for a minute to Josephus and recall what he has to say about that last person alive on Masada. Josephus describes how the rebels on Masada took their families' lives, how they

> laid all they had in a heap, and set fire to it. They then chose ten men by lot out of them, to slay the rest; every one of whom laid himself down by his wife and children on the ground, and threw his arms about them, and they offered their necks to the stroke of those who by lot executed that melancholy office; and when these ten had, without fear, slain them all, they made the same rule for casting lots for themselves, that he whose lot it was should first kill the other nine, and after all, should kill himself. . . . So, for a conclusion, the nine offered their necks to the executioner, and he who was the last of all, took a view of all the other bodies, lest perchance some or other among so many that were slain should want his assistance to be quite dispatched; and when he perceived that they were all slain, he set fire to the palace, and with the great force of his hand ran his sword entirely through himself, and fell down dead near to his own relations.[16]

Regardless of Yadin's speculation, his interpretation is not even consistent with the version provided by Josephus. To begin with, the last person alive did not kill his family and then himself; he killed the other nine survivors and then himself. Second, chances that this mass death scene took place in the lower level of the northern palace-villa are very slim. While we do not know exactly where the rebels killed one another, the lower level of the northern palace-villa hardly seems the place. They did not live there; it was far and difficult of access; and it would have been nigh-impossible to assemble 960 people there. The size of the central square is only about 18 × 18 meters. Even if we add the eastern (10 × 6 meters) and western (8 × 3 meters) wings, we are still left with a rather small area that, together with the central area, might measure 408 square meters. In fact, the first team that excavated Masada (Avigad et al. 1957, p. 64) noted that the area of the northern palace is such that "it is difficult to assume that close to a thousand people were there together." Third, the "family" Yadin mentions is not easy to understand, considering the age differences between them.

Our next stop is 1966, the year the Hebrew and English versions of Yadin's popular book on Masada were published. Both books refer to the discovery of the three skeletons in locus 8. There are, however, some differences between the two versions of the book. In the Hebrew version Yadin wrote that they found

> the remains of three skeletons. One skeleton was that of a man in his twenties who was perhaps one of the commanders of Masada. . . . Nearby, on the

> stairs, the skeletal remains of a young woman were discovered. . . . The third skeleton was that of a child. . . . Could it be that we had discovered the bones of . . . [the last] fighter [on Masada] and of his family? (1966h, p. 54)

The English version (1966e, pp. 54, 58) offers the following text:

> We were arrested by a find which is difficult to consider in archaeological terms, for such an experience is not normal in archaeological excavations. Even the veterans and the more cynical among us stood frozen, gazing in awe at what had been uncovered; for as we gazed, we relived the final and most tragic moments of the drama of Masada. Upon the steps leading to the cold-water pool and on the ground nearby were the remains of three skeletons. One was that of a man of about twenty—perhaps one of the commanders of Masada. . . . Not far off, also on the steps, was the skeleton of a young woman. . . . The third skeleton was that of a child. There could be no doubt that what our eyes beheld were the remains of some of the defenders of Masada. . . . [Yadin quotes Josephus's passage on the last person alive on Masada] Could it be that we had discovered the bones of that very fighter and of his kin? This, of course, we can never know for certain.

Now the speculation gets thicker. He is not only the last rebel, but "one of the commanders" of Masada. The November 23, 1963, transcript reveals nothing of the excitement and awe that Yadin refers to. On the contrary, Yadin's comments at that session reveal a healthy amount of humor. Moreover, finding skeletons or bones in an archaeological excavations is certainly not unusual. What makes this particular find unusual are Yadin's ad hoc and later interpretations. But this is not the end. The next time Yadin discussed the discovery in locus 8 in public was in 1970 and 1971. In 1970 (p. 382) Yadin wrote that the skeletons found in locus 8 "are probably the remnants of one of the important commanders of the revolt and his family members." In the *Encyclopaedia Judaica* (1971, vol. 11, p. 1007) he writes about the very same remains:

> The skeletons undoubtedly represent the remains of an important commander of Masada and his family.

Note how the doubts and uncertainties have gone, how Yadin moves from "probably" to "undoubtedly," and how the "important commander" and "his family" have gained entry. Nothing we know of in the form of physical evidence justifies this change.

The most intriguing interpretation of the discovery in locus 8, however, was presented on April 11, 1973, in Yadin's address atop Masada to members of the Society for the Exploration of Eretz Israel and Its Antiquities, and of the Society for the Protection of Nature:

12. Aerial view of the three levels of Masada's northern palace. (Courtesy of the Government Press Office, State of Israel)

13. Hair and sandals. (From: Gila Hurvitz, ed., *The Story of Masada: Discoveries from the Excavations*, English edition [Provo, Utah: BYU Studies, 1997], pp. 9, 20)

> I shall mention the remains of the three fighters that we found in the northern palace: a very important commander, his wife and their child, just like in the description of Josephus Flavius. (Yadin 1973)

So in the April 11, 1973, statement the three skeletons have become a family (father, mother, and child) of warriors, headed by "a very important commander." The 1973 text is much more congruent with, and can be easily interpreted within, the Masada mythical narrative. It was obviously a deliberate falsified interpretation, one that had nothing to do with the facts, and it was meant to make audiences believe in a mythical narrative.

14. Remains of hair and sandal found in locus 8. (From: Joseph Aviuram, Gideon Foerster, and Ehud Netzer, eds., *MASADA III: The Yigael Yadin Excavations 1963-1965. Final Report*, volume written by Ehud Netzer [Jerusalem: Israel Exploration Society and the Hebrew University of Jerusalem, 1991], p. 167)

In 1991 the third volume of the Final Reports of the 1963–1965 excavations was published, written by professor Ehud Netzer. On page 167 Netzer describes locus 8 (which he refers to as "Frigidarium 8"):

> Near the bottom of the pool, in the southwestern corner, were found the remains of a boy aged about 10; beneath him was a large stone covering the skull of a woman aged about 18. Another concentration of human remains was revealed in the southeastern corner, also near the bottom.

To Netzer's scientific credibility we must note how careful and factual he is. And Netzer did participate in the excavations. He does not mention an "important commander" or "family" or "last warrior" or even suggest that these skeletal remains had anything to do with the Sicarii rebels on Masada. No mention is made of the "awe" Yadin described.

Yadin's 1966 version implies that the discovery in locus 8 left the excavators mesmerized. Obviously, telling readers that professional archaeologists were awestruck by the discovery was intended to create a similar awe among the readers and further impress them with both the importance and validity of that discovery. Clearly, that mesmerization was most definitely not what was reflected either in the transcripts or in Netzer's 1991 version. How was this supposedly stunning discovery processed by the media?

Toward the end of a long report in *Ma'ariv* dated November 24, 1963, and written by Yadin himself, eight lines out of 92 were devoted to this discovery: "Here we found some evidence of their [the Zealots'] tragic end. Among more than 400 armor plates, 30 arrows and parts of a dress, we discovered two human skeletons, one of an adult, perhaps a woman, the second of a child. Nearby we found the bones of a woman . . ." (p. 15). That same day *Yediot Aharonot*[17] also has a long report about the discoveries on Masada. It also informs its readers of finding the skeletal remains of a woman and a child, but without any interpretation. A search for more references to this discovery in *Ma'ariv* yielded some later mention in 1965, when the excavations were coming to an end and summaries were issued. On page 3 of *Ma'ariv* from March 28, a report about the missing bodies can be found. The reporter, Tzvi Lavie, states: "On one of the stairs of the northern palace three [skeletons] were found—those of a man, a woman and a child, probably among the last of those committing suicide, and who went down to set the palace on fire, as described in Yoseph Ben-Matityahu's book." Lavie's source must have been Yadin. In *Ha'aretz* of the same date (p. 7), the skeletons found in locus 8 are mentioned as such, with absolutely no interpretation. *Hamodia*'s November 25 issue (p. 3) also summarized the findings from Masada. Among the many discoveries noted is mention of the fact that in the northern palace the excavators found "the skeletons of a child and of an adult . . . and 300 armor plates . . . which probably belonged to a high-ranking Roman officer." *Hatzofe* mentions nothing. Clearly, then, when the discovery in locus 8 was actually made, it most certainly did not create the stir and excitement attributed to it by Yadin in 1966 and thereafter. That later addition was unquestionably a dramatic social construction created by Yadin to support his mythical and deceptive interpretation of Josephus.

The last challenge for Yadin's interpretation of the findings of the bones in locus 8 was raised by Joe Zias.[18] In his 1998 publication he claimed that the skeletal remains were actually of different ages than those originally attributed to them. The skeleton identified as a "child" was actually that of a man aged about forty another skeleton was that of a twenty-two-year-old man, and the third skeleton was of a female some sixteen years old. This, of course, rules out the interpretation of a family of mother-father-child. Zias also points out that determining the gender of skeletal remains which are identified as an eleven-year-old child is not practical. At that age all skeletons appear to be females, because sexual characteristics appear on human skeletons only much later. Also, the skeletal fragments were found in total disarray, and thus it may not be clear whether they in fact belong to three different people. Moreover, examining the discovery in locus 8—skeletal remains of three individuals, a sandal, armor plates and arrows—Zias discounts the interpretation that the lower level of the Northern Palace was used as a burial place. Jews, he states,

> never buried an individual with his or her sandals, nor with armor and arrows which certainly suggests that if this was a cemetery, the three individuals interred here may not have been Jewish . . . but Roman. . . . Being buried with one's weapons is definitely not a Jewish custom. (Zias 1998d, p. 12)

On December 28, 1999, BBC radio channel four broadcast a program on Masada. Interviewed for that program, Zias went beyond his 1998 statements. He told the interviewer (Malcolm Billings) and producer (Hugh Levinson) that when he reexamined the field notes of the excavation, he realized that no skeleton of a woman was actually found, "only a head of hair," that the "woman exists only by her hair," and that in fact only two very partial skeletons were found. The young woman and her "husband" were only very partially represented. Moreover, Zias noted that "one gets the impression that it's lying there next to the skeleton, it's not like that at all" because contrary to the impression created by Yadin's text, the armor plates were actually scattered throughout the northern palace. Zias suggested that the skeletal remains are those of Romans because the armor was a Roman armor, and it was not a fighting armor but a parade armor, "the kind of armor which you wear when you put on all your medallions and you march down the streets in front of the cheering [crowds] . . . it's not the kind of stuff used for fighting. I think this is probably simply a Roman who died up there, but to make these Jews I find it very very difficult."

Locus 8 yielded only three skeletal remains. Even if we accept the interpretation that they reflect the presence of the rebels, where are the remains of the other 957? In at least one more case, a process somewhat similar to the one which occurred in locus 8 took place.

The transcripts of the daily meeting of October 17, 1963, already indicate that a number of human bones were found in a cave.[19] Although Yadin stated that this cave was to be explored again the following day, there is no mention of it on that day. The next mention of this discovery was not until a month later, in the daily meeting of November 17, 1963 (pp. 8–10). The discussion then focused on the discovery of a large number of human bones in a southern cave referred to as loci 2001–2002 ("Cave of the Skeletons"). At the time, the archaeologists thought that they had found at least seven skulls as well as bones. A later assessment, however, was that the remains of fifteen bodies had been uncovered. The impression which the archaeologists formed was that the bodies were not buried in an organized fashion, but were thrown into the cave in a way which could be interpreted as indicating contempt and disrespect. Nowhere does Yadin explain in detail what it was exactly that prompted him to this conclusion. The text of the transcript suggests that it might have been something in the way the bones were found: in a heap, together with clothes. And yet, while the full basis for this conclusion is very important, the reader is left in the dark. Yadin immediately raised the possibility that these skeletal remains were those of the rebels of Masada. Expressing doubt that the bodies were discarded so disrespectfully, he also raised the possibility that these skeletal remains may have been what was left of a "hasty burial by the besieged" (p. 9). In any event, although Yadin did suspect that these bones were indeed those of Masada rebels, he was definitely unsure and hesitant. On page 10 of the transcript, however, there is an interesting debate between Yadin and an unidentified archaeologist:

> -: I ask, first of all, what is the proof that the people there [in the cave] were Jews? So far I hear that there is no proof. . . .
>
> Yadin: There is one proof, not entirely decisive, but in my view it is decisive in this matter. It is the clothes that were found with the bodies . . . these are not Roman clothes but Jewish clothes. But it could be—
>
> -: This is a robe, and not a TALLITH [Jewish prayer dress. The speaker makes the point that the clothes are not specifically Jewish].
>
> Yadin: Robe or TALLITH, it does not make a difference. It is from the type of clothes we know from here.
>
> -: Are there any particularly salient signs?
>
> Yadin: They do not carry Jewish signs, but—I know. In any event, they [the clothes] are totally identical to the robes we know were collected around this environment. I do not know if these are Roman soldiers that forgot them and threw them out. This does not seem likely to me, but as a hypothesis we can accept it at this stage.[20]

Note the way Yadin wrestles with the question, trying to hold fast to his contention. It is clear that he was eager to confirm the hypothesis that these bones were of the Sicarii rebels of Masada, but the evidence was weak at best, and not specific. It did not take many questions to show the weakness of his position.

The simplest and most straightforward way to interpret Josephus's text is that the collective suicide took place at one site on Masada. Finding a few skeletal remains in locus 8 and others in loci 2001–2002 raises the questions of the missing bodies and of how the skeletal remains came to be found in different places. Yadin adopts the hypothesis that the suicides occurred not in one place, but in various locations. This enables him to solve both riddles. First, he could contend that the Romans who found the bodies "surely buried them in all sorts of different places on Masada,"[21] implying that the Romans buried the bodies where they actually found them, or wherever it was convenient. The excavations of Masada also revealed signs of many fires, some of which were very intense. This may contradict Josephus, but if the suicide took place in many places, it stands to reason that there would have been many fires as well. How far is this interpretation from the text of Josephus? We read that

> Elazar Ben-Yair . . . gathered the most courageous of his companions together, and encouraged them to take that course [kill one another] by a speech.[22]

Since not everyone was persuaded, Elazar Ben-Yair made a second speech, but as he was speaking

> They all cut him off short, and made haste to do the work, as full of an unconquerable ardour of mind, and moved with a demoniacal fury. So they went their ways . . . so great was the zeal they were in to slay their wives and children, and themselves also![23]

This description could be interpreted as Yadin did, but a more plausible interpretation is that it all happened in one spot. This leaves the question of the multiple fires open. If the rebels killed one other in one place, who set all those fires? One possibility is that the Romans did. Josephus states that after the other killings were done, the last person alive

> set fire to the palace, and with the great force of his hand ran his sword entirely through himself, and fell down dead near to his own relations.[24]

This text implies that there was a single location—the palace—where the collective suicide was carried out and where the fire was ignited.

In any event, the second time that the excavators of Masada discussed the skeletal remains was November 26, 1963 (p. 13). That was the occasion when Dr. Nicu Haas determined the type of skeletons found in locus 8. However, during that meeting Haas referred to the skeletons found in loci 2001–2002 as well:

> All in all I counted 24 or 26 people, and an additional fetus in the 6th or 7th month. If we count [them, there are]: 14 men, 6 women, 4 children, and one fetus. There are two which are difficult to identify. The women

> are all young, that is, between 15 and 22 years old. The men—from 22 to over 60, and one who was very old, [maybe] 70 or more. . . . The children—I counted as children those aged 8 to 12. There is no one under 8 except the fetus.

The question of the identity of the skeletons was not directly discussed, but Dr. Haas did state that the shape of most of the skulls resembled similar skulls which were found in Nachal Chever (south of Ein Gedi). The clear conclusion is therefore that the connection between these skulls and the ones found in Nachal Chever had already been made on November 26, 1963. This interpretation was published as such in *Ha'aretz* of March 28, 1965 (p. 7). However, it is important to note that Haas was careful to add that among the skulls discovered in loci 2001–2002 were six male skulls from an entirely different type: "All men . . . between 35 to 50 years old, very strong, both from a general physical point of view and from the point of view of the skull" (p. 13). Yadin suggested that these may have belonged to slaves.

Yadin published two reports of the discovery. In the preliminary report published in 1965 he wrote: "When found, the bones were lying in disorder, giving the impression that they had been thrown down carelessly" (1965e, p. 90), and added, "It is difficult to determine the identity of the corpses and stipulate the time they were placed into the cave" (1965e, p. 101).[25] The next year (1966, pp. 193–94), Yadin addresses the problem of the identity of the bones once again, coming to a much more definite conclusion:

> At the time we could give no accurate opinion. But now, after the bones have been carefully studied by my colleague Dr. N. Haas, of the Hebrew University Medical School, the following facts have been established: fourteen of the skeletons are of males between the ages of twenty-two and sixty; one is of a man over the age of seventy; six are females aged between fifteen and twenty-two; and four are children aged from eight to twelve; there is also one of an embryo! Most of the skulls belong to the same type as those we discovered in the caves of Bar Kochba in Nachal Chever. It seems to me that these facts conclusively rule out the possibility that the skeletons are those either of the Roman garrison or of the monks. They can be only those of the defenders of Masada.

Yadin's 1966 mind is quite determined that these bones are indeed those of the Jewish defenders of Masada, despite both his earlier reservations and his later hesitations (to be discussed below).

The explanation Yadin chose for the disrespect which he thought was reflected in the disarray of the skeletons was: "The only feasible assumption is that they were flung here irreverently by the Roman troops when they cleared the bodies after their victory" (1966e, p. 194). Of course, if this interpretation is valid, the next obvious question is, "Where are the other 935 bodies?" Weren't they discarded in a similar fashion? Why were they never found?

Following Yadin's logic is instructive. In order to establish the Jewish identity of the bones, Yadin moved from relying on the clothes to relying on the type of skeletons found, and there, by strengthening the rhetoric he used to describe the exclusions (Romans and monks), he concluded that the bones were those of Jewish defenders of Masada.

This 1966e statement is illuminating. A jarring note is that, contrary to Yadin's statements, Haas had already provided nearly all the relevant information at the staff meeting recorded on November 26, 1963! The basis for the implication in Yadin's 1966e text that something new had been added is unclear, and most probably unfounded. The fact is that the differences between the 1966e and 1963 physical analyses (if any) of the skeletal remains are, for all intents and purposes, insignificant. Haas's analysis, as mentioned above, was also part of the 1965 report.

Also interesting is the absence of Yadin's response to that part of the analysis which dealt with the stronger skulls ("It is possible that these were slaves") from the 1965 and 1966e reports. In 1966e Yadin says, "Most of the skulls belong to the same type" (p. 194), with not a single word about the nature of the skulls that are not part of the "most" (and which constitute about 43 percent of the male bones), or the possible meaning of this.

In 1965 Yadin felt that Haas's analysis probably eliminated the possibility that the bones were those of monks or Romans, but he was not sure at all whether they were of the Masada rebels. His uncertainty completely disappeared in 1966, when he more and more emphatically worded his logic of elimination. The scientific reason for his change of mind is unclear. After all, there were no additional relevant findings between 1963 and 1966. Evidently, then, the reason for the much more deterministic 1966e view is not to be found in science.

In 1970, however, Yadin wrote, "It is difficult to know if the skeletons are those of the defenders of Masada during the period of the revolt, even though this is reasonable. Most skulls are of the type found in the Nachal Chever caves, and it is plausible to assume that they are of Jews" (p. 386). It is difficult to reconcile Yadin's 1970 hesitation with his 1966e confidence. Perhaps the political turmoil surrounding the burial of the bones (to be discussed later) helped to create this shift.

A new chapter regarding the scientific aspect of the identity of the bones problem was written in 1994, when volume 4 of the final report of the Masada excavations was published. True, it was about thirty years after the major controversy, and to a very large extent irrelevant to the original debate, but it is instructive to examine it.

At the beginning of their work, Zias, Segal, and Carmi (1994) mention that "the bodies were *thrown* into the cave along with the skeletal remains

15. Locus 2001-2002 (cave of the skeletons with the skeletal remains). (Picture from Yigael Yadin, *Masada: Herod's Fortress and the Zealots' Last Stand* [London: Weidenfeld and Nicolson, 1966e], pp. 198-99)

of pigs" (p. 366). Now, this *is* a fascinating piece of information. To begin with, it is the first time that we really understand why Yadin felt that the manner in which the bones were thrown into the cave showed disrespect. Burying Jews with pigs is a desecration. Finding pig bones in loci 2001–2002 reinforces the alternative possibility that the bones there are not of Jews.

At this point I decided to reread the transcript from November 26, 1963, the session at which Haas interpreted the skeletal remains in locus 8 and in 2001–2002. Was Haas aware that pig bones were found in loci 2001–2002? At the end of the discussion (p. 13), Dr. Nicu Haas states, "I want to comment on today's bones: a lot of sheep, goats as well, some cows and a calf too, chickens, dog, rabbit, and—here's the most important—pig." Thus the proximity of pig bones to the human bones was both known and considered important already in 1963. As we shall see, this piece of information might have played a crucial role in the late 1960s, and was definitely important in 1994. However, the statement that pig bones were found in loci 2001–2002 seems to have become less salient.

Before utilizing the fact that pig bones had been found, Zias, Segal, and Israel did two things. First, they pointed out some conflicting evidence regarding the identity of the bones:

> The anthropological claim that there was a close morphological relationship between earlier "Jewish" finds from Nachal Mishmar and those of Masada proved erroneous when it was later stated that the former were *not* from the Roman period as reported . . . [b]ut from the Chalcolithic period several millennia earlier. . . . Despite the conflicting evidence and Yadin's admission that the remains in the Masada cave may not be Jewish (Yadin—personal communication), religious authorities decided that they were those of the last defenders of Masada and accorded them a proper Jewish burial. (p. 366)

Second, they tried to utilize carbon-14 analysis[26] to help determine the age of the bones. Evidently they could not apply this method to the bones for some reason. Unfortunately, they could not find the remnants of the pig bones either. They could, however, apply the carbon-14 assay to some textiles which were found in the same locus (assuming, of course, that they were from the same period as the skeletal remains). These textiles, "having been preserved by the arid environment, were amenable to carbon 14 dating," and the results of the examination were that these textiles, ergo the bones, "correspond to a calendaric age of 40–115 C.E." (p. 366). This evidently places the bones within the period of the Great Revolt (66–73 C.E.), but with a large margin on both sides. The only definite exclusions were the Byzantine monks.

The researchers' conclusion? "The carbon 14 date obtained from the textiles found in association with the skeletal remains in the northern cave therefore adds a small measure of credibility to [Josephus's] narrative," and they add that the skeletal remains "may well have been victims of the mass suicide. The fact that the skeletal remains of over nine hundred individuals were never recovered may suggest that while twenty-five of the inhabitants committed suicide, Josephus may have converted the few into all, in order to make the narrative more compelling" (p. 367). They note that it is possible that the Romans threw the twenty-five bodies they found into that cave and that the pig bones were added into the cave deliberately by the Romans, who were an "antagonistic and unsympathetic force" (p. 367). According to the researchers, such demeaning customs were prevalent at those times. It must be added that "throwing" human bodies into the "cave of the skeletons," considering the location of the cave, could not have been an easy task.

Strange as it may sound, the two pages by Zias, Segal, and Carmi (1994) suggest an altogether different interpretation of Josephus Flavius. The one new piece of hard evidence they have is the date of the textiles. The date does not contradict Josephus. Then, despite the rather large margin in the date (covering a long period before and after the Great Revolt), they construct the following account: The bones in the cave are indeed those of the Masada rebels. Only twenty-five people committed suicide on Masada and not 960 (that is, lack of evidence is interpreted as no evidence). The disrespect shown toward the bodies (pig bones) is taken as evidence of the Roman attitude towards the rebels (contradicting Josephus's account). But I find it odd to imagine the Romans staging their war campaign and siege against only twenty-five people. An alternative possibility, that of the 960 rebels on Masada only twenty-five committed suicide, leaves the question open: What happened to the rest? Were they taken prisoner and made slaves? And if so, what interest did Josephus have in falsifying the end of the siege and giving them an honorable death instead of simply recounting that they became slaves? Josephus wrote his narrative at a time when people who were witness to the events were still alive. Turning hundreds of captive slaves from Masada into respectable suicides is a fabrication that could be difficult to sell. Moreover, accusing Josephus of blatant falsification on so flimsy a lack of evidence, is equally unsettling.

Another dramatic addition to this ongoing debate about the bones saga was written in the summer of 1997. In July 1997 Joe Zias told an international Dead Sea scrolls congress held in Jerusalem that the bones found on Masada may actually have been those of Romans.[27] Zias's supporting evidence included the discovery which Yadin suppressed—that the bones of pigs had been found on the burial site. Zias declared that it was a Roman burial custom to sacrifice pigs. Thus the pig bones on the burial site should not be interpreted as a sign of disrespect for Jews (who were not buried there), but rather as a sign of respect for the Romans who were buried there.[28]

Zias continued his dispute with the interpretation of the bones found in locus 2001–2002 in 1998 as well. Meticulously reexamining the reports and photographs of the discovery in this cave structure, Zias came to some more disturbing conclusions. First, he pointed out that the original report by Haas stated that 220 bones had been found. Because an adult human skeleton has 206 bones, the report of twenty-four people in loci 2001–2002 means that about 96 percent of the skeletal material was missing and unaccounted for. Zias thus concludes that only "5 or 6 individuals" were buried there.[29] He also suggested that the presence of the bones of women and children among the bones found in locus 2001–2002 indicates that those who remained near Masada after its fall in 73 included not only soldiers, but others who stayed behind with their families (Sheri 1998). Second, Zias points out that while there are clear signs of an orderly burial in the loci, the disturbance can be clearly attributed not to human intervention but to animals (probably hyenas) that entered the loci and "ravaged the body shortly after death" (1998d, p. 5). Third, he notes that the age distribution attributed to the skeletal remains (e.g., 33 percent up to the age of sixty) is highly unlikely. Fourth, interpreting at least some of the skeletons as Jewish was based on their resemblance to remains found in nearby Nachal Chever. This, Zias explains, was an error because the Nachal Chever bones "were from the Chalcolithic period and not the Roman period as previously reported" (1998d, p. 3). In all fairness, however, we must concede that this information may not have been available to Yadin at the time. Zias even confirms that, in a personal communication in the early 1980s, Yadin told him that "he never said" that the remains found in loci 2001–2002 "were Jewish" (1998d, p. 3).

One of Zias's most dramatic evidential statements is that pig bones were unearthed in loci 2001–2002. It is patently clear that Yadin knew this and chose not to disclose it in public. Only in 1982 did he volunteer this information publicly.[30] Two relevant questions arise: What was the significance of discovering pig bones in loci 2001–2002, and why did Yadin suppress this evidence?

Zias suggests that sufficient comparative evidence from the Roman period exists that "sacrificing a pig in order to give legal status to the grave was, on occasion, practiced in the Holy Land" (1998d, p. 7) for Roman soldiers and civilians. He claims that burying pigs with humans was a custom prevalent among ancient Greeks and Romans. Moreover, the pig was one of the symbols of the Roman Tenth Legion (Fretensis) which, all seem to concur, was the force that laid siege to and conquered Masada.

Zias's work led him to conclude that the bones of the "defenders of Masada" which were buried on July 7, 1969, in a state-sponsored funeral were, in fact, the bones of Roman soldiers (1998, 1998d; Sheri 1998). If this interpretation is valid, Yadin's motivation in concealing this evidence is easily surmised, also because an entire political controversy developed around the burial of these bones.

Finally, Ladouceur points out that "archaeological excavations of the site, as one might have expected, have served neither to sustain nor [to] discredit the central suicide story," and adds that "[p]erhaps some of the defenders did in fact commit suicide, and around this historical kernel Josephus shaped an elaborate narrative influenced by literary models and political conditions of his Roman environment" (1987, p. 109).

The discovery of the bones was first mentioned in the October 17, 1963, meeting, and only three days later the daily *Yediot Aharonot* (p. 3) reported that fifteen skeletons had been found in a southern cave. The reporter, Uri Porat, actually traveled to Masada and used a rope to lower himself to the opening of the cave to see them. He reported that:

> These skeletons are some of the 960 warriors who killed one another [rather than] surrender. Their bodies were thrown into the cave by the

> Romans . . . evidently . . . with violence, without any burial ceremony, because the bones were scattered around. . . . Among the pieces of cloth [found in the cave] was one that looked like a *Tallith.*

Despite what followed, that original interpretation seemed to have held until Zias, Segal, and Carmi's 1994 report. Clearly, Yadin allowed himself much more interpretative freedom with journalists. Interestingly, when Yadin himself wrote in *Ma'ariv* on October 20, 1963, he was much more careful. He suggested that the skeletons could be some of the 960 rebels who committed suicide, but cautioned that it was too early to make such a definite conclusion.

THE SKELETON WAR

The question of the type of burial that should be accorded the bones discovered on Masada became a major political, religious, and moral issue in Israel. Should it be a Jewish burial ceremony? Of course—but only if it is

16. Symbols of the Roman Tenth Legion—Fretensis. Above are discernible "L[egio] X F[retensis]," a ship, and—very clearly—a pig. (Picture from: Kasher Arye, ed., *The Great Jewish Revolt: Factors and Circumstances Leading to Its Outbreak* [Jerusalem: Zalman Shazar Center], p. 427. [Hebrew])

certain that these bones were of Jews. If not, other ceremonies should be used. Thus, any debate regarding the question of what to do with the bones involves the issue of their identity.

To recapitulate: the Masada excavations disclosed three skeletal remains in the northern palace-villa and about twenty-five additional skeletons in a cave at the southern end of the Masada cliff. A few other skeletons and burial places were found as well (Livne 1986, p. 47).

The first shot in the "skeleton war" may have been fired on October 24, 1963, when Shabtai Ben-Dov wrote to *Ha'aretz* that:

> With a certain degree of shock I saw in *Ha'aretz* a picture of a young man examining a bucket full of bones that had been discovered on Masada. I understand that nothing can be determined about the identity of those bones without examining them first, but I contend that these skeletons are probably those of the last of the fighters of Masada who were thrown into a chaotic heap by the Roman conquerors. It is difficult today to see the bones heaped in buckets, to be sent finally—where—where? To some museum, and to some secular exhibit. It seems to me . . . truly appropriate to insist on the traditional attitude toward the bodies of our holy people. If it becomes clear that these are indeed the bones of the warriors of Masada, I cannot countenance the thought that they will not be given a Jewish burial in a state-sponsored ceremony.

The issue was raised again in March 1967 by Israeli parliament member Shlomo Lorentz of the Ultra-Orthodox Agudat Israel party. In a blazing speech in the Knesset he demanded that the remains of the skeletons found on Masada be given a Jewish burial. Aharon Yadlin, then Minister of Education and Culture, pointed out that the Jewish identity of the skeletons had not been established and suggested that the entire issue be passed on to one of the Knesset's committees. His suggestion was accepted.[31]

The Knesset Committee on Education and Culture held a discussion with Yadin about this issue in February and March of 1968 concerning the ways in which the identity of the bones could be established.[32] Yadin explained the nature of the anthropological examinations which were supposed to be performed on the skeletons in order to determine the identity of the bones. Following Yadin's report, the committee issued a statement that these examinations were of historical and national importance and value, and that the identity of the skeletons had to be established.[33] One can only wonder at a political committee in a political organization making the assessment that anthropological examinations bear national and historical value. In fact, the committee's report stated that the experts could not determine their identity, but this did not prevent the Jewish Ultra-Orthodox members of parliament (Menachem Porush and Avraham Vardiger) from demanding an immediate Jewish burial.

To its credit, the committee noted that in addition to those it labeled the "heroes of Masada," there had been Roman soldiers on top of that mountain both before the Great Revolt and after the fall of Masada, and many years later there were Christian monks as well; hence the identity of the skeletons was not so clear-cut. However, these debates and uncertainties did not deter the fundamentalist Ultra-Orthodox Agudat Israel, which kept insisting that the skeletal remains be buried immediately as Jews.[34]

A year passed, and the debate was revived again in March 1969, when it was decided that the "bones of the heroes of Masada" would be buried in an official state ceremony.[35] A few days after that announcement, the public was told that the ceremony would be delayed.[36] It was also reported that a public (Jewish) funeral for the bones discovered on Masada would take place on the Mount of Olives in Jerusalem in a week.

Two days later Yadin used the occasion of a public lecture to respond to this development, "fiercely objecting" to the idea of

> having a [Jewish] public religious funeral for the bones of the 27 dead people from Masada, which is supposed to take place next Wednesday on the Mount of Olives in Jerusalem. . . . In [my] view, there is no proof about the identity of the bones and therefore it is doubtful whether these bones are those of the Jewish heroes of Masada.[37]

Yadin's position here is very clear. In complete contradiction to the statement in his 1966e book, he states that the evidence for the identity of the skeletons was not sufficiently conclusive or definitive. Yadin also told his audience that he had tried to sway the rabbinical establishment to avoid holding the public funeral on the Mount of Olives, suggesting instead that the bones, in a quiet funeral, be buried where they were discovered. Yadin's attempts to reverse the decision failed. Consequently, a state funeral was planned.

It is interesting to note that this decision was taken out of Yadin's hands, his views were rejected, and politics overcame science. Indeed, Yadin was quite aware of this and stated, "I have a personal feeling that the public funeral will not be made in honor of the bones precisely, but against somebody." Yet Yadin did state on that occasion that he "believed that the bones were those of the people of Masada," adding that he needed proof that would dispel any doubt.[38] One wonders to what extent the discovery of pig bones together with the human bones (and the different type of bones) troubled him, because Yadin's two contradictory positions are startling. The question remains not only how these two positions developed in his mind, but also how he was able to maintain them both. The answer may be in a compartmentalization Yadin made between his self-defined roles as a mythmaker and supporter of the myth, his role as a professional archaeologist, and his Jewish identity. He may have felt comfortable with interpretations which were mythical. However, his commitment as a Jew, perhaps respectful of Orthodox Jewish traditions of burial, as well as his commitment to science (evidently partial in the case of Masada), propelled him to construct a position closer to the empirical truth.

The official response to Yadin's criticism came a day later. Responding to questions from journalists, the spokesperson for the Ministry of Religions stated, "The heroes of Masada came [to Masada] from Jerusalem, and fought in the war of the Holy City. It is therefore only natural that their bones find their final resting place on the Mount of Olives, which was already a cemetery in the period of the destruction of the Second Temple."[39] The spokesman probably had never read Josephus Flavius too carefully. But the affair of the burial was not yet over.

While the Ministry of Religions paid only scant attention to Yadin, others did. Minister Israel Yesha'yahu who was then in charge of postal services appealed the decision, stating that the burial should take place at Masada. Thus, while Yadin's doubts about the identity of the bones were ignored, his suggestion to bury the bones in Masada was gaining support. The government created a special ministerial committee[40] and authorized the committee to make recommendations about the burial of the "Masada skeletons."[41] It took the committee only a few months of deliberations to decide that the bones of "the heroes of Masada" would be buried in a full military ceremony on Masada, under the supervision of the IDF Rabbinate.[42] Apparently Yadin had won a small victory. Moreover, the ministerial committee's decision reflected their view that the "heroes of Masada" were to be regarded as soldiers.

The burial of the skeletal remains (of twenty-seven people according to one interpretation) took place on July 7, 1969. These "relics of the warriors of Masada in their war with the Romans in 73 C.E. . . . are to be buried in a special tomb near Masada which will be called the Hill of the Defenders. . . . As to the rest of the warriors of Masada, who numbered 960 people . . . their bodies were found by the Romans and destroyed, and perhaps will be found in future excavations, said Prof. Yadin." Despite his protests regarding the identity of the bones, Yadin attended the military funeral for what was presented as the "Jewish soldiers who fought the Romans."[43] The burial itself attracted an impressive array of dignitaries (Menachem Begin, Yadin, Rabbi Shlomo Goren, and many others). Photographs of the funeral feature Yadin, and one wonders what he must have been thinking.

Indeed, since no definitive proof for the identity of the skeletal remains was provided (certainly not anything new since 1963), the debate about the skeletons also found its way into the professional literature. A number of scholars attacked the identification of the remains with the Masada rebels.[44]

The Religious Point of View

Ha'aretz is a secular newspaper; I was curious to see how this debate was reflected in Jewish religious newspapers. I chose two: *Hatzofe*, sponsored by the National Religious Party, and *Hamodia*, an Ultra-Orthodox newspaper.

Hatzofe had only four reports concerning the discovery of the skeletons and the burial. The March 28, 1965, issue (p. 4) mentions that the failure to find the rest of the "fighters" is a great mystery. It states that the twenty-seven skeletons that were found were examined by Dr. Haas and that the skulls of the skeletons "are identical in their shape to the skulls of Bar Kochba's fighters found in Nachal Chever." This item is repeated in a general report about Masada which appeared in the front page of *Hatzofe* on April 2, 1965. A third report is dated March 28, 1968 (p. 2); it concerns the discussions in the Knesset committee. The report is very factual and does not express any definite stand. The last report is dated July 7, 1969, and is about the burial ceremony itself:

> The remains of the heroic Masada fighters, killed in their desperate war against the Romans in 73 [C.E.], will today be brought to a Jewish grave with full military honors—one thousand and nine hundred years after their tragic death . . . In a press conference with prof. Yadin . . . Dr. S. Z.

17. Funeral of the bones—I. Procession of the three coffins with the remains of the bones on July 7, 1969, near Masada. (Courtesy of the Government Press Office, State of Israel)

18. Funeral of the bones—II. Yadin is speaking at the burial ceremony while army chief chaplain Rabbi Goren and others are listening (July 7, 1969, near Masada). (Courtesy of the Government Press Office, State of Israel)

19. Funeral of the bones—III. Army chief chaplain Rabbi Goren speaking during the burial ceremony. Yigael Yadin, Menachem Begin, and others are listening (July 7, 1969, near Masada). (Courtesy of the Government Press Office, State of Israel)

> Kahane, general director of the Ministry of Religions . . . stated that it was decided to accept all the bones as belonging to the Jewish fighters of Masada and to bury them with appropriate military honors in Masada, where they fought and fell. He stated that, according to Jewish religious law if most of the dead are Jewish, other anonymous dead persons are considered Jewish as well and have the right to be buried as Jews. . . . In the burial ceremony, Professor Yigael Yadin . . . who was a member of the committee that made the decision on the burial, will read passages from the last speech of the commander of the besieged fighters of Masada, Elazar Ben-Yair. (p. 6)

We can learn from this passage that Yadin cooperated with the committee, accepted its decisions, and participated in the ceremonial military burial. By doing that, he relinquished his conflicting view about the identity of the skeletons. However, as he demanded publicly, the bones were buried in Masada.

Hamodia gave somewhat more extensive coverage to the affair. Its February 20, 1968, issue emphasized that Knesset Member Shlomo Lorentz, of the Ultra-Orthodox Agudat Israel party, demanded that the Knesset discuss what he termed "the disgraceful desecration of the skeletons of the fighters of Masada and [failure to accord them] burial in a proper Jewish grave" (p. 4). The March 28, 1968, issue of *Hamodia* reported the conclusions of the Knesset committee, emphasizing that the claims made by Lorentz had been accepted. However, the report expressed extreme dissatisfaction with the fact that the bones had not been brought to rest for so many years and demanded that all research focused on these skeletons be stopped immediately so that they could be buried at once. The March 4, 1969, issue of *Hamodia* (p. 4) told its readers that the bones of the "heroes of Masada" would be buried within a week on the Mount of Olives. The March 17 issue (p. 4) had already told its readers that a new ministerial committee had been appointed to decide on this issue following an appeal by Minister Yesha'yahu. The July 7, 1969, issue (p. 4) reported the burial of the remains of the "heroes" of Masada. *Hamodia*'s position is clear, consistent, and political-moralistic. The fact that this newspaper refers to the inhabitants of Masada as "heroes" is interesting, because orthodox Judaism did its best to repress the memory of Masada precisely because this branch of Judaism never considered what happened on Masada as heroism. Obviously, the affair must have served the Ultra-Orthodox as one more opportunity to get at the secular and scientific Jews who they oppose, morally and politically.

All these things relating to the identity of the bones found on Masada were written and published in 1965 and 1966. The question of why in 1968 Yadin maintained that the identity of the bones was not known is unclear, but the affair illustrates some interesting contrasts between science and politics. It also raises some historical ironies. The most glaring, of course, is the possibility that Jewish Orthodoxy was intent on providing a ceremonial Jewish and state funeral to persons who had nothing to do with Judaism.

Second, the Ultra-Orthodox interpretation of Judaism (as well as some of the Orthodox interpretation) that repressed the memory of Masada emerged as *the* protector of Masada's "heroes." Historically, the Orthodox versions of Judaism were uncomfortable with quite a few aspects of the Masada historical narrative: the suicide was problematic, the Sicarii were not well appreciated, the idea of forcefully challenging the Roman Empire was not something they identified with easily, and their conviction that Jews should devote themselves to studying and worshiping, which promoted a scholarly view of Judaism, conflicted with the aggressive, military, combatant, and challenging concept of Judaism expressed in the Great Revolt. The relevant contrast here is between two contemporary figures: Josephus Flavius and Yochanan Ben-Zakkai.

Like Josephus Flavius, Rabbi Yochanan Ben-Zakkai lived and died during the cataclysmic period of the Jewish Great Revolt. Ben-Zakkai escaped from Jerusalem (probably in 69 C.E., in the middle of Vespasian's spring offensive in the north) and found refuge with the Romans.[45] Like many other contemporary Jews, Yochanan Ben-Zakkai maintained a healthy and sober degree of skepticism in the face of increasing levels of military-political activism, zealot fervor, and false messianism. He is portrayed as a person who was not a follower of either the Zealots or the Sicarii, and supposedly questioned the wisdom of challenging the might of the Roman Empire. Discussing Yochanan Ben-Zakkai not only raises possible alternatives to the Great Revolt, but also provides an unavoidable comparison with Joseph Ben-Matityahu, later renamed Josephus Flavius.

Like Josephus, Ben-Zakkai disagreed with many of the stated goals of the Great Revolt. Being in his sixties when he defected, he apparently found a common language with Vespasian (who was more or less his age), chief commander of the Roman military machine that was crushing the Jewish rebellion (and on his way to becoming Roman emperor). Vespasian granted Ben-Zakkai his wish of establishing a small center where, together with a few other scholarly Jews, he could study and continue developing spiritual Judaism. Ben-Zakkai was sent to Yavne, where he established a renewed branch of spiritual Judaism. As so many point out, despite his defection Ben-Zakkai is definitely not considered a traitor. His way led to a renewed type of Jewish life, and his challenge to the rebels' decision to confront the Roman Empire is frequently presented as an alternative to the revolt. Apparently both Ben-Zakkai and Josephus Flavius objected to the rebellion against the Romans. Ben-Zakkai never hid his views (see Stern 1984, pp. 320–45). While Josephus does not say much about his life in Rome, he did (a) assume a new Roman name (he replaced his original Jewish name "Yoseph Ben-Matityahu" with "Josephus Flavius"); (b) divorce his second wife and marry a woman from the island of Crete (unclear whether she was Jewish or not); (c) leave Judea and go to Rome, where he wrote a historical account for the Flavians who supported him. It thus seems reasonable to question whether he practiced a Judaic lifestyle in Rome. It is clear that he elected to leave his people, their cultural geography and milieu, for a life in Rome, and that he probably preferred a Roman lifestyle to the Jewish life he practiced in Judea. Contrary to this, Ben-Zakkai remained Jewish in place and lifestyle to his last day.

Many people take Ben-Zakkai as an illustration of what could have been an alternative to the rebellion against the Romans and the resultant destruction on a massive scale, a renewed meaningful Jewish life that enabled Jews to fulfill their religious and cultural aspirations without endangering what they most cherished.[46]

So there is more than a shred of historical irony in seeing those who view themselves as Ben-Zakkai's spiritual inheritors fighting for a proper burial for Ben-Zakkai's bitter opponents more than a thousand years after the events.

Third, the state of Israel treated possible Sicarii as soldiers—a questionable act indeed.

Fourth, Yadin, who provided the Masada mythical narrative with its scientific foundation, found himself in a losing battle against some powerful fundamentalists. In that battle it was Yadin who presented the balanced and accurate view, but he was forced to compromise.

Finally, one is left puzzled by Yadin's 1968 position asserting that he could not establish the identity of the skeletons. This starkly contradicts his 1966 written account. This is also the place to recall Yadin's personal communication to Joe Zias in the early 1980s, when he told Zias that "he never said" that the skeletal remains found in loci 2001–2002 "were Jewish."

It is almost impossible to conclude without a few more words about Yadin. That he was a romantic nationalist is obvious. He lent his credibility, and his scientific reputation, to a questionable narrative, added a few imaginary elements, and persuaded the naive that the Masada mythical narrative was actual history. He did almost anything in his power to support that mythical narrative, including concealing evidence and warping interpretations of evidence. Along the way he managed to prevent other, more skeptical archaeologists from voicing their views. Unfortunately, his behavior regarding the interpretation of the Masada findings was more that of a political nationalist romantic, and a moral entrepreneur, than of a conscientious, calculated, critical, and cautious scientist. The bright side of this distortion was that his work had genuine spark to it. The price was that, in too many important aspects, his work is misleading, concealing, and creates false and empirically incorrect impressions.

NOTES

1. *Wars of the Jews*, 7.9.1, p. 603.
2. P. 1 of the transcript of the daily session.
3. P. 1 of transcript of the daily session.
4. P. 1 of the transcript of the daily session.
5. 1971; vol. 11, pp. 1078–92.
6. 1972; vol. 24, pp. 103–106.
7. Yadin's preferred use of Josephus's original Jewish name is both striking and instructive.
8. 1971; New York: Herzl Press, pp. 809–11.
9. *Wars of the Jews*, 7.9.1, p. 603.
10. In a letter to *Ha'aretz*, on April 5, 1965.
11. *Wars of the Jews*, 7.9.1, p. 603.
12. Transcript of daily meetings, November 17, 1963, p. 8.
13. In *Ha'aretz*, March 28, 1965, p. 7.
14. The cave Yadin refers to is locus 2001–2002, to be discussed below. Next, Yadin refers here to the "three" skeletal remains which were found in locus 8 in the northern palace-villa. In view of what is about to unfold below, I feel the need to call attention to Yadin's use of the word "possibly."
15. See Livne 1986, p. 47.

16. *Wars of the Jews*, 7.9.1, p. 603.

17. And in another report dated December 1, 1963.

18. Of course, the reinterpretation suggested by Zias in the 1990s could not have been known to Yadin. Also, Zias is now working on a paper which may examine the possibility that the remains found in the Northern Palace are not Jewish (personal communication, March 8, 2001).

19. P. 8. That report mentions six skeletons.

20. Possibly Yoram Tzafrir.

21. Page 8 of the transcripts for November 17, 1963.

22. *Wars of the Jews*, 7.8.6, p. 600.

23. *Wars of the Jews*, 7.9.1, p. 603.

24. Ibid.

25. It is hard to resist noting that a radioactive decay test, the carbon-14 analysis, could help solve some of the issues. The analysis was not performed. It is possible that Yadin did not request a carbon-14 examination because at the time he considered the accuracy of this test as too imprecise. Unfortunately, I could not find any deliberations on this issue. Obviously, DNA examination was not sufficiently developed at that time.

26. Carbon-14 analysis is a sophisticated physical method that helps determine absolute dating. It is based on measuring the amount of the radioactive isotope carbon-14 and comparing it to the known pace of decay of carbon atoms. All organic materials contain carbon (whose atomic number is 12). A distinct part of it is heavier and radioactive (atomic number 14), that is, it decays into ordinary carbon. When living material (e.g., vegetation, animals, humans) dies, its radioactive atoms decay at a constant rate, which is known. Thus, by measuring the ratio between the radioactive and the ordinary carbon, one can determine when the living tissue died.

27. Judging from views I heard from some archaeologists, it needs to be noted that Zias's views are not well accepted.

28. See, e.g., report in *Time* magazine, July 26, 1997, p. 12.

29. See 1998d, p. 9. In his interview with reporter Merav Sheri (1998), he revised the estimate to seven to eight individuals.

30. In an article in the *Jerusalem Post* entitled "Yadin and Goren," November 16, 1982.

31. *Ha'aretz*, March 23, 1967.

32. *Ha'aretz*, February 20, 1968, and March 28, 1968, respectively. See also *Hamodia*, February 20, 1968, p. 4; March 28, 1968, p. 1.

33. *Ha'aretz*, March 28, 1968.

34. Ibid.

35. *Ha'aretz*, March 4, 1969. See also *Hamodia*, same date, p. 4.

36. *Ha'aretz*, March 10, 1969.

37. *Ha'aretz*, March 12, 1969, p. 5.

38. Ibid.

39. *Ha'aretz*, March 13, 1969, p. 3.

40. Ya'acov Shimshon Shapira (Minister of Justice) was appointed chairman; the ministers appointed as members were Israel Yesha'yahu, Zerach Varhaftig, Moshe Kol, and Menachem Begin.

41. *Ha'aretz*, March 17, 1969.

42. *Ha'aretz*, July 1, 1969, p. 6.

43. *Ha'aretz*, July 7, 1969, p. 8. See also *Ha'aretz*, July 7, 1969, p. 3, and July 8, 1969, p. 10.

44. See Zeitlin 1965, pp. 270, 313; 1967, pp. 251–70; Shargel 1979, p. 368; Rotstein 1973, p. 16; Smallwood 1976, p. 338; Weiss-Rosmarin 1966, pp. 5–6.

45. There are a few versions of Ben-Zakkai's escape. See also Lewis 1975, pp. 20–21; Zerubavel 1980, pp. 107–16, and Kedar 1982, pp. 59–60. For further reading on Ben-Zakkai and Yavne, see Neusner 1970 and Alon 1967, pp. 219–52.

46. For a fascinating discussion about the Masada-Yavne contrast and its possible implications for Judaism generally and for contemporary Judaism particularly, see Weiss-Rosmarin 1966, 1967; *The Spirit of Masada*, 1967. Undoubtedly, the contrast between Yavne (read: "survival") and Masada (read: "death") is unavoidable. See also note 45 above.

SIX
LOGIC OF EXPLANATION

Those who have not been trained as scientists can let their imaginations run wild, unchecked by empirical realities. Scientists, however, are disciplined to pay full attention to the facts and should be both careful with, and critical toward, their interpretations. Creating false impressions, concealing or fabricating facts, contextualizing explanations in a way that contradicts known and relevant facts, and sacrificing truth are definitely bad science.

A careful reading of Josephus could not possibly have given rise to the Masada mythical narrative. Even if we take into account that what Josephus offers us is, at least in some measure, an apology by a turncoat Jew who probably became Roman in lifestyle, his narrative is the closest to the events themselves. Even if it contains distortions, there is no reason to suspect that Josephus is lying on all points and that his historical narrative is completely fabricated. Moreover, the relevant point for us is that the mythmakers, and most certainly Yadin, repeatedly attributed to Josephus purported statements that never appeared in his text, and suppressed what does appear. In other words, Yadin and others made manipulative use of Josephus, as exemplified in the presentation and interpretation of the findings in loci 8, 113, and 2001–2002, as well as about the siege ramp, the length of the siege, the battles, and the strategic value of Masada. Support for the Massada myth was not based on serious and informative questioning of Josephus's historical text leading to acceptance or rejection of different parts of it. What Josephus provides us is a sad narrative about a questionable revolt that culminated in disaster and the slaughter of the rebel Jews, and about collective suicide on Masada. The Masada mythical narrative, as a heroic tale, was constructed *despite* what Josephus tells us, not *because* of it.

How was that construction possible? In my previous work (1995) I deciphered how it was made for popular culture—literature, films, tourism, the media, and textbooks. It consisted of eliminating nonheroic and problematic element, while embellishing and fabricating other elements, weaving together a consistently heroic (and fallacious) tale.

Shmaria Guttman probably had the most influential role in shaping and formulating the Masada mythical narrative, and thus his reading of Josephus is crucial. Guttman was always careful to state that Josephus's reliability and accuracy should not be questioned. And indeed, without Josephus, no myth could be constructed. But when Josephus provides historical evidence which is not conducive to the weaving of a heroic myth, Guttman is quick to discard that evidence. Let us take the example of the massacre at Ein Gedi. Here is an excerpt from his interview (January 1987) with me:

> Now let us take Ein Gedi. . . . I am not sure that his [Josephus Flavius's] statement about exactly what they [the people of Masada] did in Ein Gedi is the most accurate. But what is entirely clear to me is that they came to Ein Gedi and took food by force, of this I am certain.
>
> So, here is a group of people on top of Masada, isolated from the world, unaware that the war with the Romans is finished, and convinced that there still may be a chance to beat . . . the Empire. . . . They are fortunate, they have water, but they need more food too. . . . They come to Ein Gedi and tell the people there, "We're asking you to give." But . . . [the people of Ein Gedi refused], so they took it by force. Look, guys, this is not a nice thing to do, but to live, people do things that are not nice. And the people of Ein Gedi could have shown more courtesy and given them something of their own. So they took it by force. He [Josephus Flavius] turns it into butchery and burning and so forth. I don't have to accept that as the absolute truth [Note how suddenly Josephus Flavius's reliability becomes questionable]. And they may have done a few things that . . . were not moral.
>
> So, on this basis I want to paint a picture of the people in Ein Gedi. . . . Who were they? They were land tenants of the Roman regime. In fact, the people of Ein Gedi almost did not have private land, it was state property, and the state then was the ruling Roman Empire. So they [the people of Masada] felt that they were taking something that the Roman Empire had robbed them of and they wanted to take it back. So they did what they did in Ein Gedi. Do we have to build mountains of arguments about types of people, etc., etc., on this act? I don't accept this. They had to reach an agreement that they [the people of Ein Gedi] would give something. They didn't reach an agreement, so the problem had to be solved. But the people [from Masada] still believed that there was hope.

This is a fascinating but shocking argument. What does Guttman say here? First, that we do not have to particularly trust Josephus concerning the Ein Gedi massacre. Second, that the people of Ein Gedi virtually deserved their victimization (that is death) by having refused to provide the Sicarii from Masada with food, in other words, that the victims of the murderous raid are to blame for it.

Just to remind ourselves what Josephus Flavius *really* says about the massacre in Ein Gedi, and how far it is from Guttman's interpretation, let me quote directly from Josephus Flavius:

> There was a fortress . . . called Masada. Those that were called Sicarii had taken possession of it formerly; but at this time they overran the neighboring countries, aiming only to procure to themselves necessaries; for the fear they were then in prevented their future ravages; but when once they were informed that the Roman army lay still, and that the Jews were divided between sedition and tyranny, they boldly undertook greater matters; and at the feast of unleavened bread, which the Jews celebrate in memory of their deliverance from their Egyptian bondage, when they were sent back into the country of their forefathers, they came down by night, without being discovered by those that could have prevented them, and overran a certain small city called Engaddi:—in which expedition they prevented those citizens that could have stopped them, before they could arm themselves and fight them. They also dispersed them, and cast them out of the city. As for such as could not run away, being women and children, they slew of them about seven hundred. Afterward, when they had carried everything out of their houses, and had seized upon all the fruits that were in a flourishing condition, they brought them into Masada. And indeed these men laid all the villages that were about the fortress waste, and made the whole country desolate.[1]

I also interviewed Ze'ev Meshel, a man who devoted much of his life to the study of the archaeology of Israel. In his interview (January 11, 1994) Meshel told me:

> There is always a problem with historical sources, and that is who they were, what they represented, and what lay behind their decision to enter specific items into historical memory and leave other items outside. Thus we have a problem with that trend in Judaism which held the key to what was entered into the historical record and what was not. The Orthodox version of Judaism decided that certain chapters in history deserved to be remembered and others needed to be repressed. This is not my version. Some of the memories repressed in this way by Orthodox Judaism were kept alive by others, for example, the Apocrypha and the history written by Josephus Flavius which was kept by Christian monks.

Meshel refers here to a few issues: first, the problem of selection in historical narratives.[2] This refers not only to what gets selected and to the construction of historical sequences, but also to who has the power to enforce specific selections. Second, the Orthodox version of Judaism had the means and opportunity to make the selection deemed proper by some of its members. Third, because those constructing historical narratives invariably make selections, it is imperative that we take a critical stand toward their decisions; in other words, there is no one, eternally true, history. Meshel continues:

> There is a common thread behind the story of Masada and the Holocaust, and that is the feeling of the rebels that the Almighty has deserted them, and consequently the feeling of religious despair and thoughts of heresy, of denying the existence of G-d. This explains why Orthodox Judaism repressed the memory of Masada.

Reading Josephus Flavius "as is" certainly gives the reader the impression that the Jewish rebellion against the Romans was futile. As a Roman historian, Josephus's moral conclusion is obvious. However, knowing this should not prevent us from listening carefully to what he has to say. The view from the Roman side need not necessarily be a falsified one. For example, the fact remains that the Roman Empire of the first century C.E. was at the peak of its power, boasting a large number of armed legions and controlling an area which stretched from Britain to the Middle East. Fearing an invasion from its eastern borders, the Roman Empire maintained a few legions in the immediate area of Judea. To challenge this military force with any reasonable chance of success requires sound military strategy, military preparations, and at least some political and military alliances. There is no evidence that the Jewish inhabitants of Judea took any serious efforts in any of these areas. What chance, then, did the Jews have of defeating the mighty Roman military machine by initiating the Great Revolt? Moreover, according to Josephus the rebellion was conceptualized and aggressively promoted by a small group of extremist rebels, against the more mature judgment of others (including Josephus himself). In this way, Josephus can be read to mean that the overwhelming majority of Jews did not support the revolt.

Inverting Josephus means, for example, that one can read his text for inconsistencies and contradictions, so that the interpretation that is made to emerge is completely opposite to that which is denoted. That is, that the overwhelming majority of Jews did indeed support the revolt, and that the doomed rebellion was an instance of nationalist pride, of heroic Jews trying to free themselves of the yoke of their Roman oppressors. For these interpreters, it was in Josephus's interest to present the rebellion as the work of a small group of extremist outcasts who forced the majority of Jews into a dead-end and doomed situation. It was Josephus's purported interest to portray the overwhelming majority of Jews as living contentedly under the Pax Romana, with few disturbances, and thus the harsh Roman reaction was basically aimed at squelching an unpopular and unjustified rebellion.

We must separate two aspects of the argument. The first is the style of this argument. More than anything else, the choice of words and tone are more consistent with an emotional political-moral debate than a scientific one, and such an argument is won or lost through the exercise of power and the strength of personal networks.[3] The second aspect is cognitive and is directed at a very serious attempt to decode the historical narrative which Josephus has left us. Both aspects, I cheerfully admit, are intrinsically interesting.

Menachem Stern was one of the most eminent scholars of the period of the Great Revolt, and his studies have earned him a well-deserved international respect. It is thus instructive to examine his response to denunciations of the Masada mythical narrative.

> I am not prepared to be a judge, neither of the Sicarii nor of the Zealots. I shall not take them as an example. I am willing to understand them, but in no way cast stones . . . at people who sacrificed themselves for ideals and to say that they were not heroes. They were heroes! Attacking Yadin on this point lowers the quality of the argument. (Stern 1983, p. 382)

If Stern does not want to act judge, how can he label the inhabitants of Masada "heroes"? And if attacking Yadin "lowers the quality of the argument," then we are evidently not dealing with competing interpretations in a legitimate academic or professional debate, but in academic politics and morality.

Inverting Josephus means taking his historical text and employing a few techniques of manipulation so that the original meaning is inverted. For example, Josephus says that the Great Revolt was initiated by a small minority of fanatics; the inverted version would have us believe that it enjoyed popular support. Josephus says that there were Sicarii on Masada; the inverted version claims that others were there. Josephus implies a brief siege of Masada with no significant battles; the inverters postulate a protracted siege and a fierce "battle of Masada." Josephus states that the Sicarii on Masada were an isolated group of marauders; for the inverters Masada was the center of regional desert guerrilla warfare, possibly the center of an autonomous Judean state.

Looking at the events of the Great Revolt strictly from Josephus's perspective does not yield a heroic tale, so one is urged instead to use a wide-angle lens rather than a telescopic one. A wide-angle lens conceals what a detailed telescopic view reveals: that the events on Masada do not make up a heroic tale.

I found the best and most detailed presentation of this logic in one of my interviews with Ze'ev Meshel (January 11, 1994). When confronted with a strict reading of Josephus, Meshel responds with a long and complicated historical narrative. In order to develop an interesting and meaningful narrative, Meshel resorts to contextualization. He weaves his narrative in two interconnected spaces, one geographical, the other temporal.

In the first place is geographical contextualization. The story of Masada is placed within the setting of the Judean Desert. According to Meshel the Judean Desert and the Dead Sea served as refuge and base for guerrilla war throughout the time of the Jewish First Temple (c. 960–586 B.C.E.) and what he refers to as the ancient Kingdom of Judea. This became very explicit during Second Temple times (515 B.C.E.–70 C.E.), and particularly so during the period of the Hasmoneans (c. 167 B.C.E.–37 C.E.). Meshel stresses that the Judean Desert served as a refuge as well as an operational and regrouping base. The desert is ideal for such purposes because it poses serious logistic problems for a regular army (water, supplies, transportation). According to Meshel the desert was a natural hiding place for different groups seeking to maintain their independence against foreign occupation. His main line of argument is to try to establish and substantiate the idea that the Judean Desert has always been a natural refuge for Jewish rebels.

We must not underestimate the role of the desert in weaving national legends and constructing a credible past. The secular Zionist interpretation of Judaism turned the barren desert of Israel's central and southern regions into a magical resource. It has typically been portrayed as providing strength and power, inspiration, and tranquility. It has been constructed as an essential component of the new, proud Jew. In Yigael Yadin's 1966 book on Masada (which is located within the Judean desert) he writes that, after the fall of Jerusalem in 70 C.E., Masada "held out till 73. . . . With Masada as their base for raiding operations, they harried the Romans for two years" (1966e, p. 11). Significantly, at the time of the excavations and when the book was published, Yadin had absolutely no empirical evidence to support this claim. His statements, much like Meshel's, are based on wishful thinking, ideology, and conjectures not founded on any direct evidence.

Thus, in order to explain Masada, Meshel first places Masada within the Judean Desert. This framing is not merely geographical; Meshel contextualizes Masada within the Judean Desert socially, militarily, and politically, with the aim of persuading the unsuspecting listener that the Judean Desert has always served as a base for rebel activities. In this way, Meshel connects the rebels of Masada to what he portrays as a long historical tradition of rebels who found the desert a natural place for their activities. However, this contextualization is insufficient.

The second contextualization is temporal. It is not adequate to contextualize Masada within a geographical location traditionally favored by rebels; it is also necessary to show that this geographical location served its function long before and even after the Jewish Great Revolt, of which Masada was only the final chapter. To do that, Meshel first jumps to the Hasmoneans, and particularly the end of their rule in Judea at 37 B.C.E.

The Hasmoneans (or Maccabees) were a priestly family living in Modi'in, in what is now central Israel. They spearheaded the successful rebellion against the Seleucid kingdom during the second century B.C.E. and established an autonomous Jewish state. The devotion and courage of the Hasmoneans have become a major symbol for heroism among Jews, credited with preferring death over bondage or violation of the Jewish religious code. Here is how Meshel describes it:

> During the days of the First Temple, the Judean Desert and the area of the Dead Sea, constituted a refuge and base for small-scale warfare for the kingdoms of Israel and Judea. This found repeated and vigorous expression especially during the period of the Second Temple (and during the period of the First Temple as well). At the low point of their rebellion, the Hasmoneans, . . . [led by Jonathan] escaped to the Judean Desert. . . . Where was his secret stronghold? In Michmash, a settlement on the border of the Judean Desert, which was connected to King Saul and . . . the war against the Philistines. Whenever there was a problem, they retreated to the Judean Desert. Simeon, the last of the Hasmoneans, built the desert fortress of Karantel, fortifying Ras-El-Karantel.[4] This does not happen in Masada. Retreating to specific topographical sites in the desert does not occur in Masada. . . . The Judean Desert is a hostile region for a foreign army seeking to penetrate it in a regular military pattern—problems of water, supplies, etc. Ma'ale Isiim[5] was built by the Romans during the period of the Bar Kochva revolt [see below] in order to lay siege to the rebels hiding in the caves in nearby Nachal Chever. War in the Judean Desert has always been war for roads, since the days of Jonathan the Hasmonean. . . . The Judean Desert and its natural fortifications, especially during Second Temple times, was used not only by refugees, Essenes and others, but also by those trying to retain their independence in the face of a foreign invader. For those who lived there, the Judean Desert did not constitute a threat; it was their back yard. Those living in settlements on the edge of the Judean Desert knew that desert. There are siege systems around Horkania[6] and Sartava.[7] Who built these siege systems? I checked Josephus and he says, as if by the way, that when the Actium war broke out (in 40 B.C.), King Herod's orientation was to the west. The Hasmoneans looked to the east, toward the Persians.[8] In 40 B.C., aided by the Persians, Aristobulus conquered Judea, and Antipater and young Herod were forced to escape from Jerusalem, which they did via the Judean Desert and Masada. Herod left his family on Masada and escaped to the Nabateans, from there to El Arish, and to Rome. In Rome

> he was crowned king, returning to Judea to fight for the crown that Rome had bestowed. Hasmonean rule ended in 37 B.C. and Herod's first year on the throne began. And Josephus writes that "at the time of the Actium war which was 6 years after this [31 B.C.] Herod thought to come and help his benefactor . . . Antonius." So, I [Meshel] discovered a siege system around Horkania. . . . So, Hasmonean rule did not end in 37 B.C., but continued in the Judean Desert and in Horkania, under what Hasmonean ruler we don't even know, and which succeeded because they had escaped to the Judean Desert, about 100 years before the Great Revolt. So what shall we call them? Sicarii? Zealots? War mongers? Who went to the Judean Desert? It didn't start with the suppression of the Great Revolt. The area of the Judean Desert became the area for Judean small-scale warfare.

In fact, Hasmonean statehood ended some years earlier than implied by Meshel, and toward the end it suffered from some nasty infighting among contestants to the throne. These fights became worse after the death of Shlomtzion in 67 B.C.E., who became ruler of the Hasmonean state after the death of her husband, Janneus (103–76 B.C.E.). Meanwhile, Roman military and political leader Gnaeus Pompeius (106–48 B.C.E.) penetrated the area which is today Syria, organized it as a Roman province, and set up supporting states around its borders. Pompeius had to formulate a meaningful response to the political and military unrest within the Hasmonean state. One should recall that he was concomitantly occupied by a campaign against the Nabateans, and coping with Hasmonean unrest certainly interfered with the Roman war effort against the Nabateans, as Pompeius had to quit his military campaign against the Nabateans in order to cope with the Hasmoneans. So it should come as no surprise that Pompeius decided to do away with the Hasmonean state politically, geographically, and militarily (63 B.C.E.). It was not really the end, because a few loyalists managed to kindle the fires of resistance against the Romans in 40 B.C.E., but three years later this revolt was quashed too, and after 37 B.C.E. the Hasmonean state was, for all practical purposes, a thing of the past.

Meshel feels that the critical historical point is the naval battle near Actium in 31 B.C.E. (not 40 B.C.E. as he mistakenly quotes), in which the good-sized navy loyal to Antony was destroyed and his large army surrendered.[9] Following that defeat, both Antony and Cleopatra retreated to the east and eventually committed suicide. Octavianus Augustus reached Alexandria that year, annexed Egypt to Rome, and effectively put an end to the Hellenistic Ptolemaic dynasty which had ruled Egypt for some three hundred years. According to Meshel that battle lies at the historical nexus of the end of Hasmonean rule and the ascent of Herod to the Judean throne.

Meshel begins his unwieldy explanation of the events on Masada at least one hundred years before they occurred. Once he completes his historical script, he continues directly to the Bar Kochva revolt, completely ignoring the Great Revolt and Masada. His next temporal is thus the next rebellion of Jews against the Romans, which took place 132–135 C.E., that is, about sixty years after the end of the Great Revolt. The Romans crushed that revolt too, but at the cost of major military efforts and heavy casualties on both sides. Again, the Judean Desert played a major role as a base of operations for the rebellion. One must note that despite Meshel's rhetoric, the Roman military machine was quite successful in battling the Jews in their own back yard, and the desert, so exalted by him, did not provide a real shield for the rebels. The Bar Kochva revolt is the upper temporal limit of Meshel's historical contextualization.

Here is what he said:

> Let's jump to Bar Kochva, an event with almost no historical sources. No effort was made to preserve the origins of that event. And, here again, is the Judean Desert. And, again, people holding on in caves and underground siege systems. . . . The Romans set almost all their military might against the Bar Kochva revolt. Those crazy people called Jews want to maintain religious independence?—that unsettles the Romans. And, again, the rebels escape to the Judean Desert's caves, and an amazing thing happens here again: the Romans take the trouble of chasing those rebels in *all over* the Judean Desert and simply destroy them. Did those few really constitute such a grave threat to the Empire?
>
> The refugees in the caves innocently believed that if they managed to survive, they would be independent Judea. Otherwise there is no reasonable historical explanation for why they were persecuted.

Thus, Meshel contextualizes Masada in the Judean Desert and between the naval battle near Actium in 31 B.C.E. and the Bar Kochva revolt of 132–135 C.E.. Within this broad contextualization Meshel states that the Great Revolt actually ended in 70 C.E., when Jerusalem was conquered and the Second Temple destroyed. Suddenly, he says, three years later the war resumes—once again a Roman army is gathered and marches to Masada. How can one explain this? For Meshel, it is simple: For three years Jews continued to maintain the political independence of Judea in the Judean Desert and the Dead Sea basin, controlling all the Judean Desert. The Romans decided that they had to conquer this Judean political entity, and thus in 73 C.E. they realized that they had to take the last three fortresses: Herodion, Macherus, and Masada.

This creative interpretation places the supposed independence of Judea within three strongholds. Meshel is quick to point out that such interpretation implies that the Roman circumvallation wall around Masada was intended not to prevent the escape of the besieged, but to keep other rebels from joining them. This narrative would have Jewish freedom fighters creating an independent political Jewish entity in the Judean Desert after the destruction of Jerusalem and the Second Temple in 70, challenging the Romans. The Romans had no choice but to meet this challenge head-on and crush this resistance as well, which they did in 73. Here is how Meshel frames his argument:

> In my view, even after the 70 [C.E.] conquest and the destruction of the Temple, Jews continued to uphold the independence of Judea in the Judean Desert and the Dead Sea basin. Who knows who came to the desert? They ruled *all* the Judean Desert. . . . In 73 [C.E.] the Romans understood that if their goal was to *destroy* the independence of Judea, they could not attain that goal as long as, and because of, Jewish independence in the Judean Desert and the Dead Sea basin. This independence coalesced around three fortresses: Herodium, Macherus and Masada. That is why the Romans returned in 73 [C.E.], to suppress this independence. After Macherus and Herodium, the refugees escaped to Masada. Guttman thought that the purpose of the siege wall which the Romans built around Masada was not to prevent escape, but to prevent refugees from entering Masada. Those fortresses were meant to preserve people from the ruling dynasty because in a monarchy, the dynasty is a symbol of independence.

It is imperative to understand how far removed this interpretation is from Josephus, and hence how misleading this wide-angle historical lens is in comparison to the more specific and accurate text provided by Josephus. Certainly Meshel's interpretation cannot be found in Josephus. On the contrary, much of what Josephus says is simply inconsistent with and contradictory to it. Two central points must be mentioned here. First, Josephus notes certain events that took place between 70 and 73 C.E.:

> Lucilius Bassus was sent as a legate into Judea, and there he received the army from Cerealis Vitellius, and took that citadel which was in Herodium . . . after which he got together all the soldiery that was there . . . with the tenth legion, and resolved to make war on Macherus; for it was highly necessary that this citadel should be demolished, lest it might be a means of drawing away many into a rebellion, by reason of its strength.[10]

Not a word about an independent Judea or Masada as an important fortress. Then:

> When Bassus was dead in Judea, Flavius Silva succeeded him as a procurator there; who when he saw that all the rest of the country was subdued in this war, and that there was but one only stronghold that was still in rebellion, he got all his army together that lay in different places, and made an expedition against it. This fortress was called Masada.[11]

Again, no word about Jewish independence. The Judean Desert is not depicted as a hiding place for some purported "independent" Jewish entity which posed a significant imminent challenge, political or military, to Roman hegemony. The passage conveys the information that Roman governor Flavius Silva was involved in a mopping-up operation, which probably did not just "happen" in 73, but extended over a longer period of time. A Roman ruler died and had to be replaced; an army had to be gathered, twice.

Second, in direct contradiction of Guttman, and implicit contradiction of Meshel, who refers to Guttman, here is what Josephus has to say about the Roman siege wall around Masada:

> [Flavius Silva] also built a wall quite round the entire fortress that none of the besieged might easily escape: he also set his men to guard the several parts of it.[12]

Let us now continue to examine how Meshel persists in weaving his panoramic-based interpretation:

> Thus, not only did those besieged on Masada believe in their power, but the Romans accepted it as well. They constituted independent Judea. There is no other explanation for the tremendous Roman effort in this God-forsaken outback. The refugees of Masada *believed* that they *were* independent Judea, and this is the only way in which I understand it. Not a thousand people, but Judean independence. And for me, in my perception, Judean independence ended there in Masada. Those one thousand people believed in it, and the Romans believed in it.

At this point in the interview I pointed out to Meshel that, while his interpretation was interesting, perhaps even true, it was most definitely *not* what Josephus said. I told Meshel that he could improve on Josephus only by using a much wider historical context within which to construct his interpretation. I also pointed out that I found it odd that we had to travel to Actium in 31 B.C.E. and to Bar Kochva in 135 C.E. to explain a few months in 73 C.E. Meshel responded by stating that "I would have phrased it differently. I am allowed to read in Josephus *more* than what is explicitly there. What you say, Nachman, is true, but I would have phrased it differently."

Another point requires reiteration here. As a Roman historian, Josephus had a vested interest in portraying Rome's enemies as powerful and aggressive. The more powerful and aggressive their portrayal, the more enhanced is Rome's conquest of them. There was no glory in conquering a band of hoodlums or marauders. If Meshel's (and Guttman's) fanciful description of an imaginary and powerful Judean entity was valid, Josephus surely would not have missed the chance to mark its presence. His failure to mention this nonexistent entity was no oversight. He does not fail to describe the battle around Macherus, or the quickly won Roman victory of Herodion. At no point does Josephus combine the three fortresses of Herodion, Macherus and Masada as Meshel does. Moreover, to crush the Great Revolt of the Jews, the Roman imperial army exerted a significant effort, sending in armed legions. To crush Macherus, Herodium, and Masada, steps had to be taken to "gather the army," the implication being of a slow process of recruiting local military forces, regrouping regular Roman army units, nothing major.

In summarizing Meshel's logic it becomes clear that this explanation was plausible only if the Great Revolt (66–73 C.E.), a period of seven fateful years, and especially the fall of Masada (a few months in 72–73) were contextualized within a historical context of almost two hundred years. Thus the events on Masada are interpreted and explained not by themselves, but within the historical context. This type of logic provides an explanation for the events on Masada within what is presented as a very long but consistent and continuous historical sequence. In this carefully crafted and enthusiastically presented sequence, the Jews are portrayed as repeatedly rebelling, in the face of all odds, against any foreign rule in the attempt to maintain their religious and national independence. During these recurrent revolts, the Judean Desert is portrayed as playing a major role. This historical sequence is presented in a persuasive and authoritative manner. In part it relies on Josephus; but what Josephus does not say becomes self-evident from this historical sequence. Hence, many of the details given by Josephus in his description of the Great Revolt are recast within this historical wide-angle view. For example, were the Sicarii in Masada? Perhaps. But even if they were, they probably were not the only ones. Just look at how many rebel groups took refuge in the desert. Was the rebellion against the Romans initiated and sustained by a small group of reckless and irresponsible bandits? Just have a look at the 31 B.C.E.–135 C.E. sequence. Jews *always* rebelled against *any* foreign yoke. It is unreasonable to assume that a small group of marauders did. No battles around Masada? That makes no sense. Just look at the historical sequence above. Not only were there battles, but it stands to reason that Masada served as a center for rebel activity against the Roman empire. If Josephus does not mention all this—well, his information must not be accurate.

It is imperative that we understand this type of logic. The expansion of the time sequence is precisely the device which enables a closer reading of Josephus to be askew. The above conclusions cannot be reached if one reads only what Josephus wrote directly about Masada.

The logic used by Meshel is fascinating and persuasive. His wide-angle view presents a long and complex period, focusing on the desert, in an integrated and compelling fashion. It is wrong, but it is also both insightful and powerful. The need for such a wide-angle view is obvious; Meshel's fanciful interpretation makes sense only when it is painted on such a broad canvas. But this view is deceptive and deliberately so. When we switch to a telephoto lens and focus on the known details, it becomes clear how far from the historical facts, and how empirically unsubstantiated this interpretation is. But Meshel's logic is that of a heroic myth, not of a factual historical narrative.

If anything, Meshel's interpretation provides one of the best illustrations of why it was so important to excavate Masada. Meshel's argument is not disconnected from a larger debate within history involving two very different conceptions of historiography. On one side are scholars such as Dilthey, Rickert, Fichte, and Collingwood. On the other side is a large group of more cautious empiricists. Thus, what we have contrasted here are historians who try to portray historical processes with a large brush on a big canvas, and those who pay careful attention to details and empirical facts. The historical development of historiography and the different scholars who nourished the heated debates about the nature of history and its presentation are obviously beyond the scope of this book. However, between the two perspectives referred to above, it is not too difficult to understand that the perspective used in this book[13] is much closer to the cautious empiricists than to the creative constructionists, interesting and provoking as their insightful statements may be. In the final analysis, I feel that we are bound to stick to facts, without which we may end up with no more than a series of competing narratives, no one any better than another—unless we reveal the values which guided the way in which the specific historiography was constructed and communicated. Despite the subversively seductive lure of postmodernism, I still believe that when we deal with real and empirical historical events (as contrasted with ideas, for example), a good way to evaluate their interpretation is by resorting to empirical criteria.

NOTES

1. *Wars of the Jews*, 4.7.2, p. 537.

2. See, e.g., Ben-Yehuda 1995, pp. 275–79.

3. See, e.g., Ben-Yehuda 1985, pp. 124–30 and 1990, pp. 181–219 for a somewhat similar controversy in the early days of radio astronomy.

4. A monastery on top of a mountain about four kilometers northwest of Jericho. The remnants of the Hasmonean fortress built there probably around 135 B.C.E. are still visible today.

5. A road about three kilometers southwest of Ein Gedi.

6. In the northern part of the Judean Desert, near an ancient road between Bethlehem and the Dead Sea. The fortress was destroyed in 63 B.C.E., rebuilt, but destroyed again in 57 B.C.E.

7. The fortress Alexandrion, built around 90 B.C.E. on top of a cone-shaped

mountain, 377 meters above sea level in the lower Jordan Valley, about six kilometers west of the Damia bridge on the Jordan River. The fortress was destroyed by Gavinius, but was rebuilt. It was excavated in 1981.

8. Meshel refers to the war fought by Octavian (Augustus) and Marc Antony against Cassius and Brutus after the assassination of Julius Caesar. Octavian and Antony won the major battle in 42 B.C.E. Then Antonius continued east to fight the Persians, but he met Cleopatra, fell in love, and neglected his duties to Rome. Eventually the Roman senate ordered Octavianus to attack Antonius. The major battle took place September 2, 31 B.C.E., near Actium. Cleopatra deserted the battle, Antony followed her, and they escaped to Egypt. Ultimately they both committed suicide.

9. For more on this naval engagement see Dupuy and Dupuy 1970, pp. 114–15; Rodgers 1964.

10. *Wars of the Jews*, 7.6.1, p. 595.

11. *Wars of the Jews*, 7.8.1, p. 598.

12. *Wars of the Jews*, 7.8.2, p. 599.

13. Contextual constructionism.

SEVEN

THE IMPACT OF THE EXCAVATIONS

Media references to the excavations of Masada are not limited to the time of the excavation (1963–65). On March 30, 1955, *Ma'ariv* (p. 2) reported that an archaeological survey expedition to Masada had made important discoveries and confirmed "almost all the descriptions of Josephus Flavius about the luxury of the fortress, palaces, and hidden paths." The report is extensive, with many superlative expressions describing the excitement of the expedition members. A day later, (March 31, p. 4) *Ma'ariv* reported that the archaeologists on Masada had discovered wall ornaments and that "on one of the walls a Roman soldier had carved his name."

As noted earlier, Yadin held tight rein over what information was given the press during the 1963–65 dig. As most sources point out, Yadin was a natural for the media. He felt comfortable with journalists and made regular appearances in the radio, as well as writing pieces for the press and giving interviews. The media provided Yadin with an important means of expressing his positions and recruiting support for his archaeological excavations of Masada, because these excavations had been deemed a "national project" and were not confined to the interests of detached professional archaeologists. Indeed, the media were a naturally cooperative and sympathetic partner for this national project.

Consequently, there was a continuous flow of information from Yadin to the media. The subject of how to present the archaeological finds to the media came up in the daily transcripts of the excavation: what to say, who to say it to, whether to agree to exclusivity or not, and so on. Yadin also used the press to make speculative interpretations that are not reflected in the daily transcripts of the archaeologists' meetings. Clearly, talking to the media became a way for him to develop his speculations unchallenged, especially when such speculations as attributing bones found in a cave to the defenders of Masada and the discovery of the synagogue did not appear directly under his name. The daily press presented such interpretations as nonproblematic, solid, and definite. In other situations, Yadin did not always demonstrate the same level of self-confidence; in the press, his hesitations tended to disappear.

The daily newspapers also occasionally published interim summaries. These are not scientific reports, but they do point out the type of information Yadin was providing the press, as well as a reflection of what he felt was important and what was not. For example, *Ma'ariv* of April 12, 1964 (p. 3), between the two seasons of excavations, published an interim summary of the major finds. The report was written by Yadin himself and it hails the scrolls discovered as most important. Of the finds mentioned in earlier chapters as important, the skeletal remains unearthed in locus 8 were barely mentioned. No mention is made of the lots, the synagogue, the *Mikve*, or the skeletal remains in loci 2001–2002, all of which Yadin himself elsewhere defined as very significant.

We have seen that the excavations of Masada were not a purely professional and academic issue. Yadin's main interest in them was patriotic, and he thus helped turn the excavations into national and international events, thereby involving himself in politics and the media. Yadin was keen on making as many key politicians as possible interested in Masada, and making them visit Masada and express support for his operation there. Great care was taken to ensure that such visits were reported in the media. The issue of burying the skeletal remains found in Masada was even discussed in the Israeli parliament and provoked some heated and bitter debates, which were extensively reported in the media.

Moreover, there is little doubt that Yadin used the media to propagate the myth and disseminate ideas that he might not have been able to publish in the academic literature. In fact, Yadin never published the full range of the findings from his excavations. His major publication on Masada was the book that appeared in 1966 in both English and Hebrew. Thus trying to capture his thoughts on what happened on Masada and his interpretations of the findings requires an examination of many sources: the daily transcripts of the excavations, the media, and his own writings in a variety of typically nonscientific outlets. In this respect what Yadin told the press about Masada is of crucial importance.

Yadin was very keen to have the Masada discoveries "star" in the news, and thus throughout the period of the archaeological digs items on the excavations regularly appeared both in newspapers and on the radio (Israel had no television at that time). In Israel, *Ma'ariv* provided the most extensive coverage of the excavations because of its agreement with the *Observer* in London, which helped sponsor the excavations. The *Observer* had exclusive rights to publishing the excavations' findings—another historical irony: the results deriving from excavations whose importance for Israelis centered on their national identity were to be published by a British newspaper.

We examined how the various newspapers presented the Masada narrative in three broad areas: (a) how the identity of the Sicarii was described, (b) how the siege, battle, and suicide were described, and (c) which values and opinions on Masada were projected.

We thoroughly examined two secular newspapers, *Ma'ariv* and *Yediot Aharonot*, which at the time were the two major Hebrew-language dailies in Israel. We emphasized the written media because a complete examination of radio broadcasts proved impractical. We did examine the radio broadcasts in which Yadin was directly involved, when they could be located in the Israeli Broadcasting Authority archives.

Most of the reports which we found in the printed press described the archaeological findings and/or the complicated logistics which made excavating in such a remote and nearly inaccessible site feasible. Only a fraction of the articles discussed the historical narrative of the events of 66–73 C.E. at any length. The few reports that did so appeared at the start of the excavations and attempted to acquaint readers with the narrative. This type of coverage seems characteristic of the period, but it reflects the Yadin touch. He was interested in disseminating the mythical narrative, but he was also interested in impressing the readers with the tremendous logistical effort required for the excavations. Thus we find some repetitions of the Masada mythical narrative, and a good deal of rather uninspired information on the environment, architecture, archaeology, and geography of the site.

The rebels on Masada were characterized by Josephus as "Sicarii"—that is, a group of extremist political assassins who committed an atrocity in Ein Gedi and refused to join the fight against the Romans in Jerusalem—a questionable band of marauders with whom one can hardly associate the term heroism. Mythologizing Masada into a tale of heroism precludes identifying the rebels of Masada as Sicarii. Indeed, the literature is replete with terms for the inhabitants of Masada: rebels, defenders, heroes, freedom fighters, and more. The most common and most misleading misnomer is "Zealots," and Yadin's use of that term is almost as persistent, and consistent, as Josephus's use of the word "Sicarii." Yadin used the term even before the excavations and throughout the daily transcripts of the archaeological venture, where the Sicarii are simply not mentioned. In *Masada: Herod's Fortress and the Zealots' Last Stand* (1966) he refers to the Sicarii only in the context of the Essenes, but without any explanation provided. The excavations on Masada produced no findings which could either confirm or disprove Josephus's assertion that the commander of Masada, Elazar Ben-Yair, was one of the Sicarii, or that the people he commanded were Sicarii. When Yadin came to Masada he already "knew" that there were "Zealots" there, which was how the mythical narrative described them. He stifled his scientific skepticism and continued to use this deliberately misleading name. It is inconceivable that Yadin was unaware of what Josephus wrote about the people on Masada; yet he deliberately and consciously chose not to use the historical evidence provided by Josephus. Yadin's transformation of the negative nature of the rebels of Masada into something positive is of course understandable. After all, Yadin's main reason for consenting to lead the excavations at Masada was to provide scientific credibility for the heroic mythical version of the tale. We really should not expect him to have done anything to undermine this intention, and telling the historical truth (that is, remaining faithful to Josephus) could not possibly have served his purpose. He probably believed the myth himself. It was Yadin the nationalist patriot, and not Yadin the scientist and professional archaeologist, who determined that there were Zealots on Masada in direct contradiction of Josephus. He felt no need to explain himself; this was the "truth."

It is not surprising, then, that all the hundreds of reports carried by the newspapers while the excavations were being carried out in 1963–65, the word *Sicarii* appeared only twice. The first mention was in *Ma'ariv* on October 13, 1963 (pp. 3 and 8). That report stated that when the Great Revolt began, Masada was conquered in a surprise attack by Menachem Ben Yehuda of the Galilee, who commanded the Sicarii. The second mention is in *Ma'ariv* on November 11, 1963, where "the leader of the Zealots, Elazar Ben-Yair the Sicarius" is referred to, leading the reader to perhaps conclude that Elazar was the only Sicarius on Masada, the rest being Zealots. In both places no explanation is given concerning the Sicarii. This is an interesting point, for in almost all the reports a clear choice has been made to use the term Zealots. If that was not enough, additional rhetorical devices were typically resorted to in order to explain who the Zealots were and also who the non-Zealots were. The expressions used for this purpose include *fighters*, *fighters of Masada*, *Hebraic warriors*, the *last fighters of the rebellion*, *freedom fighters*, *defenders of Masada* (by far the preferred expression), *the last defenders*, *the besieged*, *the besieged rebels*, *the revolutionary Jews of the First Rebellion*, *Hebraic Zealots*, and *Zealots for the freedom of Judea*. None of these terms is neutral; they all reflect a decidedly positive attitude towards the rebels of Masada, and are intended to foster awe, empathy, and identification with them. These expressions were very meaningful in the Jewish Israeli construction of reality of the early 1960s—a state under siege. The ethnic-nationalistic element of the identification is obvious (e.g., the word *Hebraic*). The open admiration for the rebels on Masada developed not only because of what they did, but because they were *constructed* as part of the Jewish people, fighting for Jewish national independence. The account was enhanced by implying that these Jewish warriors were battling for more than national independence; they were in the midst of an active ideological struggle aimed at preserving Jewish ethnic identity and religion. The social construction of heroism is supplemented by making our heroes the "last," rife with connotations of a determined group of fighters ultimately pushed into reaching a fateful decision.

This social construction achieves two goals. First, it conceals the very problematic identity of the Sicarii and the questionable reputation attributed to them in Josephus Flavius's original account. Second, it presents the Sicarii as a positively heroic group of people who may have functioned in circumstances similar in some respects to those of the State of Israel in the 1960s. For the Jewish-Israeli mind-set of those years, this particular reconstruction of reality must have made it convenient to bridge a gap of close to two thousand years and create a mystical identification with this group of "the last Jewish freedom fighters."

The actual siege of Masada was probably very short; there are no indications of any "battle," and Masada's end came by mass suicide.

Ma'ariv, of October 13, 1963, reported that

> After the fall of Herodion and Michvar [Macherus], Masada was the last fortress of the Zealots. A few of the fighters from Judea who had fled to the desert went there, among them Elazar Ben-Yair, who became the commander. Believing that the rock provided adequate protection from the Romans, the defenders of the stronghold continued to fortify it and made all the necessary preparations for battles and siege. (p. 3)

That this description is almost totally inconsistent with Josephus is evident; its implications are nevertheless interesting. This inaccurate and misleading account clearly states that the "defenders" of Masada arrived there *after* the fortresses of Macherus and Herodium had fallen, reinforcing the portrayal of the "last stand of the last heroes." Totally ignored are such facts as the moral nature of the "defenders" of Masada, the questionable circumstances of their arrival there, and the time of that arrival. The report thus creates a crucial fabrication. Later in the same article, *Ma'ariv* tells its readers,

> in 72 C.E. Silva, the Roman commander, convened a large contingent of Roman military forces in the province and began to move toward the last Jewish fortress—Masada. Among his soldiers was the famous Roman Tenth Legion. However, his first attempts to conquer the mountain failed.

Researchers indeed agree that it was the Tenth Legion that lay siege to Masada; but the phrasing of the report is misleading, suggesting that the military force sent against Masada was huge and happened to include the

Tenth Legion—clear support for the "few against the many" theme. Similarly unfounded is the statement that the "first attempts to conquer the mountain failed." Josephus does not mention any first failed attempts to conquer Masada, and there is no logical reason to assume that an experienced commander would send his troops to conquer a mountain without appropriate preparations (in this case, a siege ramp). There is no basis for the view that Flavius Silva was the kind of impatient commander which the report seems to imply he may have been.

Ma'ariv of October 13, 1963, informs its readers (p. 3) that the reason the Romans built the wall around Masada was to prevent any supplies or reinforcements from reaching it. This is definitely *not* what Josephus says. According to him, the wall "around the entire fortress" was built so "that none of the besieged might easily escape."[1] The Romans evidently wanted to eliminate the last remnants of the Jewish revolt. Moreover, judging from Josephus's description, it is very doubtful whether there was anyone who either wanted to or was able to resupply or reinforce the Sicarii. However, such a portrayal certainly helped create a double impression: first that there were other free Jews who were both willing and able to supply Masada (more a fantasy than a solidly based scientific hypothesis), and second that an (imaginary) association exists between the siege of Masada and the bitter and brutal 1948 Israeli War of Independence, which was still very much alive in the memory of so many Israelis in the early 1960s. Emphasizing the siege as a means of preventing help from arriving (rather than preventing those trapped on the mountain from escaping) played directly into this historical analogy. The crucial supplies of food, water, ammunition, and reinforcements were among the hallmarks of the 1948 war, as Jewish settlements found themselves under siege by Arab military and paramilitary forces. In fact, one of the most heroic symbols of the 1948 war was the Jewish supply caravans to besieged locations such as Jerusalem and Gush Etzion. Thus the idea of a group of besieged Jews prevented from receiving help was a construction which helped create a mystical identification.

The duration of the siege on Masada is mentioned in four reports. *Ma'ariv* reported on October 13, 1963 (p. 8), "On the first day of Pesach, April 15, in the year 73 C.E., Masada fell after months of heavy siege and desperate heroic battles." "Months" is obviously less than a year, while "heavy siege" is not a very lucid expression; what would be the opposite—"light siege"? And of course there is no mention in Josephus of any "desperate heroic battles." What seems to have actually occurred is from four to eight months of standard Roman army siege under the best of circumstances, perhaps only just a few (four to eight) weeks of siege (according to Roth's 1995 study), not accompanied by any battles and followed by collective suicide. The second reference is in *Ma'ariv*, November 11, 1963, where it is stated that the siege of Masada lasted three years. A third reference is found in

Ma'ariv, November 24, 1963, stating that the "defenders" of Masada "lived and fought" there for three years. Finally, *Yediot Aharonot* of October 20, 1963, reports that the siege on Masada lasted two and a half years. All these reports portray a long siege, accompanied by heroic battles. The construction of a fabricated protracted siege helped magnify the elements of heroism, hardship, and resistance to pressure assumed to be characteristic of the defenders of Masada. Moreover, a few reports estimate the size of the Roman military force as in excess of 10,000 soldiers, plus thousands of slaves—an enormous military array against only 967 defenders.

It is important to state once again that the archaeological excavations of Masada produced no artifacts which contradict Josephus's accounts on these issues. Moreover, there was nothing in the excavations that could provide a clue as to the duration of the siege.

Regarding the issue of the suicide the fact is that, despite searches, the excavators of Masada did not find the remains of the 960 rebel Sicarii of Masada who supposedly committed collective suicide. So that question remains open.

The suicide is cited in almost all the relevant newspaper reports. However, none of them mentions that Elazar Ben-Yair had to address his reluctant followers twice in order to persuade them to take their own lives. This complicated and painful drama is typically telescoped and edited into a short account to the effect that when Elazar Ben-Yair realized that there was no more hope of withstanding the Romans, he spoke to his people and encouraged them to commit suicide, arguing that death was preferable to surrender and slavery at the hands of the Romans. These accounts generally do not make mention of any hesitation on the part of the Sicarii.

The actual act itself is typically underplayed. The expressions usually used are "tragic heroic death," "dying," "committed suicide," "fell on their swords," and so on. The narrative given by Josephus that "they . . . slay their wives and children, and themselves also," and the long, passionate description he provides,[2] are simply ignored. Some of the reports do not even mention that there were women and children involved in the death scene, nor that those making the decision most probably did not include these same women and children in the decision-making process. Those making the decisions are typically referred to as the "defenders," "fighters," "Jews"—always using the plural male form. While this may have been standard at the time, there is no implication that noncombatants or women were consulted. Moreover, the decision to resort to, and the act of, suicide are generally mentioned in combination with what is considered to be the opposite, negative, alternative: surrender and enslavement. In this way the act of collective suicide is presented positively, as an act of true heroism.

Generally speaking, Orthodox religious Jews were not too interested in the excavations of Masada. To begin with, their historical memory from the end of the period of the Great Revolt focuses not on Josephus Flavius but rather on Yochanan Ben-Zakkai, who is viewed as the founder of modern-day Jewish scholarship. Their general lesson from the Great Revolt is that saving lives, salvaging wisdom, and studying the Scriptures are what is important, not the collective suicide on Masada. The Masada mythical narrative was never too popular with Orthodox Jews as a heroic tale.[3] Still, the excavations were progressing and yielding discoveries about Jews. Orthodox reactions to these findings centered on two areas. One has already been mentioned, i.e., the vociferous insistence of Ultra-Orthodox Jews that the bones found in Masada be given a proper Jewish burial. Another area can be discerned from the Jewish religious press, and an examination of both *Hamodia* and *Hatzofe* reveals some interesting findings.

Hatzofe is a national Orthodox Zionist newspaper. During the period of the 1963–65 excavations, it published quite a few articles reporting the various discoveries on Masada. As can be expected, these items focus on Jewish-related issues: The majority of items are about the discovery of scrolls related to the holy Jewish scriptures, ceramics with inscriptions which indicate that the inhabitants of Masada were observant Jews, and the synagogue. *Hamodia*, an Ultra-Orthodox non-Zionist newspaper, reported the Jewish-religious-oriented findings from Masada much as the *Hatzofe*. It emphasized the Jewish connection: biblical and related scrolls, the synagogue, the *Mikve*. *Hamodia*, unlike *Hatzofe*, exhibited a clearly antipathetic tone toward the Masada mythical narrative. Nonetheless, *Hamodia* also referred to the rebels on Masada as "heroes."

The religious newspapers were not the only ones reporting discoveries of Jewish religious artifacts on Masada. The secular *Ma'ariv* did as well; for example, on December 27, 1964 (p. 2), it announced the find of the traditional version of the Book of Psalms. This was hailed as "the most important discovery[4] during the second period of excavations."

Rather than exhibit some healthy criticism, the Zionist secular and Orthodox media cooperated with Yadin's drive to disseminate the Masada mythical narrative. Reports of discoveries were accompanied by the interpretations provided by Yadin. Yadin's deceptive techniques were thus amplified by an uncritical press. Much like Knightley's (1975) examination of the role of the press during war, we find that journalists and their newspapers participated in disseminating a falsified tale in society. In this respect the media certainly played a major role in creating and sustaining a questionable narrative. There is an interesting lesson here for understanding how fabrications are created and diffused into cultures. If Knightley's work showed how war correspondents helped pass on misinformation, our analysis has revealed a similar process. Undoubtedly, using the prestige and credibility of science may have helped to make willing journalists less critical and inquisitive.

Our analysis focuses on a few specific areas of contradiction between Josephus and Yadin's presentation in the press; but the press also emphasized other relevant issues, and did so consistently and repeatedly: (a) the link between the rebels of Masada and modern Israelis/Jews; (b) Masada as a heroic tale; and (c) the Masada narrative as a symbol and a positive value for Israelis/Jews.[5]

What we are seeing here is how one particular sequence of historical events is run through a series of different cultural filters, each imparting a somewhat different meaning. This is an interesting observation mainly because it supports our initial approach of first establishing the consensual factual level and then going on to examine the interpretative cultural constructions based on these historical events.

In my previous work on the development of the Masada myth (1995), I examined how the story of Masada was presented in such various spheres of Israeli cultural life as politics, literature, the arts, history, education, and tourism. The presentation of the Masada myth in these areas both preceded and followed the 1963–65 excavations. A relevant question is whether we can detect any changes in the way Masada was presented in these areas before and after the excavations, and if so, can they be linked to the excavations.

The most significant postexcavation political process involving Masada was the debate around what has become known as the Masada complex. The Masada complex may refer to a number of subjects: suicide, the "last stand," heroism, siege mentality, and perhaps more. In essence it refers to a desperate situation, to a worldview analogous to that of people on top of a remote fortress, besieged and hunted, with very few options left, and aware that time may be running out and their fate is sealed. A world outlook such as this may dictate policies, decisions, the perception of options, and behavior. From this point of view, the Masada complex is a moral lesson. It is not a positive or flattering expression, as it refers to a desperate and difficult mentality. While use of the term *Masada complex* can be traced to the early 1960s, it reached a peak in the early 1970s. At that time, major Israeli politicians were accused of following a foreign policy based on the ideology of the Masada complex.[6] But the 1970s Masada complex political controversy cannot be traced directly or exclusively to the excavations of Masada. Everything raised in that debate had been mentioned before the excavations; the theme of Masada in political service clearly preceded the archaeological excavations.

Masada was a focal point for tourists even before the excavations, but the excavations and reconstructions most certainly turned it into a major site. The construction of the cable car (which became operational in 1971) gave further impetus to this trend. Yadin himself was one of the most enthusiastic supporters of tourism to Masada. On more than one occasion he expressed support for making Masada as accessible as possible to as many people as possible. It was his idea that Masada be not only excavated but reconstructed as well, and he gave unambiguous support for the construction of the cable car. This position should not come as a surprise. As we have repeatedly noted, one of Yadin's chief motivations for his involvement in Masada was patriotic and nationalistic. He had a clear vested interest in seeing to it that as many Israelis (and others) as possible be exposed to the Masada experience: visit the site, hear the mythical tale on-site, and come away impressed.

Indeed, in *Masada: Herod's Fortress and the Zealots' Last Stand* Yadin wrote,

> Masada represents for all of us in Israel and for many elsewhere, archaeologists and laymen, a symbol of courage, a monument to our great national figures, heroes who chose death over a life of physical and moral serfdom. (p. 13)

I examined thirty-one tourist guidebooks, published from 1963 (immediately after the excavations) to 1989, which suggest sites and places to visit in Israel. In all of them Masada is highly recommended and occupies a central place. In fourteen of the books published before the excavations, Masada is mentioned as well, but with clear differences. Tourist guidebooks after the excavations typically devote more space to Masada, include many more details on the site, and make a generally stronger recommendation to visit it. Both before and after the excavations, the guidebooks present the mythical and not the historical narrative.

There is a striking difference before and after the excavations in the numbers of visitors to Masada. Before the dig, 25,000 to 40,000 tourists visited Masada annually. Following the excavations, the number more than doubled, rising to 90,000 to 120,000 each year. The most dramatic increase came in the wake of inauguration of the cable car in 1971, when the figure rose to more than 200,000 tourists annually. For the last few years that number has risen to 600,000 to 700,000 per year, 11–12 percent of whom are Israelis and the remainder foreign tourists.

A particularly grandiose tourist event was held on October 13, 1988, when the Israeli Philharmonic Orchestra, conducted by Zubin Mehta (with Yves Montand, Gregory Peck, and Martin Grey as guests of honor) played Mahler's Symphony no. 2, the Resurrection Symphony, at the foot of Masada. This concert was the last in a series of events commemorating the fortieth anniversary of the State of Israel. Israel's Prime Minister Yitzhak Shamir, President Chaim Herzog, and other dignitaries also attended. Tickets cost was between US$ 150 to $550, although some invited guests paid thousands of dollars including flight tickets and other contributions. El Al, Israel's national airline, offered special deals. The concert was attended by about three thousand guests from outside Israel and about one thousand Israelis. The reports all concluded that the concert and the evening were a most impressive production. Among other things, attractive young waitresses in Roman garb distributed food, and fireworks were displayed—the show must have been absolutely incredible. In fact, a report in *Yediot Aharonot* carried pictures of the ceremony and of the food, and contained a large article about the attire of the various VIPs who attended.[7] A 120-minute videocassette of the event is also available for anyone who is interested.

There probably can be no starker contrast than that between this hedonistic event with its ambiance of glitz and the doom-laden atmosphere of the desert as the determined Roman Tenth Legion glared at the mountaintop fortress where the desperate Sicarii counted out their days. How would these adversaries have felt if some imaginary time machine had been able to bring them to this Masada festival? Perhaps only another historical irony that Masada seems to provoke.[8]

Most foreign dignitaries coming to Israel are taken to visit the Yad Vashem Holocaust Museum in Jerusalem. Fewer are taken to Masada, although it is not uncommon for Israeli politicians to bring their foreign guests to the site.

One of the most recent dignitaries to visit the site was U.S. President Bill Clinton; his wife, Hillary; and their daughter, Chelsea, during their December 1998 trip to Israel. The Israeli guides were Benyamin Netanyahu, then Israeli prime minister, and archaeologist Prof. Ehud Netzer. Netanyahu was quoted in the press as declaring that his main reason for taking the Clintons to Masada was to show the American president what "Jewish determination" meant and to create a symbolic parallel between two-thousand-year-old Jewish resolve and the contemporary determination to obtain and maintain Israeli security.[9]

In 1995–96 the Israeli National Parks Authority began a face-lifting operation on Masada, including replacing the old cable car with a newer, large-capacity one. More visitors are expected in the future, as Masada is doubtless one of the most attractive tourist sites in Israel, and probably the most profitable one in terms of tourism-generated revenues. Now the Israeli National Parks Authority, together with the Administration for the Development of the Negev, is building an additional cable car and a new museum, reconstructing the mosaic floors, extending visiting hours, making the sight and sound show longer, and constructing a large visitors' center.[10]

Clearly, as Masada was excavated and reconstructed, and as it became increasingly accessible, it also grew increasingly commercialized, and will continue to do so. From a shrine of mythical heroism for secular Jewish Israelis, it was transformed into a profitable tourist site. This would not have been possible without the excavations at Masada, and if one looks for any decisive impact deriving from the excavations, then it is unequivocally in the area of tourism.

When I examined different forms of artistic expression following the excavations of Masada, I looked first at children's literature. There are few children's books about Masada. After 1963, only four such books were published, all of them historically inaccurate. They present a fictional account of the events on Masada, glorifying the Masada rebels. In that sense, these books adhere to the concept of heroic Masada supported by Yadin (1966e, 1966h). However, if we compare them to the few children's book written about Masada before 1963, no significant differences can be found. Both before and after 1963 they provide a spurious narrative of a few proud Jewish freedom fighters who, against tremendous odds, fought the Imperial Roman army and, when faced with what they felt was a certain life of slavery, chose death.[11] The Jews are portrayed not as passively going to their deaths like sheep to the slaughter (an image from the early period of Holocaust commemorations), but as fighting to the end in what Yadin called "the last stand." In summary, the excavations of Masada did not have a decisive or even discernible effect here.

I also looked at artistic endeavor in fiction, science fiction, poetry, the theater, and film after the excavations at Masada. Generally, I found that not many artists were inspired by Masada, and it has not been a major theme in any of these art forms. I uncovered no significant differences in content before and after the excavations, which do not seem to have inspired much in these areas, not even the relatively famous (but terribly boring) Universal movie *Masada*, first broadcast by ABC as a miniseries on American television in 1981.[12] Although a few (mainly unknown) artists used Masada in their work, we could not establish a direct connection between their artistic artifacts and the archaeological excavations as such.

To try and assess the impact of the Masada excavations in education, I looked at history textbooks in schools and general reference history books. I examined twenty-one textbooks for intermediate school students, ten texts for eleventh and twelfth grades, and fifteen general reference books. I compared how these texts presented the Masada narrative before and after 1963, and found no significant differences. Thus the excavations of Masada do not seem to have had any tangible impact on the presentation of the Masada narrative. For all practical purposes, we can say that the Masada mythical narrative remained more or less consistent from the 1920s to the late 1980s.

For many years Masada was the focal point of pilgrimage of various groups and individuals. Secular Israeli youth movements made the trek to Masada an annual event. The Israeli army used to have many of its new recruits (mostly from armor units) trek to Masada and there stage a dramatic swearing-in ceremony. Israeli schools have also made Masada a focal point for pilgrimages. They usually involve a long hike at night, a climb to the top of Masada before sunrise, and there, as the sun rises from the east, some sort of dramatic representation of the meaning of Masada.

Masada has also become a place to celebrate Bar and Bat Mitzvas, the traditional Jewish coming-of-age rites for twelve- and thirteen-years-olds. Students from the Hebrew University (mostly non-Israelis) often mark the beginning of the academic year by trekking to the site. As such events develop, the commercialization of the place increases, as the rock concerts and other musical events of the past few years attest.

The excavations of Masada did not have a discernible impact on many areas of Israeli culture. The Masada mythical narrative was prevalent in Israeli culture before the excavations; the excavations did not challenge the myth, and thus did not change what the public knew about Masada. However, the excavations most certainly provided the mythical version with strong scientific credibility. Thus the patterns of the cultural utilization of the myth that antedated the excavations continued during and after them as well, reinforced, unchallenged, and unaltered.

One illustrative contemporary reaction to the excavations deserves some attention. Hano'ar Ha'oved Vehalomed (the Working and Studying Youth) is an Israeli youth movement that has made Masada a major site for pilgrimages for many years. In 1964 the movement's magazine, *Bama'ale*, expressed explicit anxiety regarding the archaeological excavations. An article entitled "Masada—History or Existence?" (vol. 23) indicated concern that the excavations might uncover findings incongruent with the accepted beliefs held by the movement, that is, the myth. If that happens, the report cautions against surrendering to archaeological authority, recommending instead continued adherence to what was accepted as absolute truth up to that point:

> [T]he important thing is not to lose [a] sense of proportion and not to become enslaved to . . . authority. With all due respect, there are things greater than archaeology. For the human truth which we create, archaeology is but one ingredient. (p. 112)

At the very least, this statement indicates that the youth movement had created a Masada of its own, in complete disregard of whether or not their social construction of a mythical Masada corresponded to objective, external findings.

But the writers had nothing to fear. As noted earlier, the archaeological excavations were not intended to, nor did they, challenge or compromise the mythical narrative of Masada. If anything, the archaeological discoveries were used to amplify, magnify, and give scientific credibility to that myth.

Of the two cultural areas which were most affected by the excavations, tourism was the one on which the impact was decisive. Masada was eventually transformed from a shrine to heroism, the site of pilgrimages for hundreds of thousands of Israeli secular Jews, into a most profitable tourist attraction for mostly non-Jewish tourists, in fact, one of the best tourist attractions Israel has to offer. The other area clearly affected was the media. During the excavations, frequent reports about them appeared in the daily press and on Israeli radio.

NOTES

1. *Wars of the Jews*, 7.8.2, p. 599.
2. *Wars of the Jews*, 7.9.1, p. 603.
3. Of course, there were always individual exceptions such as Rabbi Goren's misleading interpretation. See my 1995 analysis.
4. One cannot escape noting the inflationary use of this expression for a variety of findings in Masada—scrolls, the *Mikve*, the synagogue, the lots, the skeletal remains in locus 8, etc.
5. This part was partially based on Ben-Yehuda 1995, pp. 184–88; and Tal Ben-Shatz and Yossi Bar-Nachum's 1990 paper, "The Masada Myth in the Written Media," a seminar paper submitted in my 1990 course Culture, Myth and Deviance.
6. For a detailed discussion see Ben-Yehuda 1995, pp. 243–49.
7. See also, for example, *Ha'aretz*, October 14, 1988, p. 2; *Hadashot*, October 16, 1988, p. 17. The most intensive coverage was by *Yediot Aharonot*'s weekly magazine, October 21, 1988, pp. 28–29, 30–31. Sculptor Yigael Tomarkin had some sarcastic and acid remarks about that event; see his 1988 article in *Ha'aretz*.
8. A less dramatic, more commercial, but nevertheless interesting event occurred in September 1993, when American entertainer Michael Jackson visited Israel. He was flown by a helicopter to Masada, where he was photographed drinking cans of Coca Cola. His sister LaToya also visited Israel in December and, naturally, also visited Masada (on the eleventh).
9. *Ha'aretz*, December 16, 1998, pp. 1A, 5A; *Yediot Aharonot*, December 16, p. 9.
10. *Yediot Aharonot*, July 20, 1994, p. 10, in the financial supplement.
11. An interesting example is the book written by Yoram Tzafrir, an archaeologist who participated in the 1963–65 excavations, who published his book under the pseudonym "Yoram Avi-Tamar" (1989). Tzafrir's experience as part of the dig does not seem to have spurred him to depart from the standard formula of other similar books.
12. The first episode was aired April 5, 1981, and converted into a 131-minute feature film in 1984. Connecting it to the excavations is not obvious.

EIGHT

POLITICS AND HISTORY

The Social Construction of Knowledge Engineering

ARCHAEOLOGY, HISTORY, AND POLITICS IN THE CONTEXT OF MASADA

In 1966, Moses Finley wrote in his review of one of Yadin's books that Masada was a prime example of the politics of modern archaeology. And it is clear that archaeology can be used for political purposes. Israel's special circumstance is the ongoing perception of immense threat to the survival of the state, resulting in the tremendous investment of national resources in security (to the point where some have referred to it as a "garrison state"). Can an objective program for the study of history, free of nationalistic or patriotic bias, be put into effect in a state where the selection of what is considered appropriate history is dictated by political and national considerations as determined by the Minister of Education? Obviously not.

That different cultures have different interpretative histories is no great revelation. Different versions exist for many selective historical sequences because, by definition, these versions select different facts and contextualize them in different terms. Therefore, the contrast between genuine and deceptive historical sequences is not always an easy one to establish.

The general problem here can be divided into two issues. The first concerns where we look for the genuine/false boundary: Is it in the facts quoted or in the interpretations generated? It is one thing to falsify and fabricate findings, and it is an entirely different enterprise to play with the interpretations. Undoubtedly, claims for falsification are much easier to establish when the deception is on the factual level, when one can use the facts to settle a possible dispute between different versions. Separating true from false on the interpretative level is more difficult. To do that, one must pay careful attention to the selection of the facts, their sequencing, the choice of words. Some of the major deceptions in archaeology—and Masada—were on the level not of the factual findings, but of interpretations.

The second issue to which we need to pay attention in this context is the *reason* for carrying out a study—any study—in sociology, history, archaeology or in other areas. That many Jews in Israel are interested in archaeology for what they see as political and national reasons, is, I believe, legitimate. Two essays are relevant in this context. The first is Shavit's (1986) documentation of the important and central place that archaeology (in the broader sense of the term, including history) assumed in shaping the national modern historical consciousness of Israelis. Shavit's paper, "Truth Will Rise from the Land," is witness to how archaeology found itself caught up in various ideological debates (e.g., biblical archaeology), and points out that most of the intense public excitement was created by archaeology which focused its efforts precisely around the period of the Second Temple (and not, for example, biblical archaeology). It was precisely this period that provides the symbols so badly sought by the moral entrepreneurs engaged in forging the emerging national Zionist Jewish identity (Shavit 1986, p. 54). Masada was most certainly a major ingredient in this process.

The second essay, "Israeli Biblical Archaeology at Its Beginning," was written by Shulamit Geva (1992) and focuses on biblical archaeology in Israel. Geva knows Yadin's work in Hatzor well, and her paper very strongly supports the claim that biblical archaeology was used by Zionism in order to help legitimize the establishment of the State of Israel. According to Geva, this exploitation of biblical archaeology helped transform it from an independent scientific field into an ideology, ultimately degrading its quality.

It is well worth noting that the one hundredth issue of *Cathedra* (August 2001), celebrating the twenty-fifth anniversary of this important Hebrew-language journal devoted to the study of Eretz Israel, devotes a major portion of its space to archaeological issues. Five of seventeen articles involve archaeology.

It is, perhaps, educational at this point to examine in detail some of the expressions used by the person who became so identified with the excavations of Masada, Yigael Yadin. Learning what he had to say about the excavations, how he justified them and how he presented them to the public can give us some powerful clues as to how "Mr. Masada" conceptualized the Masada narrative. As will become evident, Yadin made some unmistakable ideological/political statements.

We have very little from the period preceding the excavations of Masada, and almost all of it is indirect. The most reliable account is that by Shmaria Guttman,[1] who states that he had to invest a great deal of time and effort into persuading Yadin to get involved in excavating Masada. Joseph Aviram (interview, December 1993) and Neil Asher Silberman (1993, pp. 273–74) both confirm Yadin's reluctance, which was also supported by some of the archaeologists we interviewed as well. We should not be surprised at Yadin's resistance. After all, according to Aviram and Silberman, Yadin was busy with other projects, and Yadin the archaeologist saw no reason for the dig on Masada. But Guttman was a powerfully persuasive fellow and he appealed to Yadin the politician, the Zionist nationalist, the educator, and he succeeded in making a convert. Coupled with Joseph Aviram's similar appeal to Yadin, Guttman's efforts culminated in Yadin's wholehearted adoption of the project.

We cannot stress enough that during the 1963–65 excavations of Masada Yadin had tight control over what information was given to which newspapers. He had an exclusive agreement with the British *Observer* and the local daily *Ma'ariv*. From the very beginning journalists were interested in Masada; in fact, the transcripts of the archaeologists' daily meetings include quite a few comments, notes, and instructions from Yadin concerning when journalists or dignitaries were expected to visit, as well as how to treat them. The daily transcripts of November 4, 1963, for instance, reveal that a visit by David Ben-Gurion was imminent. Although he had agreed to come to Masada, Ben-Gurion was not too keen on the project, Yadin noted, but, "I hope that following his visit—his appetite [for Masada] will grow" (p. 16). When Ben-Gurion visited Masada again on March 29, 1965, the transcripts bear evidence of similar care before his arrival. Securing Ben-Gurion's support was clearly on Yadin's agenda. On November 7, 1963, Yadin prepared his team again, and very carefully, for a visit of other VIPs.

It is worth our attention to examine a report of a visit by journalists to Masada. The following is based on a transcript made by the author of the report titled *Discovering the Secrets of Masada*, which was broadcast on August 11, 1963, during the evening news by the state-controlled radio:

> A few journalists climbed Masada and began interviewing some volunteers. Apparently, independently. It did not take long, and after a few minutes the interviewers are told, "I'm sorry to interrupt you. I have to ask you to leave the place. Go to Professor Yadin, he will receive you, will tell you what are the possibilities and limitations. You are making us sick and tired of letting journalists arrive here." The journalist intervened and said, "Here too there is censorship." And, our disciplined reporter went to Yadin.

Whatever provoked this exchange, it is very obvious that Yadin exercised tight control over what journalists were exposed to while visiting Masada, thus insuring that his interpretations were the ones that were published.

20. VIPs visit Masada. Yigael Yadin (with a stick) accompanies David Ben-Gurion in a November 10, 1963, visit to Masada. They walk down the stairs leading to the lower level of the northern palace. (Courtesy of the Government Press Office, State of Israel)

In 1964 Yadin lectured journalists on Masada and stated that the most glorious chapters in Jewish history were uncovered there. He added that Masada constituted a national and religious symbol of Jewish heroism (*Ma'ariv*, May 18). On November 11, 1964, he stated explicitly to *Ha'aretz* that Masada was going to become a place for national pilgrimage. These early statements[2] clearly reveal the nationalism that permeated Yadin's motivation in involving himself in the Masada excavations.

All these points are noteworthy because on page 15 of *Masada: Herod's Fortress and the Zealots' Last Stand* (1966) Yadin writes, "It would be one of the tasks of our archaeological expedition to see what evidence we could find to support the Josephus record." Yadin, of course, was not looking for corroboration of Josephus, but rather for evidence to support his interpretation of Josephus: a protracted siege, Zealots bravely fighting the Romans, a heroic last stand, and so on. Indeed, Yadin's statement on page 17 of the book—"It is not my purpose to offer a dry scientific record; rather it is to enable the reader to share our remarkable experience"—only reinforces this.

In an interview which he gave to the official IDF weekly magazine, *Bamachane*, published in March 18, 1969, Yadin said,

> The public's interest in the antiquities of Israel is . . . almost phenomenal. . . . This intense interest does not stem from interest in archaeology as such; everyone feels and knows that he is discovering and excavating findings and artifacts from the days of his forefathers. And every finding bears witness to the connection and covenant between the people and the land. From this aspect archaeological research has added an important national dimension. There is an element of curiosity as far as the unknown is concerned. There is the wish to decipher the past. This is a natural tendency that most certainly helped the revival of interest in archaeology. But, as far as Israel is concerned, it seems to me that the factor I mentioned—the search for and construction of the connection between people and the land—must be taken into consideration. [Archaeology] in my view reinforces the Hebraic consciousness, let us say—the identification and the connection with ancient Judaism and Jewish consciousness. When Torah scrolls, synagogues, ritual phylacteries and prayer shawls are discovered—it reinforces Jewish consciousness." (vol. 26, pp. 14–15)

In a filmed interview Yadin justifies the excavations of Masada because they help attain the goal of Jews living "again as the People of the Book in the Land of the Book."[3]

Shavit (1986) documented the tremendous interest in archaeology as early as the 1930s. In 1973 Yadin wrote in the daily *Ma'ariv*,

> One of the hallmarks of archaeological research in Israel is that it . . . brought us close to our past, as if with a huge magnifying glass. . . . From a distance of 2000 years, it is as if it had all happened only yesterday. And so, our life here became one that goes against the laws of grammar, indecipherable to strangers, in which past, present and future blend together in a whirling mix. . . . *The* taste of life here is the feeling of an ancient nation returning to its homeland. Without this feeling it is difficult to live here.

Regarding Masada, he wrote,

> There is no doubt that as Jews, and not just as archaeologists, the most important findings are those from the last eight years on Masada . . . at the end of which Masada fell and became a symbol. . . . Indeed, there is no doubt that the findings from this period were the high point of our discoveries. (Yadin 1973, p. 15)

Yadin's selection of Masada as excavation site, the tremendous effort he expended in organizing the excavations, his decision to reconstruct the site as well as excavate it, and his later support for the construction of a cable car to the top of the fortress, which made Masada very easily accessible, all support the contention that patriotism was a motivating force. True, there were indeed scientific reasons for excavating Masada, but they were not particularly compelling and certainly cannot explain the choice of the site and sheer amount of effort involved in those excavations.

That Yigael Yadin was the man behind the major excavations of Masada is beyond any doubt. His organizational skills and talents, the networks he was party to, his eminence and his energy made the old dream of excavating Masada into a reality. Before, during, and after the excavations, Yadin emerged as Mr. Masada. However, it is also very clear that when the decision was made to excavate Masada, as well as during the excavation itself, the absence of any compelling scientific rationale was more than compensated for by *compelling* political, ideological, and national reasons and motivations. Providing the Jewish-Israeli tale of heroism with scientific credibility, grounded in archaeological facts, is indeed a powerfully wild and fantastic move.

Yadin's statements and published work on Masada provide an insightful glimpse into his integrated view of Masada, which was mythical-political and not scientific. By succumbing to the mythical view, Yadin set himself on to a dubious road which was to include suppressing information, concealing evidence, and structuring a historical tale of Masada which was falsified and deceptive. The road Yadin chose led not to cool and skeptical scientific explanations of Masada, but to the concoction of a purportedly scientific reinforcement for a twentieth-century myth of Jewish heroism.

YADIN'S MAIN PUBLICATIONS ON THE EXCAVATIONS

In 1966 Yadin published his popular book on Masada in both Hebrew and English. Significantly, the name Yadin chose for the English version of his book, *MASADA: Herod's Fortress and the Zealots' Last Stand*, is not identical to the name of the Hebrew book, *MASADA: In Those Days—At This Time* (*Metzada: Bayamim Hahem Bazman Haze*). The last four words in Hebrew are from the traditional Hannukah recitation to denote the miraculous occurrences of that holiday. Among other things, it may be taken to imply that the same miracles that happened then may happen now—again an attempt to bridge an abyss of close to two thousand years. It is nearly impossible to resist commenting that both book titles vividly project Yadin's personal bias. For the Zealots, at least according to Josephus Flavius, were never on Masada, the Hannukah-Masada connection is elusive, for what exactly was the "miracle" of Masada?

Yadin did publish some bits and pieces here and there about Masada (e.g., in the *Encyclopedia Judaica*), but there can be very little doubt that his 1966 books contain his central views on Masada. In 1966 Yadin had enough time to ponder and mull over the physical findings from Masada vis-à-vis the Masada mythical narrative and Josephus's version.

How did Yadin project the events on Masada in his book? This is well worth a close examination. Pages 11–13 of the book begin with the following description:

> The rock of Masada . . . is also the site of one of the most dramatic episodes in Jewish history. In the 1st century [C.E.] Palestine was under the occupation of the Romans, who had overthrown the Jewish Maccabean kingdom in the middle of the previous century. . . . But in the year 66 [C.E.] the Jewish revolt flared up into a full-scale country-wide war, which raged with fierce bitterness for four years, the Romans having to bring in legion after legion in reinforcements to suppress the insurgents. In 70 [C.E.] the Roman general Titus conquered Jerusalem, sacked the city, destroyed the Temple, and expelled the bulk of the Jewish survivors from the country.
>
> One outpost alone held out till 73 [C.E.]—the fortress of Masada.
>
> At the beginning of the 66 [C.E.] rebellion, a group of Jewish zealots had destroyed the Roman garrison at Masada and held it throughout the war. They were now—after the fall of Jerusalem—joined by a few surviving patriots from the Jewish capital who had evaded capture and made the long arduous trek across the Judean wilderness, determined to continue their battle for freedom. With Masada as their base for raiding operations, they harried the Romans for two years. In 72 [C.E.], Flavius Silva, the Roman Governor, resolved to crush this outpost of resistance. He marched on Masada with his Tenth Legion, its auxiliary troops and thousands of prisoners of war carrying water, timber and provisions across

> the stretch of barren plateau. The Jews at the top of the rock, commanded by Elazar Ben Yair, prepared themselves for defense, making use of the natural and man-made fortifications, and rationing their supplies in the storehouses and cisterns.
>
> Silva's men prepared for a long siege. They established camps at the base of the rock, built a circumvallation round the fortress, and on a rocky site near the western approach to Masada they constructed a ramp of beaten earth and large stones. On this they threw up a siege tower and under covering fire from its top they moved a battering ram up the ramp and directed it against the fortress wall. They finally succeeded in making a breach. This was the beginning of the end. That night, at the top of Masada, Elazar Ben Yair reviewed the fateful position. The defensive wall was now consumed by fire. The Romans would overrun them on the morrow. There was no hope of relief, and none of escape. Only two alternatives were open: surrender or death. He resolved "that a death of glory was preferable to a life of infamy, and that the most magnanimous resolution would be to disdain the idea of surviving the loss of their liberty." Rather than become slaves to their conquerors, the defenders—960 men, women and children—thereupon ended their lives at their own hands. When the Romans reached the height next morning, they were met with silence. And thus says Josephus at the end of his description: "And so met [the Romans] with the multitude of the slain, but could take no pleasure in the fact, though it were done to their enemies. Nor could they do other than wonder at the courage of their resolution, and at the immovable contempt of death which so great a number of them had shown, when they went through with such an action as that was."

One needs to read these passages carefully to realize how unsubstantiated, archaeologically and factually, some of the claims are. For example, Yadin begins his description by contextualizing the Great Revolt with the Maccabeans, telescoping more than one hundred years of complex history into a simple "Jews have always disliked foreign yokes." The "full-scale country-wide war" implies that the revolt against the Romans was a popular one and encompassed all the Jewish population. This is not what Josephus states, nor can it be supported from the excavations of Masada. The statement that there was "one outpost" which "held out till 73 [C.E.]" is misleading because unsuspecting and innocent readers may be led to believe that this "holding out" was against repeated attacks. But nothing in the excavations (or elsewhere) supports this surmise. There is no indication, anywhere, that there was any Roman military attempt to subdue Masada between 70 C.E. and when the Roman siege began (end of 72 C.E.? or perhaps even spring 73 C.E.?). Thus, there was nothing that threatened Masada directly and that the rebels on Masada had to "hold out" against before the Roman siege actually began. Ignoring Josephus's accounts, Yadin makes no mention of the Sicarii. There exists absolutely no archaeological empirical support or evidence for Yadin's claim that any group of Jews "held" Masada (that is, against repeated attacks) "throughout the war."[4] There is no evidence to support the view that survivors of the destruction of Jerusalem in 70 C.E. reached Masada "determined to continue their battle for freedom." On the contrary, remembering that the Sicarii were chased out of Jerusalem before the Roman siege and destruction of the city, their inhospitality and hostility to other Jews, all imply that even if there were survivors from Jerusalem, the last place they would find refuge in was Masada. Yadin's claim that Masada served as "a base for raiding operations, [and] they harried the Romans for two years" may or may not be true, but there is not a shred of direct textual or empirical archaeological evidence in the Masada excavations to support this fantastic assertion. The rebels of Masada had more than the two options Yadin attributes to them; even if they did not want to be captured alive by the Romans, they could also choose a Samson or Kamikaze death.

In chapter 15 of the English version his 1966 book, Yadin discusses "The defenders of Masada" (p. 197):

> It is thanks to Ben-Yair and his comrades, to their heroic stand, to their choice of death over slavery, and to the burning of their humble chattels as a final act of defiance to the enemy, that they elevated Masada to an undying symbol of desperate courage, a symbol which has stirred hearts throughout the last nineteen centuries. It is this which moved scholars and laymen to make the ascent to Masada. It is this which moved the modern Hebrew poet [Lamdan] to cry: "Masada shall not fall again!" It is this which has drawn the Jewish youth of our generation in their thousands to climb to its summit in a solemn pilgrimage. And it is this which brings the recruits of the armored units of the Defense Forces of modern Israel to swear the oath of allegiance on Masada's heights: "Masada shall not fall again!"

This passage must be recontextualized in, and confronted with, Josephus's historical narrative. Yadin systematically ignores Josephus's insistence that the rebels on Masada were the Sicarii. He uses the term "defenders," but much more frequently "Zealots." The reason is obvious; the Sicarii were a group of Jews described by Josephus in very negative terms: bandits, assassins, and thieves led by ruthless tyrants, following an ideology that culminated in disaster. For the same fastidiousness Yadin ignored the massacre at Ein Gedi, the absence of battles, and unchosen option of fighting to the end.[5] Finally, Yadin took no heed of the fact that the story of Masada was virtually repressed by religiously orthodox Judaism, among other reasons because of the suicide angle, and that it most definitely did *not* stir hearts "throughout the last nineteen centuries."

Thus, regardless of the archaeological evidence which was *not* found in Masada, Yadin felt no obligation to scientific truth and preferred to lend his name and scientific credibility in support of a mythical tale unsupported empirically by findings from the excavation, thereby helping deceive unsuspecting readers.

It is now more than thirty years since the excavations, and it is instructive to explore some of the perceptions of Yadin by archaeologists who worked with him. In the fall of 1994 the Institute of Archaeology at the Hebrew University inaugurated a Masada exhibit in which some of the findings from the 1963 excavations were displayed for the public. The Hebrew University publication *Universita* included a short unattributed report on the exhibit in its fall 1994 issue:

> The story of Masada has become one of the national symbols of Jewish revival in the State of Israel. The last Jewish stronghold in the Great Revolt against the Roman oppressors exemplifies courage and tenacity. The identification of archaeologist Yadin, the military man and the statesman, with Masada was no mere coincidence. His approach to archaeology went far beyond the interest of experts and scholars immersed in their field. He felt it proper that the public should be interested in the excavations and discoveries of Masada.[6]

The text makes it clear, then, that Yadin's interest in Masada stemmed from nationalistic, political, moral-ideological reasons implying an emotional involvement as well.

In the brochure that was published specifically for the exhibit (Hurvitz 1993), Yadin is referred to several times. Gila Hurvitz, the talented and sensitive editor of the brochure, states that "Yadin's attitude to archaeology went beyond the narrow scientific investigation of the past. He wanted to emphasize the broader implication of exposing the history of Israel. Yadin considered the public interest which accompanied the different excavations in which he was involved as important" (from the foreword). Professor Amnon Ben-Tor, head of the Institute of Archaeology at the time, wrote the introduction to the brochure: "Yadin saw in Masada much more than an archaeological excavation. . . . [T]he lesson from those days [when Masada fell] was important for him . . . and that was that we, Israelis, must do everything so that Masada—that is, the State of Israel—shall not fall again."

CAREERS OF ARCHAEOLOGISTS

Livne (1986, p. 130) implies that the excavations of Masada were a turning point in the careers of several archaeologists, an implication readily believable in light of the effort involved in the excavations and the noise they made locally and internationally. However, nearly all the archaeologists we interviewed[7] averred that the excavations of Masada had no major impact on their professional careers. However, they also pointed out that their experience of participating in the excavations of Masada influenced their personal acquaintances (that is, individual networks—friends, romantic involvements, etc.) and it facilitated, reinforced, and helped to sustain their individual national identity and consciousness. Their enthusiasm and personal interest in the excavations is readily evident in the transcripts of the daily sessions. However, any professional ramifications are denied, almost all stating that in terms of scientific importance, the excavations of Hatzor were the crucial and important ones.

The reasons for the interest in archaeology say little about the quality of research; this issue is, however, at the heart of our question as to whether the reason for conducting the research colors the data collection and the interpretation of that data. If so, such coloring definitely provides a basis for the accusation implied by Geva's (1992) work.

We have already discussed the ideological-political impetus behind the interest in Masada. It is not too difficult to understand that secular Zionism, dealing with the unprecedented concept of a people returning to its homeland after almost two thousand years of living elsewhere, was only too happy to embrace a scientific endeavor that could potentially validate and reinforce its moral claim to the land (against increasing Arab resistance, one must add). Moreover, the possibility of discovering ancient Jews who physically worked the land and who were willing to fight and die for it was a rather healthy antidote to the traditional stereotypical anti-Semitic view of Jews in Europe as lazy and cowardly. As the political and social leadership of the Jewish community in Palestine and of Zionism at that time came largely from Europe, the temptation of relying on archaeology for the dual purposes of forging a link with the past while countering anti-Semitic prejudice must have been simply irresistible.

Furthermore, Shapira (1992) has pointed out that the use of the Masada mythical narrative also helped resolve an internal controversy concerning the legitimization of the use of violence and force by secular Zionists. The Masada mythical narrative was most certainly utilized to give credence to the view that the use of force was indeed justifiable (Shapira 1992, pp. 45, 269, 421–33).

This meant that some elements of Israeli archaeology, certainly up to the 1960s, cannot be viewed properly outside the context of nation-building. Indeed, in July 1994 an organization called "the Council for a Good Land of Israel," also incorporating the *Ma'ariv* daily, the El Al national airline, and the association of performing artists (EMI), held special festivities in which distinctive recognition and appreciation to Israeli archaeologists was acknowledged for their contribution in "revealing the secrets of the Land, its antiquities and heritage."[8] No such recognition on the part of such a collection of organizations was ever offered to, say, Israeli physicists, mathematicians, biologists, economists, or sociologists.

That Yadin had both a personal and a national interest in Masada is obvious. He used all the advantages at his disposal: his military career, his standing as a professional archaeologist and powerful position within Hebrew University, a vast network of social, political and economic professional and media connections. Thus it is obvious that he became extremely and powerfully effective in helping to spread the Masada mythical narrative.[9] Both he and Shmaria Guttman, no doubt, knew the original narrative, yet chose deliberately to tailor their creatively invented version to what they felt were personal and national needs. They both deliberately suppressed competing and powerful hypotheses, ignored evidence, and suppressed findings (Yadin would not publish, or let others publish, the full report of the findings). By being involved in such a process, of course, they participated in a scheme of distortion which was aimed at providing Israelis with a spurious historical narrative of heroism. Did that basic motivation cause Shmaria Guttman and/or Yadin to falsify excavation findings? Did their bias affect the physical results of their excavations? The answer must be *no*. Yadin was so careful with the findings that even the daily meetings of his staff of archaeologists were recorded and later transcribed. That, as Magness (1992) pointed out, was quite unusual, and very helpful.

Even without Josephus Flavius, the archaeologists could have established some facts. For example, it would have been possible to determine that Herod was involved in the main building of Masada, that a Roman siege array surrounded Masada, and that the Roman army was there. The archaeological findings regarding the history of the Jewish Great Revolt are meager. One salient archaeological finding is of some poor-quality construction over some of the Herodian structures, and these constructions are interpreted to have been made by the Masada rebels. In fact, Yadin and Guttman must have been quite disappointed that the findings did not unequivocally confirm the narrative provided by Josephus Flavius. So, again, we see that the motivation for the study is separated from the actual scientific findings, and that scientific findings can be separated from interpretations of these findings. The warping of the historical narrative both by Guttman and by Yadin was not at the level of the excavations or the findings themselves, but at the level of the interpretation, that is, the social construction, of the findings.

NOTES

1. My interviews with him in 1987 and 1993.

2. As well as his 1969 interview to the official IDF weekly, *Bamachane*, his 1973 statements to *Ma'ariv*, and his own writings from 1973.

3. Open University's illustrative documentary video series *Archaeology*, chapter on the Masada myth.

4. On this issue see also Cotton and Preiss 1990.

5. Pointed out in Weiss-Rosmarin's 1967 article as well.

6. No. 9, pp. 30–31.

7. We interviewed nineteen people: Joseph Aviram, Dan Bahat, Meir Ben-Dov, Amnon Ben-Tor, Amir Drori, Avi Eitan, Shmaria Guttman, Moshe Kochavi, Gideon Foerster, Malka Hershkovitz, Gila Hurvitz, Aharon Kampinski, Micha Livne, Menachem Magen, Ze'ev Meshel, Ehud Netzer, Beno Rotenberg, Yoram Tzafrir, and David Usishkin. Most interviews were conducted by Iris Wolf. The majority of interviewees were archaeologists who had participated in the excavations; some are very prominent archaeologists today, while others are involved in archaeology-oriented occupations.

8. *Ma'ariv*, July 22, 1994, p. 7.

9. See also Silberman 1993, pp. 270–93.

NINE

REALITY CONSTRUCTIONS AND DECEPTIONS

The nature of social realities and the ways in which individuals define and construct them is of crucial theoretical and practical importance. Social realities form the cement with which we construct our conception of what is real and what is not, what is important and what is not. It is thus important to frame the more specific riddle of this book within the analytical structure of reality constructions.

THE OBJECTIVE AND CONSTRUCTIVIST APPROACHES

Two major analytical approaches which offer solutions for the mystery regarding the social construction of reality have crystallized in sociology. One approach can be called the objectivist or essentialist. It is the older one, and is less accepted these days than it was some twenty years ago. The objective view is a variant of the positivist approach, actually quite close to functionalism. It assumes that such things as deviance or, more generally, social issues and problems, constitute an objective and measurable reality which, according to this perspective, is nonproblematic. It is "out there" for us to observe, record, and analyze.

The other approach is the constructionist perspective (also referred to as subjective or relativist). This approach maintains that such things as deviance, social issues and problems do not present the characteristics of a so-called objective reality. Constructionists maintain that what is, and what is not, viewed as deviance, social problems, myths, even science, are the results of complex collective social definitions of what some organized members of a culture view as such. For example, what some of these members define as a problematic, harmful, or dangerous condition(s) may become defined as "social problems." In this perspective the nature of what is, and what is not, defined as reality is not a result of some objective conditions but is rather socially constructed. As Goode puts it, "to the subjectivist, a given condition need not even exist in the objective sense to be defined as a social problem."[1]

The debate between objectivists and constructionists, of course, goes much deeper than this controversy. The argument here genuinely revolves around what we view as the nature of reality, about how we make sense of the social and physical environment in which we live and die. That is, the question which lurks behind this painful dilemma is whether there is a real, objective reality, what the meaning of that reality is, how we explain or interpret it—or is it that all we have are only images and all we do is relate to these eternally evasive and elusive images? This problem is particularly acute for construction theory. As we shall see below, modern construction theory indeed offers a solution to this problem.

Construction Theory: Strict and Contextual

The theory of social constructionism is not new, and its parameters have been delineated since at least Berger and Luckmann's definitive book *The Social Construction of Reality* (1966).[2]

Both Best (1995) and Goode (1989) point to two very different variants of the constructionist perspective. One is strict constructionism, the other contextual constructionism. The difference between the two is significant. The first variant assumes that constructionism encompasses all social processes, including facts. It argues that the expert, or scientific, evaluation of such a thing as deviance represents only one "claim-making" activity out of many. This view argues that scientific claims are also socially constructed, as are other claims, and should be studied as such. That is, there are many versions of what reality is, and the scientific version is only another version, intrinsically no better or worse than any other. Since this approach does not, and cannot, use criteria to attach more significance to any of the possible different versions which define reality, all versions become equalized: political, scientific, religious, artistic, romantic. What may explain the hegemony of a particular version may simply be the use of power in order to guarantee the supremacy of one version over others. The second variant bases its perspective on the assumption that experts can reach a consensus regarding the nature of objective facts. This consensus is based on empirically testable processes and driven by facts and (scientific) evidence. It argues that while such things as science, deviance, and social problems are the result of claim-making activities, the so-called objective dimension can be assessed and evaluated by an expert on the basis of some agreed-upon evidence. Sociologists working from this second perspective typically contrast the "objective" with the "constructed" versions of reality. Contextual constructionism most certainly provides a solution to the problem focusing on the nature of reality because it sets defining parameters for reality and thus hands the researcher a powerful analytical anchor which is altogether absent from strict constructionism.[3]

Contextual constructionism does not claim to know absolute truth or to be objective. Rather, it tries to bypass the epistemological problematics involved in deciding on objectivity by establishing a consensus of relevant experts based on careful examination of empirical facts. Thus the problem faced by contextual constructionism is not of making distinctions between what some postmodernists describe as "real" and "unreal" facts, but of making an informed and intelligent selection from among the relevant and important facts for specified narratives. While this agreed-upon, fact-based consensus is temporary and relative, it provides a powerful base line which we can use to evaluate a variety of claim-making activities. In fact, my use of the term "objective" (to the extent that I use it at all) should be placed within quotation marks, precisely because of the above. Strict constructionism *assumes* the equality of all narratives (including the scientific), regardless of the validity, reliability, or even usefulness of empirical evidence. Contextual constructionists cannot accept this extreme relativist position, simply because the empirical world does not behave in this fashion. Thus the contextual interpretation of construction theory does not try to pretend that those making the analysis have some impossible (and probably also undesirable) magical spell that somehow emancipates them from being themselves part—or prisoners—of a constructed thought. Rather, it acknowledges the context of these constructions, attempts to offer some good critical sense of how and why we make constructions, and contrasts what come to be accepted as "facts" with their interpretation.

Substantively and methodologically, contextual constructionism requires that we examine the ways in which people construct meaning by relating to facts. The very existence of physical realities is not denied. Rather, we examine how people interpret and utilize that reality in order to manufacture meaning. Looking at the disparity between facts and the social construction of those facts, if it exists, is a fascinating challenge for any investigator,[4] and frequently constitutes an exercise in debunking and in understanding the very nature of the process of manufacturing meaning. Those cases where large gaps exist between the facts and their social construction provide us with a golden opportunity to comprehend how deviating from the facts helps us maintain an illusion of order.[5] The nature of this exercise has the potential of destabilizing systems of meanings, hence of order, and thus it should not surprise us to find that these exercises may elicit a negative emotional reaction.[6]

Deviance and Contextual Constructionism: Lies and Deceptions

Three decades ago, Liazos (1972) noted that sociologists of deviance were too narrowly focused on case studies of "nuts, sluts and perverts," as if these studies on little or narrow topics somehow prevent us from making larger or more sweeping generalizations. Surely there is much more to the study of deviance than that. Using analytical frameworks which utilize frames of interpretation taken from the study of deviance can very easily focus on such areas as power, science, religion, assassinations, and even mythology.[7] Within this expanded sphere of investigation, even the possibility of examining the promising concept of positive deviance can be evoked.[8]

This book is both based on and reflects contextual constructionism. The main line of argumentation which I used focused on presenting the facts, the empirical evidence, and then contrasted it with the different constructions and interpretations for which these facts were used as a base. Indeed, the way in which we examined Yadin's interpretations of his archaeological discoveries at Masada followed contextual constructionism very strictly.

From a contextual constructionist's perspective, opportunities to contrast reality with its constructions are precious.[9] They permit us to conceptualize reality through inverse opposites and thus gain a better understanding. This theoretical commitment was reflected in the actual structure of this book, when the concepts of truth and its nature were contrasted with those of deceptions and false presentations.

Examining the ways in which representations of realities are negotiated and compromised can give us some strong clues about the nature of cultures. If we take "truth" to be the known and accepted factual level, we can look at straying from that truth as deviance. That is, we can examine the nature of, and the degrees to which, particular constructions of social realities diverge from the factual level.

This approach tells us something important about the nature of the cultures in which we live. First, it tells us how we establish the factual level, that is, the truth level. Second, it tells us exactly how and why people deviate from that factual level, which paths they choose to follow when they stray from that factual level, and where these paths lead them. The importance of examining reality and its constructions in this way is focused on a few considerations. First, it enables and forces us to examine the social and moral boundaries between right and wrong in an empirically specific way (Ben-Yehuda 1985) and, more generally, the way in which we construct lines and boundaries, thereby creating and forcing categories upon the world (Zerubavel 1991). One example is the way we draw boundaries between the use and criminalization of psychoactive substances.[10] Second, it helps us examine reality and conceptualizations of deviance within major processes of social change and stability. In this way, we observe the deviant in order to understand the nondeviant, which forms another interesting contrast. For example, looking at the deceptive techniques used by Nazi Germany to present itself generally, or in specific incidences it was involved in, is instructive for the nature of Nazi culture and society.

My 1995 study examined the creation of the Masada mythical narrative within the context of collective memory. A major controversy in the area of collective memory has been between those claiming that "the past" is there and is utilized in the present for a variety of reasons (the "continuity perspective"), and those claiming that there is no "past" because the "past" is socially constructed for a variety of reasons in the present (the "discontinuity perspective"). The second perspective has clearly dominated the field (Schwartz 1991). It implies that constructing the "past" so as to create collective memories must almost always involve deception and fabrication (for more see Schwartz 2000, pp. 8–25). In fact, my Masada study showed what type of deceptive techniques were used, why, and how. Looking at the way archaeology was involved in the Masada excavations, and the ways it supported and generated a deceptive myth by using the present to explain the past, will give us some powerful empirical and analytical tools with which we can understand how science is involved in creating, sustaining, and diffusing deceptive myths.

The empirical case used in this book—the connection between archaeology and political ideology—pointed out how questionable and dubious behavior could be utilized in central processes of nation-building, in helping to construct an imagined community (B. Anderson 1991) within which new personal and national identities and moral boundaries were forged.

Morality and Power

One way to explore this issue is via a normal cultural prism—examining relationships such as trust, integration, degree of inner conflicts, and cultural wars. Another, perhaps more interesting, way is to look at the deviant. By definition, the deviant differentiates that which is not. Examining deviance can give us good and powerful insights not only into deviance, but into nondeviance as well. Reaching a solid understanding of what light is necessitates looking at darkness. Understanding truth and trust requires looking at lies and violations of trust (Ben-Yehuda 2001). In other words, if we are to understand the morality underlying social orders, we need to look at the moral boundaries which separate the morally right and the morally wrong. Understanding how social realities such as truth and trust are created and maintained, as well as how they change, is looking exactly at this issue. How we socially construct right and wrong, the moral universe which we create and in which we live and function and how we come to believe in this moral universe are very central issues.

Belief in the validity and morality of a culture is an essential ingredient in creating and maintaining social cohesion and integration, and thus enables meaningful, purposeful, and directional social action. Durkheim's "collective conscience," Shils's "center," and Parsons's "societal community" are all terms that were created in order to help us conceptualize that part of cultures which guarantees social continuity (and hence is conservative), and in which innovations and social changes take place. The moral realms, and the rhetoric used to conceptualize them, are the loci of conflict as well as of consensus. These are the realms we need to examine if we are interested in processes of social change and social stability. These are the loci where deviance and conformity are, and these are the cultural areas we need to examine if we want to understand the relations between morality, change, and stability (Ben-Yehuda 1985).

It is indeed morality which lies at the root of the distinction between good and bad and between deviance and that which is not. However, while morality itself is a sufficient variable to contend with, it is not enough. The other major element is power. It is the combination of power and morality which lies at the basis of what is defined as deviance and what is not.[11] The eternal play between competing moral entrepreneurs, the symbolic moral universes which they help to create, define, and maintain (and in which they are trapped), and the power which they are able to generate, mobilize, and utilize—these have always determined the demarcation between deviance and nondeviance, and hence, between conservatism and innovation, between evil and good, between right and wrong. This conceptual structure does not require us to make any moral assumptions regarding the type of power or morality. These are to be determined empirically.

It must be clear by now that our ability to socially construct realities, weave meaning, and concoct imaginary realms and symbolic universes of meaning may pose an interesting dilemma for drawing boundaries between false and true. Now we shall dive deep into the topic of lies, truth, and deception and try to clarify and limit the parameters of this topic so that we can continue our discussion within manageable dimensions.

TYPES OF DECEPTIONS

Lies, deceptions, "con" games, cheating, scheming—are all intriguing terms which relate to a situation which involves some form of untruth. These terms, and a few others, assume that some establishable "truth" exists and that when this "truth" is subverted, the result is some form of lie or deception. The inquiry presented in this book is directed at clarifying precisely this issue: the boundaries between "truth" and "untruth." To illuminate some of the issues involved, as well as to whet our appetite and curiosity, let us look at some illustrative cases.

An "Imaginary" Romantic Case

Imagine Noram and Tanie, two fictional characters, who are emotionally involved, holding hands and sitting on the banks of an enchanted pond. The moon shines brightly on a penetratingly crisp night while the sounds of darkness, the call of frogs, and the cool breeze structure the romantic setting. The couple hold hands and whisper softly to each other. Tanie likes the touch of Noram, she does not feel particularly talkative and enjoys the magical moments. Noram feels more like talking. He wants to express his deeply felt love for the intelligent, warm, and soft Tanie. Like so many males before and after him, he tells his sweetheart that he loves her, so much so that he is about to let the whole world know.

Sound familiar? Of course; lines like these appear again and again in books and movies depicting such romantic situations, and the above situation is played and replayed almost on a daily basis. In this respect, this is not an imaginary tale at all. Is Noram lying? Not in the sense that he is sincere; he is simply repeating cultural clichés. And yet the probability that the "whole world" will know about the couple's love is virtually nil. It is inconceivable that Noram is unaware of this. Even such famous Western love stories as King Edward VIII and Mrs. Simpson, Antony and Cleopatra, even Romeo and Juliet, are not known to the "whole world," meaning the entire planet with its billions of inhabitants. Many of them, perhaps even most, may have never heard of these love stories. While from the empirical point of view Noram is feeding Tanie a fabricated line, hardly anyone could accuse him of deception and lying. Most people would feel that the line may actually be appropriate, expected, and culturally conventional in that romantic context.

However, and despite the lure of the illustration, this book is not about romantic love stories but about another type of love—that of archaeology and excavations. Creating deceptions in archaeology should not be separated from a broader context of deviance and deceptions in science.

Some Cases from Science

The history of science provides us with numerous illustrations of deceit.[12] Let us look briefly at some famous illustrations. At the annual meeting on tumor viruses at Cold Spring Laboratory in May 1980, Mark Spector, a twenty-four-year-old graduate student in biochemistry from Cornell University, presented a revolutionary paper. Spector suggested a new explanation of how viruses work and cause cancer. Steven O'Neal, a postdoctoral researcher in Cornell's biochemical laboratory, had worked unsuccessfully for more than two years in order to isolate a specific protein (sodium-potassium ATPase). Spector came to Cornell in December 1979, and was assigned the task of isolating the protein. He accomplished it in less than a month. This discovery was the first milestone in Spector's development of a new, innovative theory about viruses and cancer. The news of his findings spread rapidly in the scientific community, and in July 1980 some of his work was published in respected journals such as *Science* and *Cell.*

In the fall of 1980, however, signs of fraud were already apparent. At that time Raymond Erikson, a virologist at the University of Colorado Medical Center in Denver, found that a sample serum from Spector's experiments contained certain antibodies which, if the theory was correct, should not and could not be present. Another warning sign was that a few of the experiments worked only under Spector's very personal supervision. By late July some of Spector's own laboratory colleagues began to be suspicious. During the summer of 1980 Spector was asked to stay away from the laboratory while his supervisor, Professor Racker, tried to replicate Spector's studies. New discrepancies appeared. In September 1980 Racker sent letters to both *Science* and *Cell* partly retracting the previous reports; he also withdrew papers which were scheduled to appear in two other journals. The university began to investigate Spector's past and discovered that he had never received a bachelor or masters degree. Spector withdrew from Cornell and denied all the allegations. His claim seems to be supported by the puzzling fact that some of his work does indeed seem to be valid and replicable.

A second case involved a young scientist in desperate need of publication: Vijay Soman, whose case also received much publicity. It appeared in the November 1, 1981, issue of the *New York Times Magazine.* The Soman case occurred in 1980 at the Yale Medical School when, during the course of a scientific audit, Soman admitted to having falsified work in a paper. After an investigation, twelve papers involving Soman as a researcher were retracted. The Soman case, perhaps more than any other, reflects how pressure to "publish or perish" led to plagiarism, falsifications, fraud, forgery, widespread destruction of laboratory data, and everything else that could happen because no effective social control mechanism existed.

A third case is the famous painted mice affair in which William Summerlin, a scientist at Sloan-Kettering Institute, painted the skin of a mouse with simple ink and claimed that he had successfully completed skin grafts between genetically different animals. The discovery of this fraud was rapid but uncomfortable. Peter Medewar, who was well aware of what was going on, found himself, by his own confession (Zuckerman 1977, p. 96), "Lacking in moral courage . . . to say at the time that . . . we were the victims of a hoax or confidence trick." A scientific investigation into this case found Summerlin guilty of misrepresentation. Summerlin himself admitted he had inked the back of a mouse, making this clearly a case of intentional fraud. But Summerlin had been determined to prove that skin grafts between genetically different animals are possible—a clear case of a scientist who resorted to fraudulent practices in order to "prove" something he believed in.

Three additional cases will end this part of the illustrations. One concerns the "discovery" of N rays. The reputable French physicist from the University of Nancy, Prosper Blondlot, claimed in 1903 that he had detected N rays about eight years after the German physicist Wilhelm Konrad Roentgen discovered X rays (for which he received the first Nobel Prize in physics in 1901). The period was rife with all sorts of discoveries focused on rays, and Blondlot had apparently pressured himself to discover some new form of ray. This "discovery" was well received in France and the French Academy even awarded Blondlot a prize, but American physicist Robert Wood was skeptical. He visited Blondlot in his French laboratory and while "Blondlot was observing and describing an N-ray spectrum, Wood slyly removed an essential prism from the apparatus. This had no effect on what poor Blondlot fancied he was seeing" (Gardner 1952, 345). As Asimov (1979) stated, Blondlot "wanted to believe in something desperately—and he did" (p. 137).

Our second case is the famous Lysenko case. As Gardner (1952, 149–51) stated, "Seldom in the history of modern science has a crackpot achieved the eminence, adulation, and power achieved by Troffim D. Lysenko, the Soviet Union's leading authority on evolution and heredity. Not only have his opinions been pronounced dogma by the Kremlin, but his Russian opponents (whose views are held everywhere but in the USSR) . . . have been systematically eliminated from their posts" (p. 140). Lysenko, a former peasant and plant-breeder, publicly defended and endorsed the debunked Lamarkian view, i.e., that the mechanism by which evolution works is the inheritance of traits which various organisms acquired when responding to their environment—inheritance of acquired characteristics. Lysenko's views accorded fully with the political views of the Soviet Communist party at that time. The year 1948 marked a decisive victory for Lysenko and the agonizing end of his opponents.

We shall delve, with many more details, into the third and more recent case, that of Alfred Kinsey. This can help us gain a better insight into this issue, as it indicates that Yadin was not the only scientist who let his ideological convictions color his scientific work.

As many of us may remember, the 1948 publication of Alfred C. Kinsey's book on the sexual behavior of males (known better as the *Kinsey Report*), and of another book on the sexual behavior of females in 1953, helped bring a revolution into being. The 1948 work by the Indiana University professor indicated that a very large proportion of males were engaged in masturbating and premarital sex and utilized the sexual services of prostitutes. It showed that close to 40 percent had experienced homosexual contacts leading to orgasms, and that 30 to 45 percent of married males had extramarital sex. Similarly sensational findings were produced in 1953 about females. Within a rather puritanical social context, Kinsey's books came as a shock. Basically, his research indicated that the sexual behavior of both males and females presented significantly richer, more varied, and complex patterns than those allowed (or thought to be existing) by prevailing conservative morality. Kinsey, of course, was viewed as a dry, detached, and pedantic academic whose data collection was not something to be questioned on moral grounds.

Jones's 1997 work, *Afred Kinsey: A Public/Private Life*, casts dark shadows on this. He claims that

> Kinsey . . . was not quite what he appears to be—the genial academic in baggy tweeds and bow tie, the simple empiricist disinterestedly reporting his data. . . . [H]e was, in reality, a covert crusader who was determined to use science to free American society from what he saw as the crippling legacy of Victorian repression. And he was a strong-willed patriarch who created around himself a kind of utopian community in which sexual experimentation was encouraged. . . . In his obsessive energies and powers of persuasion, Kinsey resembled a late twentieth-century cult leader . . . with a burning belief in his mission. (1997a, p. 100)

Jones's work reveals the considerable disparity between the private and public lives, and presentations, of Alfred Kinsey. In public—the presentation of a cold, calculating, and careful scientist. In private, Kinsey was a domineering man, interested in and mastering many areas (entomology, biology, education, classical music, designing a house and elaborate flower garden); but above all he had a remarkably free and rather wild sexual lifestyle. It included experimentation with various sexual behaviors—homosexuality, masochism, promiscuity—all the while maintaining his role as (heterosexual) husband and father. Much of the sexual experimentation, by the way, was justified on the grounds of being "needed for research." Jones has no hesitation in concluding that Kinsey's private life and morality

> almost certainly did affect the objectivity and detachment of his work as a scientist; his celebrated findings, I now believe, may have been skewed. From the very beginning of his research into sexual behavior, the Ameri-

> cans who most persistently engaged Kinsey's attention were people who were either on the margins or beyond the pale: homosexuals, sadomasochists, voyeurs, exhibitionists, pedophiles, transsexuals, transvestites, fetishists. (1997a, p. 101)

Jones points out that Kinsey was involved in outright deception when he had to justify how and why his interest in human sexuality developed. His presentations always gave the impression that he became involved in the topic quite by accident, and in response to demands from his students. That presentation both concealed and falsified the truth—that Kinsey had been involved in sexual experimentation throughout his entire life, some of which was considered by contemporaries as esoteric, marginal, and negative, and that his private life certainly affected both how and why he became involved in sexual research (1997a, p. 105). The clear implication is that Kinsey was strongly motivated to show American society as extremely unconventional in sexual practice but very condemnatory in principle, and therefore hypocritical. His crusade was to eliminate this hypocrisy, and to this end he used his scientific status and credibility.

Although the media's attention to Kinsey's work was very favorable, the academic professional reaction was mixed. While no one knew about the formidable disparity between the public appearances Kinsey gave and the private realities he lived, his sampling methods drew sharp criticism, his book was described as confusing, and he was accused (by no less than Margaret Mead) of decontextualizing sexual acts from relevant contexts.

Finally, let me note that similar accounts about deceptions and hoaxes are easily found in many areas (MacDougall 1940), such as the media (Fedler 1989) and geographical explorations (Roberts 1982).

These examples illustrate that when the relevant information is available, a clear line between truth and deception can be drawn. This is probably valid as well for other areas of life where deception may occur. Another conclusion is the *intention* to falsify, lie, and deceive an audience. The fact that the deceivers *know* that they are involved in telling deliberate untruths is a distinguishing hallmark of deception. The lack of such intention is typically taken to indicate that no bona fide lie exists. However, to illustrate how complex this issue can be, I introduced the case of Blondlot. Did he intentionally fabricate his apparatus? On one level, yes, he certainly did. The lenses he put in his contraption were aimed to capture something that was not there. And, indeed, they did not capture the elusive and nonexistent N rays. On another level, it appears that Blondlot genuinely believed that his contraption did capture those rays, and therefore he may have lacked the intention to falsify evidence.

The problem, of course, resides with our difficulties in establishing intent. Moreover, the case of Blondlot illustrates another difficulty so common in construction theory. Blondlot was working in a paradigmatic context that was conducive to belief in the existence of N rays. As the famous scholar Bertrand Russell has noted, the application of a mathematicised astronomy leads to a mathematized universe. Likewise, optical astronomy created severe obstacles for the acceptance of radio astronomy as a bona fide science.[13] In other words, what we see, perceive, and understand is mediated by filters, one of which is culture, or a paradigm in the case of science. If you like, this is another illustration of Thomas's now classical dictum that if situations are defined as real, they are real in their consequences. But the solution to this problem is found in the N-rays story itself. When a hard, cold, empirical test was applied to Blondlot's experiment, the reality that was based on falsehood simply collapsed into nothingness, regardless of what Blondlot believed. So ultimately even the case of Blondlot can be used as an illustration of how a reality based on falsehoods can be collapsed.

The above cases illustrate that lies and deceptions range from the unclear and problematic to the clear and obvious. Deception is a behavior which occurs among individuals, groups, and nations. Thus, infidelity; military deception; national lying; faking orgasms; a variety of such white-collar crimes as counterfeiting money, fashion products, music CDs, and art; computer crime; embezzlement; insurance fraud; con games; worthless medications; plagiarism; environmental crimes; consumer fraud; and a host of similar phenomena are all deceptions. Moreover, our language allows us to make fine distinctions among different lies and deceptions, for example, "blatant lies," "deceptions," "white lies," and "exaggerations." The specific term which we choose to use in specific instances is context-dependent. Such issues as those pertaining to the nature of the lie, its impact, the intentions of the liar, the audience—all are variables which help us decide, case by case, how to classify the tale—innocent lie, exaggeration, blatant lie, and so on.

Various deceptions are thus part of our culture, and we are involved in deceptive schemes almost all the time. We live in a cultural ecology which is permeated by lies and deceptions to its very core. Lies and deceptions are therefore to be found almost everywhere and anytime. The crucial variable in this context is one of degree and quality, not of principle. Consequently we need to examine the nature of lies.

WHAT ARE LIES AND DECEPTIONS?

Academic interest in lies and deceptions has not been strong, but it seems to have gained momentum in recent years, yielding some interesting formulations.[14]

We humans are capable of using means of communications which are symbolic and enable us to transcend the limits of time and space. There can be little doubt that the ability to fantasize is intimately associated with the ability to lie and deceive, and that these capabilities are greatly facilitated by the acquisition of language skills, oral and written. Thus we are capable of creating legends, myths, and fairy tales; we can fabricate, cheat, deceive, and lie—in other words, relate to things whose empirical reality is partial, imaginary, nonexistent, or even deliberately falsified. We all tell lies. And there are different types of lies and deceptions. There are defensive lies, political lies, romantic lies, and so on. The list of types of lies which Cohen (1999, p. 124) constructs is impressively long. Robinson even states that "lies have great potential for preserving the status quo" (1996, p. 299). These researchers also note that the construction of truth is meaningful only when we contrast it with lies and falsehood. For example, the so-called Witness Protection Program in the United States, in which official bureaucratic agencies are involved in a coordinated activity whose aim it is to falsify identities and keep those falsified identities secret for as long as possible.

The last example tells us that not every act of telling a deliberate lie is considered culturally negative. In fact, some such activities are not usually even thought of as telling lies. Storytelling in the form of creating fictional stories, characters, plots and places, movies, and other forms of art which are loosely connected (if at all) to reality as we recognize it, can be rewarded very generously. Obviously one of the major differences between Tom Clancy's or Alistair MacLean's fictional suspense and fantasy war stories and criminal con artists is the intention. Creating fiction for the sake of fiction, deliberately but openly, can be a socially gratifying activity. However, telling deliberate lies which create a nonfactually based reality with an intent to conceal the truth and lead unsuspectful victims into suspending disbelief and to manipulate those victims in a way which is detrimental to their well-being is typically condemned as negative and deserving of punishment. Hence the activity of telling lies, in itself, is not universally banned. It is the context of that activity which will help us determine what the appropriate reaction to telling these lies will be. Intention seems to be the crucial factor. Some diplomats are engaged in fabricating deliberate lies in an explicit attempt to conceal the truth; they are expected to lie, and to repeat those lies in public—part of the profession, we are told.

For most people, truth means something nonproblematic, simple, straightforward, and objective, something which is "out there" and which can be looked at, measured, described, perhaps photographed, an entity which manifests a genuine existence regardless of human folly and manipulations. This perception of truth is a cultural belief which is also translated into special institutions dedicated to the discovery and establishment of truth—for example, courts and science. However, the type of "truth" which is constructed in courts can be very problematic. Courts are much more concerned with the application of a complicated set of rules in order to create a version of reality which sometimes may be as far from the truth as is possible. Consequently, sometimes innocent people are convicted for doing things that in fact they have never done, or guilty ones are exonerated of crimes they have actually committed. The language of justice and fairness is dominant in court, and it may sometimes contradict truth. Likewise, the history of science teaches us that truth was (and probably still is) a problematic issue there as well.

The increasingly digital age can make the reproduction of truth even more problematic. This technology enables the fabrication of reproductions representing different versions of reality on a mass scale. And yet even with this technology, the belief in the existence of truth marks a solid foundation of our culture. We are looking for genuine art, not fabricated products. We do not like to be told that a plagiarized product is a genuine one. We do not take kindly to claims which try to take false credit. Thus while the modern age of digital and electronic technology may blur the difference between falsehoods and genuine artifacts or facts, we are still interested in the genuine, the authentic, and the truth. Without truth as a baseline, the existence of lies cannot be established. A culture which harbors truthless social realities must be wilder than Alice's Wonderland. We will be lost in a twilight zone where no clear boundaries between lies and truth exist, only different versions of "reality." In this strange universe, reality will become a choice commodity. To me, it is inconceivable that anyone could live any meaningful or appreciable period of time in such a culture and remain sane (again, assuming that "sane" exists).

FACTUAL VERSUS INTERPRETATIVE TRUTH

There are blatant lies, those whose existence can be established because they typically contrast empirical facts, both on the personal and collective (sometimes national) levels. However, what happens when the lie is not so evident or easy to detect and verify? When the lie is structured along slight but significant distortions? What about the motivation to mislead?

In wars, armies like deceptions. By fooling the enemy they can achieve better and cheaper victories. Military history has a few such fantastic episodes: the Japanese attack on Pearl Harbor, Egypt and Syria's surprise attack on Israel in October 1973, the complete surprise of the Nazi counterattack in the Ardennes (Battle of the Bulge) in December 1944. A spouse who is not faithful to his/her mate is involved in such a deliberate deception as well. But what if a person, or a group of persons, believes that the nature of reality has a certain form, and they discard or twist evidence to the contrary, not out of a desire to deceive, but out of a deep belief in their own fabricated reality? In "their truth," shall we say? How about parents telling their children some "white lies" because they feel that facing the truth is beyond their children's power and ability to process? How about physicians who avoid telling some patients the true nature of their diseases for similar reasons?

It is beneficial to distinguish between at least two types of truths. One type is *factual truth*. This is the truth involved in finding out whether something happened or existed or not. This type of truth typically does not involve interpretations, and if all the facts are known, is easy to establish. Such questions as "Who sank the *Lusitania* on May 7, 1915?" or "Do we inherit acquired traits?" have factual answers. There is, however, a type of truth which is more difficult to establish, and that is *interpretative truth*. This type of truth, as its name implies, may be based on combining facts in different ways. Political claims, ideologies, social identities, romantic involvements—these are all illustrative of this type of truth. Interpretative truth typically takes as building blocks some factual truths and integrates them into what looks like a coherent, systematic, and credible narrative. Issues regarding the type of facts taken into account (that is, selection), their differential weights and the way in which they are combined are at the foundation of many mythologies, fairy tales, legends, fiction, and a few other forms of collective behavior. The play between factual truth and interpretative truth forms much of the empirical focus of this book. How and why cultures take factual truth and socially construct meaning from it is an intriguing topic.

Power and Truth

Bailey adds a fascinating dimension: "truth and deceit are inextricably entangled with power" (1991, p. xviii). For example, he points out that lies protect the weak from the strong, and thus myth is something which is actually developed as a weapon by the weak. Here we need to point out that there may actually be significant differences between the reasons for the invention of a myth (or a tradition) and its strategic deployment. Revel's work (1991), in which he claims that we live in an "age of lies," supports Bailey's claim that power plays a major part in deciding what is and what is not "truth." Truth, according to Bailey, can imply "authority, dominance, an unyielding absolutism" (p. 3). He states that the only way in which we "can understand 'truth' and 'untruth' is to see them as rhetoric, as concepts used primarily for persuasion. They are political words, weapons for use in competition for power. In that context 'truth' and 'untruth' represent a tension, a tug of war, a dialogue between adversaries, who use these words in the contest, each striving to make their own ideas and values prevail" (p. 128). This, of course, is a fantastic claim. It can be taken to imply that making a distinction between truth and untruth depends only on power, and that truth and deceit are completely context-dependent. But to sustain this assertion one must restrict oneself to *interpretative truth* and not to *factual truth*.

Truth and Belief, Myth and Master Frames

What if people have such a strong belief in something that they are willing to discard, or deliberately ignore, contradictory (or not supportive) evidence? It is not too difficult to bring numerous illustrations of this. Intelligence failures are one good area; for example, the American failure to discover in time the impending Japanese attack on Pearl Harbor (December 7, 1941), and the failure of Israeli intelligence to expose the Egyptian-Syrian attack of October 3, 1973 (the Yom Kippur War). In both cases the attackers inflicted temporary military catastrophes. Many observers point out that in both cases intelligence was a prisoner of its own concept. While this concept assumed that the attackers had hostile intentions, it did not include an imminent war. Thus despite enough intelligence information that a military strike was indeed imminent, this information was ignored. In other words, Japan and Syria and Egypt were highly successful in deceiving their opponents.

Science, too, has its share. For example, while physicists had enough evidence that it was possible to view the universe through radio waves, this information was discarded as unreliable in favor of an optical view, which did not allow radio astronomy to develop.[15] The Ptolemaic view of the solar system was accepted as a dogmatic (even sacred) truth despite accumulating evidence to the contrary. The acceptance of quantum mechanics and plate tectonics suffered a similar fate. Each scientific discipline constitutes a belief system; within this belief system puzzles are raised, anomalies are recognized or denied, and the plausibility of various types of explanations and knowledge claims is weighed. The acceptance of some new ideas and the rejection of others, as well as the problem of resistance to innovation in science, are all directly linked both to science as a belief system and to the fact that every scientist operates on the basis of, and within, an extensive and complex matrix of existing beliefs. This matrix includes the prevailing disciplinary paradigm and the scientists' criteria for evaluating knowledge claims.[16]

Focusing on illustrations from areas such as religion, science, and politics, the issue of people believing falsehoods occupied much of

Robinson's work (1996). Mythology certainly plays an important part there. "Societies constructed myths about the creation of the world and their place in it. . . . People with aspirations for achieving or sustaining their power would attach themselves to creation myths" (pp. 291–94). The term Robinson chooses to describe these myths is quite instructive: "noble lies" (p. 295). However, his analysis proceeds from creation myth to heroic legend (p. 296), stating that both "are but two examples of major cultural institutions where truth was initially received truth" (p. 299). Robinson takes the fact that people believe major falsehoods as a very central trait of contemporary cultures. Indeed, these beliefs create difficulties for anyone trying to establish clear lines between truth and falsehoods.

Some researchers working in the area of social movements have developed the concept of a "master frame" (and processes), attempting to conceptualize the ways in which the ideologies of various such movements are translated into the individual level. These master frames act as experience organizers and as paradigms in science. That is, they are utilized by individuals in order to make sense of their empirical reality, transforming factual truths into interpretative truths. These frames produce criteria for, and sensitize individuals to, what to pay attention to, what to ignore, and how to combine one's knowledge into a systematic, consistent, and coherent worldview.[17] Thus Yael Zerubavel (1995) tries to understand the processes by which a new culture invents itself. She proposes use of the concept of commemoration as a central key to understand these processes, and she suggests that "each act of commemoration reproduces a *commemorative narrative*, a story about a particular past that accounts for this ritualized remembrance and provides a moral passage for the group members" (p. 6). Zerubavel argues that, when put together, commemorative narratives form what she refers to as "*master commemorative narrative* that structures collective memory. With this concept I refer to a broader view of history, a basic 'story line' that is culturally constructed and provides the group members with a general notion of their shared past" (p. 6). The temporary hegemony of master commemorative narratives provides members of cultures with an organizing principle. This narrative is used to organize experience, explain the past and the present, and helps shape identities. It is no coincidence that both Zerubavel's study (which is focused on collective memory) and the new studies in collective behavior focusing on the concept of a master frame converge on the issue of identity formation. Whether a "master frame" or a "master commemorative narrative," what we have here are suggestions for key conceptual ideas which individuals acquire and which they use when they need to manufacture meaning, forge identities, and delineate social and moral boundaries. When any specific person uses these cultural organizing principles, that person will accept and reject information as it fits those principles. An effect of deception can be easily created when these cognitive processes are set in motion. However, deception requires more than choosing selective information. This act of choosing must be made consciously, by deliberately suppressing or concealing other and possibly contradictory facts, and with the explicit intent to deceive unsuspecting audiences.

Prevalence of Deceit and Its Cultural Meaning

Claiming that deception is a cultural trait which we all share still requires some attention to its prevalence. Indeed, Bailey (1991), Barnes (1994), and Robinson (1996) all note that lies and deceit are ubiquitous and that individuals and governments are involved in deceptive schemes on a routine and regular basis.

Charting the history of public presentations of falsehoods, Robinson (1996) concludes that in the distant past public representations did not draw very clear or sharp boundaries between truth and falsehood. Only in the modern era have such distinctions become important and significant, and the contrast between true and false came into being. Areas where lies, deceptions, and misinformation are part of the normal conduct are military conflicts,[18] politics,[19] and that period called the Cold War (Charters and Tugwell 1990; Friedman 2000). Indeed, Knightley finds it appropriate to quote Sen. Hyram Johnson's 1917 proclamation, "The first casualty when war comes is truth," as the motto for his 1975 book.

Jones edited a fascinatingly instructive volume (1990) which shows how widespread different forms of deception (e.g., copying, transforming, embellishing, forging, faking) are in the arts,[20] as well as charting their causes, types and modes of detection. Because it is difficult to estimate accurately the amount of deception, one is necessarily forced to examine its various manifestations. As pointed out earlier, the range of deceptions is impressively large and encompasses areas of human conduct from the personal to the collective, from pranks to military, from the noncriminal to the criminal. Such a profound range must simply be taken as an indication of how prevalent deceptive behavior is.

Ekman devotes an entire chapter in his book (1992) to examining the question of why lies fail.[21] The reasons he gives include: bad lines, lying about feelings is very difficult to maintain, fear of being caught, guilt about deceiving. Of course, maintaining that lies fail accords well with our Western ideas about the immorality of lies. However, it is clear that not all lies fail. Certainly they do sometimes, but not always. The systematic and persuasive empirical evidence for deciding whether lies fail or succeed is still not available, and what we have most of the time are instructive but nonrepresentative anecdotes.[22] Nevertheless, as so many authors have pointed out, lies and deceptions form such an intimate part of Western culture that it is reasonable to assume that most lies probably do not fail. Besides, how are we to explain the fact that lies are so prevalent if they tend to fail so often? However we refer to them, situations in which there is a considerable disparity between factual reality and its presentation are extremely common. And this disparity is not a random and innocent occurrence, but the result of deliberate intent to deceive. In fact, I am willing to risk contradicting Ekman by suggesting that lies and deceptions fail far less than we would like to assume. In other words, "most liars can fool most people most of the time."[23]

Defining Lies: The Literature and the Conclusion

Having made some distinctions and discussed the issue of prevalence, we are now in an advantageous position to clarify the very nature of the phenomenon we are looking at—lies and deceptions. Barnes refers to a lie as "a statement intended to deceive a dupe about the state of the world, including intentions and attitudes of the liar" (p. 11), disregarding the success or failure of the lie. Bailey contrasts "truth" with "untruth," pointing out that "untruth" has three basic forms: deceit, error, and fiction. He characterizes deceit as the "deliberate statement of what is known not to be the case" (p. 127). This definition obviously relies heavily on intention, which in itself is another difficult concept, among other things because honest mistakes and misunderstandings should not be included, not to mention the problem of measuring intent. Barnes suggests, "If we intend to deceive, we are acting untruthfully; if our untruthful act consists of making a statement intended to mislead, we are lying" (p. 12), making the distinction between "lie" and "deceit" distinguishable by the intention involved and not by the state of the world. Vasek (1986) sharpens this approach further and notes that "almost all writers include a definition of deception as the intentional communication of falsehood. . . . Deception occurs when the content of a message is untruthful" (p. 272).

While truth may seem rather straightforward, in fact it is not always easy to establish. Barnes apparently enjoys quoting an 1897 statement which he attributed to Mark Twain: "Truth is the most valuable thing we have. Let us economize it" (1994, p. 37). Bailey (1991, p. 128) notes that truth is always contextualized, negotiated, and dependent on power. The idea of truth being problematic, negotiated, and forever changing is typical of many contemporary, popular, and powerful paradigms such as postmodernism and relativism. Some of the works of such contemporary cultural heroes as Michel Foucault, Hayden White, and Richard Rorty seem to blur the lines between truth and untruth. Indeed, Norris's work (1996) very strongly criticizes such works for failing to provide clear lines of demarcation between untruth and truth.

In view of these developments it becomes important to note that "the world" is not composed merely of equally valid "versions," but that there are numerous forms of lying and deceptions, and that there is indeed a "truth." In fact, without truth such words as deception, hoax, concealment, lying, and cheating become devoid of any meaning. Truth and untruth span a wide range indeed, from simple acts like dyeing one's hair, using makeup, and resorting to plastic surgery, to masking the signs of one's real age, through a physician's hiding the true nature of their diseases from patients, to major military and political deceptions, as well as deceptions on the interpersonal level.

One of the better and more thoughtful definitions of, and approaches to, lies and deceptions was developed by Ekman. He states that a lie or deceit occurs when "one person intends to mislead another, doing so deliberately, without prior notification of this purpose, and without having been explicitly asked to do so by the target." He then distinguishes between *conceal*—when a "liar withholds some information without actually saying anything untrue"—and *falsify*—when the liar not only withholds information but "presents false information as if it were true" (1992, p. 28). While concealment may seem to be less disreputable because it may not involve inventing untrue accounts, it is quite capable of misleading audiences to believe in a false reality.

For example, while the late cellist Jacqueline du Pré has been portrayed as "the golden girl of classical music: beautiful, talented and irresistibly vivacious . . . known to her fans as 'St. Jackie,'" that portrayal may have actually been mythical. According to a new report based on accounts provided by her brother and sister, Piers and Hilary du Pré, she was "spoilt, manipulative and emotionally dangerous to know. . . . [Her] family are tired of the image of her saintliness and want to set the record straight. . . . After Jacqueline's death her family came close to burning all her possessions in an attempt to 'exorcise' her influence." If that is true, the concealment of du Pré's behavior was, at the very least, certainly helpful in crystallizing her image as a "saint." Indeed, du Pré's fans are reported to be concerned that while no one challenges her musical talents, her saintly image may now be replaced by that of a monster.[24] Interestingly, what we have here are two diametrically opposed versions about du Pré; an outside observer could quite possibly produce a third version, which might lie somewhere between the two. In other words, the empirical basis behind the different constructions could provide other than two discrete black/white interpretations of du Pré.

In our context, for example, Yadin's concealment of the fact that pig bones had been found in loci 2001–2002 is a good illustration. Some of the interpretations of the discoveries in the cave of the skeletons and in locus 8 (the three skeletal remains) were based not only on concealment but on falsifications as well.

Ekman bases his inclusive definition on a few elements. First, an *intent* to deceive must exist. This element is mentioned by almost everyone who has done work in this area and provides a good handle for distinguishing between benevolent and malicious lies. While intention is not always easy or simple to measure, it appears that defining lies without it may be too difficult. It needs to be pointed out that a possible alternative criterion to intention can be based on outcome. Second, this intention means that the deceiver or liar had a *choice* to make (whether to lie or not). Third, the target of a lie or a deception did not give his or her *consent* to be misled and the liar did not give any *prior notification* of the intent to make a false presentation. No one would consider calling film or theater actors liars, despite the fact that they, by both choice and intent, make false presentations. Finally, the distinction between concealment and falsification is indeed illuminating. As Ekman points out, given a choice, liars will always choose concealment over falsification, because concealment is much easier to accomplish, and because liars tend to assume that it is less reprehensible than falsification (1992, p. 29). Ekman notes that there are many social situations in which we need to conceal; for example, poker or other and similar games, commercial and political negotiations, embezzlers who conceal the fact that they steal money, plagiarists who conceal the fact that the work they present as their own really is not so. As is easily seen, these very same situations may give rise to falsifications as well.[25] Ekman is quick to note that in some situations concealment is crucial for survival; for example, Jews hiding their identity under Nazi rule and occupation, or spies. Such mass concealment of identity has been historically documented, such as the "Marranos" or "Anusim"—Jews who pretended to convert to Christianity to avoid death during the Spanish Inquisition, while maintaining some aspects of their Jewish identity in secret.[26]

Ekman's definition accords well with the observations made in previous chapters. Yadin had the choice of telling the whole truth (and explaining why he preferred one interpretation over another) and not concealing evidence, falsifying or fabricating interpretations. He chose not to. He certainly seems to have intended to deceive his audiences, and the outcome of his actions was that the Masada mythical narrative, and not the historical narrative, received a credible boost. Yadin's audiences certainly did not express a wish or consent to be deceived and were not notified about being part of a deception.

Robinson's meticulous work (1996) is focused on the role of lies and deceit in representing realities and creating the illusion that a coherent culture in fact exists. This work views lies and deceptions as main characteristics of cultures. Relying on Schwarz et al.'s 1988 dictionary, he maintains that to lie means "to utter a falsehood with an intention to deceive; to give a false impression" (1996, p. 26), and that the "contrast between truth and falsity is the crucial distinction for the utility of the representational function of language" (p. 27). He then distinguishes among five different approaches to defining lies. One measures the deviations from truth (characteristic of this book). The second focuses on a lingual analysis of words of deception. The third examines prototypical cultural lies. The fourth approach takes a wide-angle view to include all possible forms of deceit and concealment, stressing that free will is essential to deception—that is, the liar must have the choice not to lie. The last approach is philosophical, exploring those acts which are intended "to make others believe what we ourselves do not believe" (p. 34), and trying to understand the historical development of lying. Robinson himself is quick to warn us to beware of this approach because philosophy "is prone to develop a paralysis through analysis, and its practitioners are liable to forget the ultimate importance of synthesis, decision making and action" (p. 38). If anything, his work needs to be taken as an indication of the complexity of this topic.

Robinson (1996) points out that there are some deliberate fabrications and deceptions at the very core of our cultures, for example, mythmaking or legends. It is one thing to provide an imaginary and fabricated tale when everyone knows its nature (e.g., fictional movies, books, tales), but it is an entirely different thing to know that one is providing a questionable, fabricated tale and to deceive audiences into believing that this fable is actually the truth.

Using the criterion of intention, one can classify types of lies and deceptions.[27] For example, Barnes points out that the last place we would expect to find deceit is science, and yet deception has existed in science in at least two forms,[28] as a deliberate act in the research itself, and as deliberately falsified reports. Such reports can range from reports on observations which have never been made to manipulative, selective, and suggestive interpretations of data which are intended to deceive audiences into believing that a particular reality construction is *the* valid one. Both of these forms can be found in the excavations at Masada.

Relying on systems theory, Myrdene Anderson suggests that deception "can be understood as simply the sending and/or receiving of misleading information in open cybernetic systems" (p. 324). Anderson points out that there is an interesting interaction between deceit and secrecy. Thus deception can result from providing partial information, hiding crucial information, or telling factual information in such a way that no one will actually believe it (M. Anderson 1986, p. 325).

It is important to note that faked information can sometimes fall into an area where it is difficult to establish intent to deceive. For example, faked memories of imaginary traumas include many instances not only of untruths, but of tales which, despite their dubious validity, may receive full support from clinicians.[29] This is certainly not the case with the excavations of Masada.

Using usefulness as a defining criterion, Barnes (1994, p. 147) points out that lies "are a mixed blessing"; and Bailey adds that "some forms of untruth are admired" (1991, p. xvii). This may be so because the ability to lie and deceive may have some advantages in an evolutionary context among humans, animals, and plants.[30] Indeed, Mitchell and Thompson (1986) devote their work to examining deceptions among humans and nonhumans alike from that perspective.

Since deception is so prevalent, why should we object to the imputation of deception? Plainly, because a value incommensurability (Cohen and Ben-Ari, 1991) is created. On the one hand, practicing deceptions is useful; on the other hand, we praise truth as a highly important value. It is this contradiction which fuels our ambivalent attitudes toward deception, including our hesitation even to use the term. Moreover, the use of the terms *deception* and *truth* must be contextualized. Deception in science, or using the cloak of science to deceive, creates an incommensurability. Science is not a conducive context for deception.

Summarizing the different definitions and approaches, I would say that lies and deceptions have occurred when the following conditions are met: the existence of the intent to present a false front based on a choice to do so; an unsuspecting and uninformed audience; and a presentation based on both concealment and falsification. Once the existence of deception is established, we will need to distinguish between factual and interpretative lies.

Functional Importance of Truth

Bailey (1991) states that the psychological, functional reason we need truth is "a universal psychological need to be sure of something, to put an end to the questioning, to know where one stands" (p. 124). Put differently, the insecurity, powerlessness, and uncertainty which seem to plague modern life propel us to search for objective, perhaps eternal, truths, a truth capable of establishing trust and integration.[31] The quest for truth can be thought of as a quest for meaning (and religion as a sort of ultimate truth not to be questioned). Accepting Bailey's idea that on the personal level we are prone to fall prey to deceptive persuasive schemes means that we may have answered the question of why we are willing to accept some of the most bizarre belief systems, whose truth claims are certainly not empirically based. Many so-called religions and ideologies, based totally on pure belief, fall into this category. The ability of these religious forms and ideologies to attract new recruits depends on the ability of recruiting agents to contextualize and tailor the specific solution they market as a remedy for uncertainty to specific innocent buyers. Much of their recruiting tactics must rely on deception: telling only part of their "truth," hiding information, creating an atmosphere where suspension of natural disbelief occurs, and creating trust in the converting agents. For example, the typical price of specified salvation solutions in economic, social, and psychological terms is hardly, if ever, disclosed or discussed. Regardless of this need, cultures are characterized by maintaining some level of lies and deception by relying on such schemes as mythologies.

Cultures and Deception

The ability to lie and deceive is a hallmark of human and nonhuman species alike, and deceit has emerged as a major characterization of human cultures, substantively and historically.

Since deceit is correlated negatively with trust, we can expect deceit to increase as trust declines. This means that as our interest in understanding trust and its violations increases,[32] we may also benefit from exploring the parallel and complementary concept of deceit and untruth. What does the prevalence of deceit mean in cultural terms? Prima facie, and using a Durkheimian prism, it could mean that cultural deceit, truth, and untruth are linked to processes of cultural integration and disintegration.

Can cultures based on lies exist for long? To answer that question, we must first answer a few other crucial questions. To begin with, what *type* of lies are prevalent? Are these lies about factual matters? About interpretations of facts? Do members of a particular culture *know* that they are being constantly lied to and deceived? Both Bailey (1991) and Barnes (1994) provide anthropological evidence for cultures which are characterized by high levels of deception and lies. Historically, moreover, living with false ideologies is nothing new. Indeed, Zagorin (1996) offers further evidence for the historical significance of lying and dissimulation. Many cultures did, and still do, live with central untruths and their members believe, for example, in deceitful mythologies. But, as the literature on myth points out,[33] regardless of their truthfulness, myths have played a central role as powerful cultural integrative forces, capable of providing a strong sense of an imagined community (B. Anderson 1991), i.e., forging personal and national identities and shaping collective memories. Once believed in, mythologies bind members of cultures together, furnishing them with a constructed common heritage and belief system. At the beginning of the twentieth century Georges Sorel stated that myth was the exclusive force which was capable of driving people to action. He identified myth with the beliefs of a group and he felt that those strongly felt beliefs propelled people both into forming movements and to direct action.

It is in many cases virtually impossible to establish the empirical basis of a myth and thus determine to what degree it is based on falsehood. Furthermore, falsehood does not always mean deception, because the intention to deliberately falsify must be first established. Both the present book and Kohl and Fawcett's 1995 work document cases in which archaeological support was given to mythologies and where falsehoods could be verified.

What happens when the basis of falsely based mythologies is exposed and the myth becomes questionable? The immediate essence which is being threatened is obviously trust. If members of a culture become aware that central elements of the beliefs and moral code which define them as a particular culture may be based on falsehood, this could threaten the faith of these members in the validity of the ways in which their culture weaves meaning, constructs reality claims, and interprets the cultural cosmos in which they live. In short, such a revelation could create distrust and cynicism and may either set in motion or reflect disintegrative forces of social change. A distinctive factor in such a process, I believe, lies in the power of knowledge. As long as members of cultures are unaware that they live in lies, no disintegrative forces are set in motion, and trust can be maintained. But such cultures are characterized by a chronic tension. Once members discover that some meaningful aspects of their life have been deceitful—the older construction of national and personal identity, that is—their sense of an "imagined community" may crumble and give rise to a new one, perhaps equally deceitful. Mythologies seemed to have always characterized cultures. Therefore discounting old mythologies on the grounds that they are based on falsehoods may actually make room for new mythologies emphasizing different moralities and reflecting new cultural ambiences.

This conceptualization makes it clear that a central characteristic of cultures, the ideological symbolic level, is in fact a major source for tensions and a powerful motivator for setting processes of change in motion, as well as setting in motion very powerful forces aimed at keeping the status quo. Indeed, Bailey points out that

> Untruth—the whole range from outright lies to fantasy—is the mover . . . when we want to move the world . . . we need deceit and fictions. . . . Deceit and fictions are Max Weber's magic—creativity, imagination, fantasy, ingenuity, charisma—all those denials of the iron cage which he saw in rational bureaucracy and which are constitutive of any basic lie. (p. 126)

And he also notes that

> grand designs like capitalism or communism or Islam or Christianity, or lesser designs like functionalism or structuralism or postmodernism, and other such basic lies, might all in the end be subject to the same kind of empirical test. . . . The ultimate control on a design (that is, a purported truth) is whether or not it copes with a real world of fundamental problems. . . . Truth, perhaps, is what works. (1991, pp. 122–23)

Without explaining why, Bailey conveys his conviction that in the long run a basic lie stands a good chance of being exposed, even though it may often be presented as a basic truth.

A potentially relevant issue to our discussion is the observation that a main theme in contemporary Western culture, and especially so in the United States, concerns deceitful conspiracies.[34] As Goode and Ben-Yehuda (1994) noted, moral panics are based on either deceitful and fabricated or very severely exaggerated claims. Some of these conspiracy theories are of monstrous proportions. The most famous of these is probably the claim that governments conceal the "fact" that extraterrestrial aliens have been visiting Earth and are in touch with earthly governments.

One of this culture's most powerful modes of expression, visual arts in the form of movies and television series, capitalizes on such theories.[35] These theories assume that normal, innocent humans are constantly being lied to, deceived, and manipulated by powerful forces. It seems that more and more individuals are inclined to believe that gigantic cover-ups, deceptive schemes, and national and international conspiracies are lurking behind almost every corner.

Lest we get too immersed in the idea that conspiracies are a thing of our imagination, let me quickly point out that there have been some genuine conspiracies in the past. One glaring example is the Watergate conspiracy. Examining this conspiracy, both Rasberry (1981) and Wise (1973) conclude that the U.S. government has always been involved in deceiving and lying to the public.

Conspiracy theories lead us to note the intimate connections between politics and deceptions. Indeed, Ekman's main discussion is devoted to enumerating—almost tediously—the long list of lies made by major American politicians (including presidents). Clearly, the phenomenon of politicians who lie right and left is most definitely not confined to the United States. The obvious conclusion is that politicians almost everywhere are routinely involved in lies. This observation is connected to the fact that different agencies of states, as a matter of course, are involved in concealment and lies on an everyday basis. For example, intelligence services, both for military and criminal purposes, by their very nature conceal information and lie. Many aspects of foreign policy conducted by different countries are carried out in a way which conceals their true nature and presents a false representation to the public. This includes cooperation between different countries in military or intelligence covert action, support for terrorist (sometimes referred to as "freedom fighter") organizations, questionable and corrupt commercial transactions, and more. Israeli governments have lied repeatedly. The nuclear reactor near Dimona, explicitly constructed to create nuclear weapons, was presented as a textile factory. Israel distanced itself from a few assassinations in which it almost certainly was involved.[36]

Despite the almost obvious temptation, I do not claim that the Masada mythical narrative and the archaeological excavations which supported it should be examined as a conspiracy committed by a few conniving individuals against the innocent many. The devious, paranoid, secret, and cynical character so distinctive of conspiracies seems to be lacking altogether there.

We cannot conclude such a discussion without mentioning Hamilton's intriguing work (1996). If we claim that cultures present an almost magical ability to maintain lies and deceptions despite all contradictory evidence, we should note that Hamilton analyzes how some major social theories have been accepted despite accumulating evidence against them. Hamilton points out that even in social science, supposedly based on the search for and presentation of empirical evidence, truth does not always prevail. In very many respects, the archaeological backing given to the Masada mythical narrative supports Hamilton's ideas. Moreover, as my 1985 work indicated, this state of affairs characterizes not only social sciences, but other disciplines as well.

Deception as a Generic Quality

The human ability to use a highly symbolic form of communication enables us to transcend the limitations of time and place. This ability also means that we are quite capable of being involved in lies and deceptions. Although in itself this is not a good reason to utilize these abilities, most researchers of lies and deceptions are convinced that all of us have been involved in various forms of lying and deceit. The reason is that the cultures we have constructed have lies and deceptions built into them. In other words, any process of socialization involves acquiring the ability, reasons, and practices of lying and deceiving. The boundaries between deceiving and not deceiving are not set as absolute qualities. Rather, we learn more about how much to deceive, in which situations it is appropriate to utilize what type of deceptions, to whom one is allowed to lie, and the like. Lying is thus a matter not of principle, but of degree and quality. The answer to the question of why people lie can be found in its opposite. That is, people lie because they can and because we live in cultures that incorporate and normalize the practice of lying and deceiving into everyday life as a useful and accepted behavior. Lying and deceiving are therefore both a personal ability and a salient cultural structural characteristic. Perhaps the more interesting and proper questions to study are why and when people do not lie.

The General Research Question in Context

Two earlier research directions gave rise to this project. One was my previous study of the Masada myth (1995), in which I charted how and why the Masada myth was created. That myth was clearly based on untruth. The 1963–65 archaeological excavations of Masada made a real contribution to myth by providing authoritative scientific credibility to a fabricated and mostly factless tale. The other direction is my older interest in the sociology and philosophy of science (1985, 1990). There I was interested in the way scientific knowledge is constructed, evolved, and fabricated. Combining these two lines of research led me into trying to understand how and why archaeology supported the Masada myth. More generally, the question is one relating to the complex relations between science, power, ideology, and politics. How (if at all) does science support national politics? What is the nature of the connection between science and politics? The way in which this possible connection is conceptualized, in theory and in practice, forms the axis around which this book revolves. Answering this question requires some serious and meticulous empirical work in specific areas. My past involvement in studying the Masada myth, as well as my continuous interest in and commitment to social constructionism theory, propelled me to formulate the research question in a much more specific manner, using one particular scientific discipline—archaeology—in one specific case—the excavations of Masada—and to examine in detail how and to what extent ideology and politics were involved in it.

Rather than devise a formal theory, in the manner of Parsons's paradigm or others (e.g., Turner 1991), my work is much more focused on the "sociological imagination" (C. Wright Mills). This imagination provides us with a particular consciousness, defined by a set of analytical concepts, which enables us to describe, interpret, understand, and generalize from the factual world which we and others observe (see also Bash 1995). If anything, this is the single most important variable that distinguishes sociological work from journalism. What, then, is the "sociological imagination" presented in this book, and on what set of concepts is it structured?

Contextual constructionism is our base line. On the one hand, this theoretical perspective requires that we pay careful and close attention to agreed-upon empirical facts which we generate, discover, and cite. Setting the factual level up front is a must. On the other hand, once we have the facts, we need to examine the social constructions of reality which utilize these facts for their presentations. Having done this, we can generate broader generalizations. Indeed, there is an almost built-in element of debunking in contextual constructionism. It forces us into a detached, critical, and perhaps somewhat cynical view of social processes.

The theoretical infrastructure of this book is based on a few other concepts. If contextual constructionism relies on the potential disparities and contradictions between appearances and realities, then the rest of the conceptual set follows suit. In a very major sense, we examine the deviations from factual reality. Contradictions and boundaries are an inherent device in my inquiry. Thus, contradictions such as those between truth and untruth, fact and fiction, trust and its violations, integrity and deception, form a central focus of this book, as they did in my other works. Consequently, the boundaries between deviance and that which is not are at the center of my inquiry. Examining such contrasts as deviance and nondeviance provides a genuine glimpse at fine lines (Zerubavel 1991). Looking at deviance within its broader cultural context of processes of change and stability, are the formatting and configuring parameters of my "sociological imagination" (1985). Processes which define the nature of deviance and which select and determine the nature of the societal reactions to that deviance always involve making fine distinctions which are focused on symbolic moral boundaries and which utilize power to enforce these moral decisions. Therefore, deviance and nondeviance involve understanding not only of morality, but of generating and utilizing power as well.

This book uses a conceptual framework from the study of deviance to interpret an interesting empirical area not touched before by scholars studying deviance, and hardly, if ever, touched by other sociologists: politics and archaeology within the context of deception. Our interpretation requires that we review processes of deviance not as discrete and atomized events, but as processes which are culturally integrated. This cultural integration is of crucial importance. Looking at deviance within this complex cultural context is exactly what forms the sociological imagination within which the empirical observations made for this study were conducted. It explains the choice of the cases, as well as the way we go about interpreting them.

The examination of politics and archaeology within the context of deception and culture also requires that we examine the ways some scientific claims are made in support of either scientific or political belief systems. This is done by socially constructing claims which are tailored to particular belief systems. These constructions can deviate quite significantly from what a cold examination of the tested and agreed-upon facts would produce. In some cases we observed some warping of interpretations, in others we observed sheer and deliberate fabrications. Naturally, discussing this issue necessitated some immersion in understanding the nature of deception and of the sociology of science.

Becker's work (1963) implied that deviance is in the eye of the beholder. The archaeology-politics-deviance connection is *not* merely in the eye of the beholder. In this connection we can see that truth is compromised. Doing this in science can have serious ramifications regarding our image of what science is all about and how it helps us shape our comprehension of the reality in which we live. The fact that in this case we can refer to an agreed-upon truth, based on facts, is fully consistent with contextual constructionism. We can thus utilize the conceptualization of deviance within the context of social constructionism in order to examine how and why social realities are created, maintained, negotiated, and changed.

Finally, because a major and broad analytical axis of this work is deception, it became imperative to be able to distinguish between truth and that which is not. Our ability to make a distinction between deception and truth depends not only on knowledge, but on *detailed* knowledge. Truth, if you will, resides in the details. And indeed, in the previous chapters particular attention was paid to the details.

NOTES

1. Goode 1989, p. 328; see also Best 1995.
2. This is the proper place to note that one should contextualize this work within that of Alfred Schutz; see also Searle 1995; for an update on various developments in this approach, see Potter 1996.
3. See Ben-Yehuda 1995, pp. 20–21 for a short review.
4. See, e.g., Goode and Ben-Yehuda 1994; Best 2001.
5. See, e.g., Goode and Ben-Yehuda 1994; Ben-Yehuda 1995; Best 2001.
6. See, e.g., Ben-Yehuda 1995.
7. See, e.g., Ben-Yehuda 1985, 1990, 1993, 1995. This issue has attracted much attention in philosophy as well. For a midway position see, for one example, the works by philosopher Richard Rorty.
8. See, e.g., Ben-Yehuda 1990 and Goode 1991.
9. My previous works (1985, 1990, 1993, 1995; and Goode and Ben-Yehuda 1994) utilized such contrasts in a variety of areas: witchcraft, deviant sciences and scientists, assassinations, moral panics, mythmaking, and collective memory.
10. See, e.g., Goode and Ben-Yehuda 1994.
11. See, e.g., Ben-Yehuda 1990.
12. Illustrations are from Ben-Yehuda 1985, pp. 179–80, 182–83, 190–93. For

more on similar cases see Ben-Yehuda 1985, 168–207, Ben-Yehuda 1986; Broad and Wade 1982; Kohn 1986; Pallone and Hennessey 1995; Weiner 1980. Deception in social science research, especially in psychology (e.g., work on dissonance theory, on mental illness) and sociology (e.g., Humphreys's work on homosexuals), has captured the imagination. On the related issue of the ethics of research, see also Erich Goode's work-in-progress tentatively titled *Unauthorized Experiences: Sex, Drugs, and Social Research*, particularly his excellent summary in the "Reflection" chapter, as well as his 1996 paper.

13. See Ben-Yehuda 1990, pp. 181–219.

14. E.g., Robinson's 1996 very comprehensive study; and the fall 1996 issue of *Social Research*, which was devoted entirely to truth, lies, and deception.

15. See Ben-Yehuda 1990, pp. 181–219.

16. See Ben-Yehuda 1985, pp. 106–67.

17. See, e.g., Hunt, Benford, and Snow 1994; Snow and Benford 1992.

18. See Barnes 1994, pp. 23–29; Broad 1992; Brown 1975; Dear and Foot 1995, 283–86; Dunningan and Nofi 1995; Handel 1987; Lloyd 1997; Mure 1980; Reit 1978; Sexton 1986; Sykes 1990; Wheatley 1980; Young and Stamp 1989.

19. Barnes 1994, pp. 30–35; Robinson 1996, p. 8.

20. The Israel Museum devoted a whole issue of its quarterly, *Mishkafaim* ("Eyeglasses"), to the subject of forgery in the arts and related topics of forgery in the sciences, politics, in police work, and in nature (issue no. 23, February 1995, in Hebrew).

21. And substantial discussion to the question of whether it is possible to detect if a person is lying or not.

22. Detecting if a person lies or not is a major issue in such areas as: police investigative techniques, which look at alibis, results of "lie detector" tests, facial expressions and body language, as well as simple advice on how to be a successful "lie catcher" (e.g., Ekman 1991; Zebrowitz 1997).

23. To paraphrase Ekman 1992, p. 162. Almost naturally, the topic of lies and deception elicits considerable interest in the popular press. Let me bring a few illustrations. In April 1997 both the *Sunday Telegraph* and the Israeli *Ha'aretz* (April 7, 1998, p. 12A) reported on Jerald M. Jellison's work-in-progress, which purportedly concluded that every person in the United States lies, on the average, two hundred times a day. Most of these lies are "small," for example, saying something like "I'm sorry to interrupt, but . . ." when the person making the apology does not really care, or blaming traffic for being late for a meeting when it is not the real reason. Jellison was quoted as stating that lies were essential because someone who does not lie would probably be perceived as subversive. *Ma'ariv* devoted its entire April 10, 1998, supplement, more than one hundred pages, to lies, deceptions, and secrets. The competing *Yediot Aharonot* carried two long reports (July 5, 1998, pp. 12–13, *Yours* supplement; and September 24, 1998, pp. 10–11, *24 Hours* supplement) focusing on lying. The conclusion in both was clear: we lie frequently, lies are not so bad after all, and we couldn't live in a culture in which people do not lie because it would be nightmarish. The problem would then seem to be not whether or not we lie, or how frequently, but the type, content, and context of the lies we tell. Some lies are accepted and excused as a matter of daily routine, others are strictly unacceptable and their exposure is typically followed by the application of sanctions.

Adir Cohen's "Lies" (1999) supports the view that lies are prevalent and provides an overwhelming amount of anecdotes and illustrations for this assertion in such diverse areas as psychology, politics, love, business, sex, art, literature, and science.

24. Harlow 1997. In the autumn of 1997, newspapers in London (*Times*, *Guardian*) gave readers details and offered interpretations. See also the 1998 biographical drama *Hilary and Jackie.*

25. Ekman's definition is consistent with another popular form of deception, the hoax, which, however, is not relevant to the case of Masada (see Fedler 1989; MacDougall 1958; and Roberts 1982).

26. For a short reference, see *Encyclopedia Judaica*, vol. 3 (1971), pp. 169–74.

27. See Barnes's 1994 reviews.

28. See 1994, pp. 55–64; Ben-Yehuda 1985, pp. 168–207; Kohn 1986; Sisemondo 1996.

29. For example, abductions by UFOs, early life sexual traumas, etc. See, for one example, Ofshe and Watters 1994.

30. See M. Anderson 1986; Bailey 1991, p. xvii.

31. For a philosophical discussion on the nature of truth in the context of Semantic Truth Theories, and using techniques of mathematical logic, see Yael Cohen 1994.

32. See for example my 2001 work on betrayals and treason as violations of trust and loyalty.

33. For a short review see Ben-Yehuda 1995, pp. 279–81, or, for a much fuller review, Doty 1986.

34. See, e.g., Ben-Itto 1998; Gaon 1998; Gardiner and van der Vat 1995; Pipes 1997; see also Vankin and Whalen 1997 and Moen 1995 for popular and comic reviews, respectively.

35. E.g., TV series such as *The X-Files* or *Darkskies* and movies such as *Chain Reaction* (1996), *Independence Day* (1996), *Conspiracy Theory* (1997), *Men in Black* (1997), and the excellent *The Matrix* (1999), to name only a few.

36. E.g., Ali Hassan Salame in Beirut, January 22, 1979; Khalil El Wazir, April 16, 1988.

TEN

THE PAST

Integrated Cultures, History, and Archaeology

Complex societies, characterized by multiculturalism, must invest a great deal of effort into creating and sustaining a consciousness of togetherness among their members. The danger of not doing so risks cultural and social disintegration. Such complex cultures are characterized by the different and the divergent. Creating a consciousness of togetherness in such complex cultures is a major effort (see McCarthy 1997). These cultures must help into existence, cultivate, and nurture personal and national identities that are made to encompass common, significant, and shared elements. Such major cultural ingredients as a common language and a shared past and future have thus become major foci for efforts to create an impression and feelings of a unified and integrated culture. For example, in Israel the debate on the revival of the Hebrew language is well documented and is referred to as the "language war." That war came to a peak in 1913 with the decisive victory of the Hebrew language.[1]

USING HISTORY

History and memory focus a major cultural effort on the creation of a consciousness of likeness among individuals. Concentrating on history in an attempt to integrate cultures constitutes an effort which is aimed at creating and sustaining personal and collective identities. These identities are helped into being by establishing boundaries which separate between "us"—sharing what is presented as a common past and hence future as well—and "them"—who do not share it. Consequently, the type of historical sequences, events, and facts which are selected, taught, and memorized in cultural transmissions are of crucial importance. These histories do indeed serve as boundary markers and as setting the context in which personal and collective identities are established.

Establishing links with a real or fabricated past is anything but new. The deposed shah of Iran tried to present himself as continuing what was presented as a majestic and glorious past of the kings of ancient Persia. Thus some elaborate and extravagant ceremonies were constructed in order to establish this link (e.g., the celebrations in Persopolis in 1971).[2] Likewise, Iraqi ruler Saddam Hussein tried to present twentieth-century Iraq as the natural continuation of ancient Babylon. Modern-day Egypt most certainly presents itself as the keeper, guardian, and rightful heir to what is presented as the cultural treasures of the ancient Egypt of the pharaohs. This claim-making activity is translated into an empirically specific content when, for example, Egypt demands that ancient Egyptian artifacts be returned to it from British museums, or that Israel return archaeological artifacts taken when Israel occupied the Sinai peninsula.[2] Likewise the 1996 discovery near Kennewick, Washington, of a nine-thousand-year-old Caucasoid skeleton created quite a controversy about the rightful ownership of these remnants (see Thomas 2001). It is important to note that a nation which presents itself as the rightful owner of cultural products and artifacts of cultures which no longer exist is, in and of itself, an interesting and instructive phenomenon. The justifications which are formulated for such claims of ownership rights create a link between two cultures, sometimes separated by thousands of years. The parameters of making such claims are of prime interest. Does sharing the same territory give the right for such claims? Does it authenticate them? Are there non-geographical links used in this claim-making activity? While sharing the same geography seems to be a major ingredient in such claim-making activities, it is not the only one. The same geographical location could serve as host to many cultures. Which two cultures specifically are presented and constructed as related and linked is a major question.

Let us examine some cases. The area that is now Israel was occupied in the past by such diverse cultures as the ancient Hebrews, the Greek and Roman empires, some of it was occupied by Nabateans, the Ottoman empire, the Arabs, the British empire—to name only some of the major occupiers. The choice of the modern Jewish state of Israel to identify with the ancient Hebrews has a profound cultural meaning. It creates and emphasizes a mythical and mystical connection between two very different cultures, across an abyss of thousands of years. However, this choice also denies the connection to thousands of years of Jewish existence in the Diaspora, some of which was characterized by a tremendous cultural blossom, some by misery and death.

One of the most interesting studies in this area is Herzfeld's (1986) illustrative and suggestive work:

> In 1821, the Greeks rose in revolt against the rule of Turkey and declared themselves an independent nation. . . . [T]hey proclaimed the resurrection of an ancient vision in which liberty was but a single component. . . . [T]he new Greek revolutionaries went one step further . . . they proposed to embody their entire vision in a unified, independent polity. This unique nation-state would represent the ultimate achievement of the Hellenic ideal and, as such, would lead all Europe to the highest levels of culture yet known. (p. 3)

He continues to argue that his book attempts

> to show how Greek scholars constructed cultural continuity in defense of their national identity. It is *not* intended to suggest that they did so in defiance of the facts. Rather, they assembled what they considered to be the relevant cultural materials and used them to state their case. In the process, they also created a national discipline of folklore studies, providing intellectual reinforcement for the political process of nation building that was already well under way. (p. 4)
>
> The central tenet of cultural continuity provided an organizing principle for the collection, classification, and ranking of all ethnographic items. Although the folklorists' emergent discipline was mainly concerned with nonmaterial artifacts, they were unusually fortunate in the wealth of historical evidence to which they could turn. . . . In Greece, by contrast, a rich archaeological record enhanced an already surprisingly large assortment of scraps of oral literature preserved (or at least mentioned) in ancient and medieval writings.
>
> The archaeological aspect of this historical perspective was extremely important; indeed, it provided the dominant model for the whole enterprise. (p. 10)
>
> In order to justify their special ancestral status, the Greeks relied heavily upon their archaeological model. (p. 11)

For a somewhat different illustration, let us look briefly at Knightley's sobering work. Examining media reports of wars can be instructive. For many people, the media are how they learn about what is going on, and actually shape their sense of history. For millions of individuals their sense of history, and to some extent their own self-contextualization in those wars and hence sense of identity, is shaped by what they know from what they have read in the newspapers, or saw and heard in the electronic media. For many of them that media-transmitted information indeed becomes history. Knightley's work (1975) provides quite a few cases in which such "history in the making" was completely fabricated: battles that did not occur but were reported anyway, other battles that did take place but went unreported, magnitude of casualties suppressed, and so on. He focused on the disparities between facts and myths, suggesting that what we think we know about history, or our attitudes toward it, are molded to a very large extent by information we are exposed to during war. That information, maintains Knightley (with a great many very persuasive illustrative cases), "bears little resemblance to reality." Knightley points out that the First World War was where these deceptive reports were most prominent. Let us look at one of the more recent illustrations he provides—the Japanese surprise attack on Pearl Harbor on December 7, 1941 (1975, p. 273).

> After flying to Hawaii on a tour of inspection, the Secretary of the Navy, Colonel Frank Knox, held a press conference in New York at which, with President Roosevelt's approval, he gave the impression he was revealing the full extent of the American losses at Pearl Harbor. Colonel Knox told correspondents that one United States battleship, the *Arizona*, had been lost and the battleship *Oklahoma* had capsized but could be righted. This must have made strange reading for anyone at Pearl Harbor, who had only to lift his eyes from the newspaper to see five United States battleships—the *Arizona*, the *Oklahoma*, the *California*, the *Nevada* and the *West Virginia*—resting on the bottom. Colonel Knox then went on to say that the entire balance of the Pacific Fleet "with its aircraft carriers, heavy cruisers, light cruisers, destroyers and submarines is uninjured and is all at sea seeking contact with the enemy."
>
> This list did not mention battleships because, of the nine in the Pacific Fleet, five had been sunk and three damaged, and one was in a navy shipyard unready for sea. . . . When asked whether the fleet seeking contact with the Japanese also included battleships, Colonel Knox answered that it did.

At a footnote on the page, Knightley adds that:

> British readers were even worse served. Early newspaper reports actually gave the impression that Pearl Harbor had been an American victory. "'Jap Plane Carrier and U-Boats Sunk'" said a *Daily Express* headline on December 8. "The main U.S. Pacific Fleet is heavily engaged with a Japanese battle fleet, which includes several carriers, just off Pearl Harbor, its Hawaii base. Washington reports late tonight say that one Japanese aircraft carrier and four submarines have already been destroyed by the American forces off Hawaii."

Robinson (1996, p. 187) notes dryly that "The reality was more devastating: five battleships sunk and three badly damaged, three cruisers and three destroyers badly damaged, 200 planes destroyed, and 2,344 people killed. The full extent of the damage was never released officially. At various times up to 1967, occasional communiques and leaks raised the figures. Even today, the official guidebook at the memorial of the Arizona omits the data." Robinson adds (p. 274) that "As late as 1945 . . . the semiofficial *War in Outline*, published by the *Infantry Journal* for members of the United States armed forces, perpetuated the legend that the only battleship sunk at Pearl Harbor was the *Arizona*." Lest somebody get the false impression that it was only the United States which was engaged in such falsifications, he adds, "Somewhat earlier in Europe, [in] the 'Battle of Britain' . . . [t]he British Air Ministry reported shooting down 2,698 German planes; the final revised figure was 1,733. Without a touch of irony, in 1945 the Ministry appeared to be boasting of British honesty when it noted that the British exaggeration was 55 percent whereas the German overestimated British losses by 220 percent" (p. 187).

Malcolm (1990) went a step beyond Knightley. Questioning journalistic objectivity, she states that journalists can—indeed *should*—be conceptualized as traitors (and assassins) because journalists falsify and betray the truth.

There can be little doubt that from 1963 to 1965 Israelis were exposed to a rather large dose of the Masada mythical narrative from the noncritical printed and electronic press. In this sense, this study supports Knightley's main line of argument.

The use of history in constructing boundaries can also be illustrated vividly in another region of Europe, and in the modern period. In November 1997 the *New York Times* reported about the "boundary maintenance" function served by the study of history in schools in some parts of what used to be Yugoslavia. Following the civil war there, three main cultural groups remained: Moslem Bosnians, Orthodox Serbs, and Catholic Croats. Each one of these groups gained control over some of its main formatting cultural institutions, so children were sent to separate classes (as determined by their ethnic origin) and learned different versions of language, art, and history. This certainly affects in a most fundamental way social integration, a sense of purpose, and community, directs sympathies and hostilities, and in short gives pupils a sense of identity. History certainly serves as a major source for constructing boundaries for these different imagined communities. For example, while Moslem history textbooks describe the five hundred years of the rule of the Ottoman Empire in Bosnia as a "golden age" of culture and progress, both Serbs and Croats refer to the very same period as a cruel occupation and as a dark and backward period in the history of Bosnia.[3]

One of the most interesting debates in recent years focused on issues concerning the nature of history and its relation to memory, as well as truthfulness and validity in history and memory.[4] The heated debate in these areas, and more so in the area of collective memory and its relation to identity, illustrate the complexity of the problems involved here. Suffice it to say here that there seems to be a consensus that moral entrepreneurs in the present tend to utilize the past (real or imagined) in order to forge personal and national identities and introduce meaning and order into everyday realities.

THE ISRAELI CONTEXT

The topic of history in the context of Israel and its politics came to the attention of academics and nonacademics alike in recent years. The debate about this intriguing and puzzling connection was part of a more general discussion about the nature, and role, of the historical narratives in nation-building processes generally, and more particularly, that of Israel.

That history can be, and has been, falsified is a well-established fact.[5] The issue here is not one of different, sometimes legitimate, versions of historical sequences based on different selections of events or emphases, but of lies, fabrications, misinformation, and false presentations.

Summarizing the evidence on historical false presentations, Robinson notes that:

> If God is invoked, then He (!) is on our side. If justice is invoked, she is on our side. The answer to any question about who started any war is them. If the facts just cannot be constructed to allow this accusation, then it is possible to invent and use ideas of "preemptive counterattacks" or make out how we were "forced" to act because "vital interests" or "security" were threatened. If it is asked why they are fighting us, then there is reasonably high probability that their leaders are mad, bad, or both. If a list is drawn up of the major opponents of the Western alliances since the 1930s, it is difficult to recall enemy leaders who were not so categorized. . . . At the least they have been portrayed as fanatics who contrast with our moderation and reasonableness. (1996, p. 188)

The presentation of history in Israel is no exception. Briefly stated, a major focus of the controversy is between the so-called new historians (and/or new sociologists) and, for lack of a better term, what we can call the conservatives. The latter are described by the former as politically, ideologically, and scientifically conservative; ignoring (or actively suppressing) noncomplimentary information about Zionism and Israel; and portraying a positive, heroic, nonproblematic history of the State of Israel. The new historians tend to be more critical, more reflexive, and much more willing to take into account problematic and noncomplimentary facts. The reality they construct is problematic, nonconsensual, and one which requires explanations and interpretations. Among other issues, this debate has brought to focus discussions about the political nature of Israeli sociology and history, as well as accusations and counteraccusations about ideological biases.[6] The older group is accused, among other things, of being insensitive to state-sponsored discrimination and repression of minorities. The newer group is accused, among other things, of selective focusing (and decontextualization), and of being biased, hostile, and disloyal to the state. The debate between these two groups has heated up, professionally and personally, and serves as a major focus of debate among some Israeli sociologists and historians. It is frequently emotional and bitter, and accusations seemed to be flying in all directions throughout the 1990s. It was not confined to academic circles, but diffused to the general public.[7] A significant part of this debate is about issues of patriotism and loyalty. Thus the "new historians" tend to accuse the other historians of deliberate fabrication, censorship, and suppression of important historical facts with the political goal of portraying Zionism in a favorable light. Those accused deny the accusations and tend to accuse the new historians of anti-Zionism, treason, and betrayal. The debate, then, is about the interpretation of the past, of the social construction of the collective memory, and the meaning of loyalty.

Reverberations of this debate could be found in both the English-language *Newsweek* and the Hebrew-language *Ha'aretz* during 1992.

The May 18, 1992, issue of *Newsweek* (p. 38) carried a fascinating article about how history is taught to Israelis. The major criticism was that this history is focused on the most negative aspects of that history, emphasizing how Jews were persecuted, at the expense of explaining periods of Jewish renaissance and the real complexity of the history of the Jews. If you like, the article implied that Israelis learn a "whining (and *kvetching*) history." While Bartal (1992) tried to show that the *Newsweek* article was too simplistic and biased, Raz-Krakotzkin's (1992) critique of the studies of history in Israel implicitly supported the critique voiced in *Newsweek*. Raz-Krakotzkin argued that the study of Jewish history in Israeli schools has been reduced to a study of Zionism, emphasizing national power and aggressiveness as crucial factors.

The issue of an ideologically charged history was brought up again in *Ha'aretz* in 1995 and 1996. In January 1995 (see Elgazi 1995) the charge of such an indoctrinated history was raised within the midst of a heated debate about the curriculum on the Holocaust in Israeli schools. In April 1996 a joint Israeli-Polish professional review committee examined history textbooks used in Israeli schools. The committee's review focused on the way Jewish existence in Poland between the two world wars was presented, and the committee's findings supported the positions taken by *Newsweek* and Raz-Krakotzkin. The main recommendation was that rather then focus on anti-Semitism, the historical narrative should look at Jewish life in its Polish context, including anti-Semitism but also looking at cultural achievements. The committee could not help pointing out that the way in which the history of the Jews was presented in Israeli texts projected an image of a persecuted, discriminated minority with poor cultural achievements, a very biased and inaccurate image indeed (Kashti 1996).

Three recent cases are illustrative. The first is the special issue of *History and Memory*,[8] which was devoted to "Israeli Historiography Revisited."[9] The second is Giora Eilon's work (1995), which touched off a bitter debate about the department of history in the Israeli Defense Forces. The accusation was that this department has been rewriting and reconstructing a nonproblematic and favorable official history of the Israeli army. Again, the issues of manipulation of images (of key commanders, battles, and decisions) came to the fore. Finally, one can look at Dr. Eli Podeh's work, which examined how the Israeli-Arab conflict was represented in Israeli school textbooks. The main conclusion of the study is that the way the Israeli educational system described the conflict was oversimplistic, one-sided, inaccurate, and sometimes verged on falsification, and that facts which could make Israeli society and state look bad were blurred or censored (see Kashti 1997). Sa'ar's (1998) review of the teaching of history in Israeli schools documents the conflict between different historical narratives: Zionist, Palestinian, Ashkenazi, Sephardi, religious, secular, modern, conservative, universal, ethnic, and more.

Looking at four recent books published on the construction of history in Israel seems appropriate at this point. One is by Yael Zerubavel (1995), who examines the creation of Israeli national tradition by the focusing and construction of different mythical tales, and in fact rewriting history. My own 1995 book focused on one specific myth in depth, the Masada mythical narrative, and showed how and why it was created (1995).

One of the ways through which a people transmits and interprets its past, shapes its perception about itself and creates its national and cultural identity[10] can be found in the ways school textbooks present critical issues; thus examining the rhetoric used in them is a major way to comprehend processes of social integration into specific cultural beliefs. In my work on the Masada myth (1995) I used this approach quite intensively, showing how a mythical perception of Masada was created and maintained in these texts. In the third book Podeh (1997) does a somewhat similar study on the Israeli-Arab conflict, focusing on twelve issues which express this conflict in a powerful way and examining how these issues are presented in different textbooks (see also his paper "History and Memory in the Israeli Educational System" [2000]). He shows empirically how the Israeli educational system was recruited to shape a unitary and simplistic view of the Israeli-Arab conflict, and how questionable facts and views, filtered and corrected (sometimes even falsified), were disseminated in these texts. Podeh points out that these processes created a delegitimization of, and negative attitudes toward, the Arabs and enhanced ethnocentrism at the expense of universalistic values. Finally, in May 2000 Hazony published his book which presented a scathing criticism—from a conservative, right-wing ideological prism—of the way history was presented in history textbooks, and the role Hebrew University supposedly played in this subversion. Naturally, a heated controversy erupted (see, for just one illustration, Eldar 2000).

The last episode in this ongoing saga of debates about Israel's past I shall use took place when a new government was formed in Israel in March 2001. One of the first acts by the new Minister of Education, Mrs. Limor Livnat (Likkud party), was to ban the use of a specific history textbook for schools (*Olam Shel Temurot*, "a world of changes" in Hebrew) because, she claimed, it was not Zionist enough and portrayed a warped and biased history. Her action took place when she assumed office and was based, among other factors, on the recommendation of a committee of historians that suggested some major revisions in that book (see, e.g., Sa'ar 2001; Trabelsi-Hadad 2001).

In essence, the argument on the nature of history is about moral and political legitimacy and about constructions and forgings of personal and national identities.[11] While drawing on narratives about the past is a common way to forge identities, archaeological artifacts prove a more powerful resource for the same process. These artifacts provide tangible and empirical proof for, and are presented as genuine and authentic remnants of, a past which is utilized in the present. The authenticity of these artifacts is guaranteed by the science of archaeology. For example, in August 1996 London newspapers[12] told their readers that "one of Scotland's most romantic legends is to be placed under archaeological scrutiny with a dig to find the lead casket said to contain the heart of Robert the Bruce." The price of the excavation was estimated at some £30,000 (around U.S. $50,000), perhaps not so a high price to pay for finding that symbolically important part of Scotland's national hero. In September it was reported that the 650-year-old casket with the heart had been found and displayed to journalists. However, no proof was provided that the artifact was genuine or contained the said heart.[13]

Two additional recent examples from Britain and Israel should suffice to illustrate this point. Looking at the crystallization of the European Economic Community, and raising questions about the place of Britain vis-à-vis Europe, Sir Roy Stone (1996) asks in a long essay the inevitable question, "Who are we?" (the British):

> What is, in fact, holding us together, if anything? No educated person can make a contribution to any of those debates without a knowledge of history. . . . And recent reports and polls keep on demonstrating that people know less and less at a time when they need to know more. When the answers eventually come through we shall move towards some new kind of collective identity. No society in Britain over the centuries has been without one and, without exception, it has been based on a reading or, rather, recasting of history, even though, in retrospect, it will be deconstructed as myth. Indeed, Tonkin notes that "we are our memories." (1990, p. 25)

The other illustration involves Israel and Masada. In a very long report on the eve of Israel's 1995 Independence Day (May 4), a Jerusalem reporter touched many of the myths and complexes that in his view characterized Israel. Archaeology and the Masada mythical narrative starred at the beginning of the report. As Falk shows, he had no qualms about the true nature of the Masada historical (not mythical) narrative:

> The highlight of the recruited Zionist archaeology is, of course, Masada. It became the symbol of, and the focus for, the crystallization of the national identity since the 1920s. This myth had, from its very beginning, a threatening ambivalence: the heroism of the defenders of Masada, an illustration for the Zionist "new man," against the desperate solution these defenders chose. Zionism usually opted to emphasize the optimistic interpretation of the myth: "Masada shall not fall again. . . ." Moreover, Elazar Ben-Yair's big heroes were nothing but a gang of murderous hoodlums, but their stand against the Pharisees' establishment on the eve of the Great Revolt must have captured the new Zionist imagination which portrayed them as noble non-conformist rioters. (Falk 1995, pp. 34–35)

That many cultures are engaged in various activities of reconstructing their past in order to achieve some political and ideological ends in the present is well established.[14] For some relevant analysis of the Israeli case, all one needs to do is look at Zerubavel's (1995) and my own (1995) works. All these works suggest that the process which typically takes place is one in which some elements of the original narrative are retained, others are discarded, and new elements are fabricated and added to the account. In this way "history" is reconstructed. The relevant question for us is how this process works when scientists such as archaeologists are faced with a mythologized past? Critically examining nationally constructed and accepted "pasts" can yield some amusing and unexpected results. For example, a debate has risen as to whether the biblical King David—certainly one of the most important figures in the construction of Israeli-Jewish identity—ever existed at all, whether his existence may be as real as that of, say, King Arthur (see Shea 1997), even whether what we refer to as the "City of David" existed as a glorious city.[15]

NATIONALISTIC ARCHAEOLOGY: DIFFERENT CASES AND THE ISRAELI CONTEXT

The place of archaeology in linking cultures that are separated by a gap in time should not be underestimated. Archaeological artifacts can be made to provide tangible and physical proof for a once glorious past. I know; I was born and raised and lived most of my life in Jerusalem. The visible reactions of visitors to the city when they are shown artifacts thousands of years old is daily proof of the power of tangible, physical remnants of the distant past. And some horror and/or science-fiction films have elevated archaeological artifacts to an almost sacred status: the *Indiana Jones* trilogy, "Mummy" films, *Forbidden Planet*, *Stargate*, and a few others. Examining a physical remnant of a culture which disappeared thousands of years ago has an irresistible and enchanted appeal. It is almost like holding a key to cosmic riddles. Hence, the mystical appeal of archaeology as a science which is dedicated to uncover physical remains of cultures long gone is powerful. An added charm is the detective work so stereotypically associated with archaeology and the deciphering effort which surrounds the artifacts, and which is supposed to help us reveal what is referred to as the "secrets of the past."

Archaeology, simply put, attempts to make inferences from physical materials, remnants, and artifacts about the nonmaterial aspects of cultures. It tries to weave a credible story by using these artifacts. In the case of Masada, two such stories existed: the historical and the mythical. As we made abundantly clear, the choice of the archaeologists in this case was clear: myth over history.

Archaeology and politics are distinct pursuits, but they are not mutually exclusive. Archaeology seems to have a built-in political dimension. Some would argue that a totally scientific, perfectly objective archaeology is an impossibility. In this sense archaeology resembles history, although there are some important epistemological differences between the two. For example, archaeologists through their excavations create (and necessarily also destroy) their own historical record. What they find (or do not find) is directly related to the methods they have developed. These methods, as well as the problems involved in selection, have a subjective component which is related to the interests and concerns of particular archaeologists. Thus the didactic dichotomy must be seen to be relative, not absolute.

Moreover, one important virtue of historical archaeology is that it can correct and supplement the historical record. This has been demonstrated numerous times (e.g., the archaeological record of Gen. George A. Custer's Seventh Cavalry's "last stand" at the Little Bighorn in 1876 and the excavations of slave plantations in the American South). Thus archaeology can and does modify and correct what is known historically. In our case, the excavations of Masada could modify and correct Josephus's historical record. Indeed, to some extent they did (e.g., finding some inaccuracies in his description of the place). However, in the case of Masada, Yadin felt rather free to create associations and interpretations that were not based on the artifacts he found, or to deliberately ignore competing interpretations which were just as good as the ones he preferred without explaining why. The interpretations developed by Yadin for Masada should be viewed in this context. On the one hand he had Josephus's account, on the other hand he was highly influenced by the Masada myth, which was a nationalistic, ideologically driven interpretation of Masada, and which was based on a distortion of Josephus's work. Yadin chose to interpret some of the findings as supporting the mythical interpretation, and presented these interpretations in his books on Masada and in other publications as approving the myth.

Ayalon (1972) already noted (pp. 283–92) how important archaeology was to the construction of the newly created secular Israeli Jewish culture. "Israeli archaeologists, professionals and amateurs, do not excavate just for the sake of knowledge and findings, but for reconfirmation of their roots [p. 283]. . . . Patriotic archaeology is devoted to the study of the Jewish past, sometimes ignoring other periods, Hellenist, Roman, Persian, Byzantine, Muslim and crusaders" (p. 285). Shavit (1986) reinforced this view and pointed out that the central place archaeology (in the broader sense of the term, including history) occupies in shaping the national modern historical consciousness is undisputable.[16] In fact, in one of the interviews with Yadin mentioned in a previous chapter, he made similar statements.

Tongue in cheek, one can claim that to substantiate national claims one had better start digging. One of the interesting questions, of course, is how deep to dig. Different strata can substantiate different national claims. Shavit's paper attests to how archaeology was in the midst of various ideological debates (e.g., biblical archaeology). As he points out, recruiting archaeology for the service of Zionism is a later development. The involvement in archaeology had a few goals:

1. To confirm the biblical historic description, particularly from the conquest of the land by the Hebrew tribes;
2. To prove the continuity of Jewish settlement in the Land of Israel, as well as its size;
3. To emphasize the attitude of the Jewish settlers to the land, as distinguished from the attitude of the non-Jewish settlers;
4. To emphasize the "down-to-earth" side of the Jewish life in the Land of Israel;
5. To give the new Jewish presence a deep structural-historical meaning;
6. To provide the new Jewish presence with concrete symbols from the past which can be transformed into symbols of historical legitimization and presence. (1986, p. 54)

As Shavit points out, most of the intense public excitement was created by archaeology that focused its efforts precisely on the period of the

Second Temple (and not, for example, biblical archaeology). It was this period that could, and did, provide the symbols that the moral entrepreneurs for the newly emerging national Zionist Jewish identity needed the most (Shavit 1986, p. 54). The story of Masada, so deeply connected to that period, was most certainly a major component in this process.[17] I must note that contrary to Shavit's approach, I was more interested in focusing on one particular case through which the complex relationships between archaeology, politics, and ideology could be explored in depth.

Indeed, even though many Israeli archaeologists have distanced themselves from past political and ideological influences, in 1986 an accusation was made that Israeli archaeologists (and historians) were distorting facts for political purposes.[18]

Geva's 1992 and 1994 essays focus on biblical archaeology in Israel. Geva is familiar with Yadin's work in Hatzor well, and her paper strongly supports the claim that biblical archaeology was used by Zionism in order to help legitimize the establishment of the State of Israel. According to Geva, this use of biblical archaeology helped transform it from an independent scientific field into an ideology and thereby degrade its quality. The issue raised here for the sociology of science is truly fascinating. Geva's critical stance elicited counterclaims. Amnon Ben-Tor, at that time chairman of the Institute of Archaeology, responded (1994) by stating that many of Dr. Geva's claims actually lacked factual foundation.

Yotam Benziman, reporter for a local Jerusalem newspaper, surveyed this debate about an ideologically recruited archaeology (1994). His report shows how Yigael Yadin, Yochanan Aharoni, Aharon Kampinsky, Shulamit Geva, and other archaeologists have been immersed in this acrimonious debate on biblical archaeology and the nature of the Israelite conquest of the land from the Canaanites. The debate focused on the accuracy of the biblical version of that conquest.

Michael Feige[19] examined the annual meetings of the Israeli Exploration Society, which have been taking place during the Sukkot holiday every year from 1944 to the present. Feige focused his inquiry on the 1950s and 1960s. He discovered that these meetings attracted large audiences, some as large as three thousand participants. Many of the conferences were attended by Israeli presidents and prime ministers. The meetings focused on archaeology and were tailored to the specific archaeology of the geographical area in which they were held. Since they were held in the geographical periphery of Israel, Feige's interpretation is that the meetings were used not only to create historical continuity between different parts of Israel, and to establish historical territorial and moral rights over these areas, but also to show that although they were peripheral, all these areas join together to form the much larger historical and geographical jigsaw puzzle that is Israel. The annual meetings were thus a locus for the forging of a national consciousness based on the construction of a common past. They were used to help bring into being that sense of community in which national and personal identities are embedded. In other words, archaeology was nationalized in two major aspects: the topics it chose to focus on, and the structure and site of the annual meetings. For example, Ben-Gurion said at the annual meeting of 1950, "In the general wisdom of Israel, archaeology will take its proper place. Its [archaeology's] conquests make our past relevant and reify our historical continuity in the land" (Sheri 1998b).[20]

Clearly, much of the new interest in what can be called ideologized archaeology in Israel in the last decades of the twentieth century was focused among right-wing and religious Jewish settlers in the territories occupied by Israel after the 1967 war. Many of these settlers, mostly in the West Bank (also referred to as Judea and Samaria), used narratives which constructed their right to settle these regions by resorting to biblical times and references, as well as to later periods. Using archaeology to find ancient Jewish remnants and thus present material evidence as a nucleus for a narrative which argues that a Jewish presence characterized the area, and thus establish legal rights to it as well, has become common. In an interesting twist, in January 1999 a fierce argument developed around these and other issues in the context of archaeological excavations in Tel Rumeida, near Hebron. Dr. Avi Ofer, an archaeologist who was excavating the site and was identified with the Israeli left and with the "Peace Now" movement (ideologically, a position diametrically opposed to that of the settlers) accused Jewish settlers there of interfering in the excavations. According to Ofer, the settlers did whatever they could, with the tacit backing of a sympathetic government, to prevent him from excavating. The possibility of finding ancient remnants in Tel Rumeida could mean that the settlers would be prevented from building there.

While Israeli archaeology was recruited, mostly in the past, for nationalistic goals, this engagement has weakened considerably in recent years[21] and has become characteristic of mostly right-wing and religious Jewish settlers who are trying to establish their "historical right" to areas populated by Arabs in both the West Bank and the Gaza Strip. Nonetheless, attempts to present Israeli archaeology as neutral still exist. For example, in 1998 Gideon Avni, an archaeologist with Israel's official state-sponsored and controlled Archaeological Authority, felt it necessary to deny in writing that archaeological excavations have anything to do with politics.[22] Interestingly, Avni's letter does not deny that *other* archaeologists are indeed recruited, or that in the past Israeli archaeology was recruited for political purposes, but seems to need to point out that, in the 1990s, this no longer applied to Israeli archaeology.

Some background information is in order. In June 1998 a group of Jewish right-wing fundamentalists decided that it was time for them to establish a Jewish settlement in the "Gate of the Flowers" area of the Old City of Jerusalem, which is a predominately Moslem area. So severe was their provocation that even Ehud Olmert, right-wing mayor of Jerusalem, put a stop to it. The picture of the Jewish settlers on one side, the Moslem residents of the area on the other, and the Israeli security forces in the middle was broadcast quite frequently during the crisis. The solution? The archaeologists were conjured up and brought in. Before any building was done, the archaeologists would perform a so-called emergency (or salvage) excavation to ascertain the archaeological value of the area.

So the connection of archaeology to the forging of nationalism and identities is not new. In a fascinating and remarkable book, Kohl and Fawcett (1995) chart how different political and ideological cultures utilized archaeology "in the service of the state": Europe, Spain, Portugal, the Soviet Union, China, Korea, Japan. Perhaps one of the most interesting chapters in the book concentrates on Nazi Germany's efforts to create and substantiate an imaginary past for the fabricated "superior race." While Kohl and Fawcett show how complex the relationship between politics and archaeology can be, they also confirm that such a connection exists, and they explore its different manifestations. Kohl and Fawcett's work is not the only one examining national archaeology. *Archaeology Under Fire* (ed. Meskell, 1998) examines archaeology in the context of nationalism and politics in various countries, including Cyprus, Greece, Bulgaria, Turkey, Lebenon, Egypt, and the Gulf Arab states. The British journal *Nations and Nationalism* devoted its entire October 2001 special issue (vol. 7, pt. 4) to nationalism and archaeology, both theoretically and empirically. The aim of my book is to continue this trend. What this work provides, and previous works lack, is focused in two areas. First, while it maintains the established connection between archaeology, ideology, and politics, it also shows how this connection is made. In the cases presented in this book, we can see that the connection was made on the level not of the physical findings, but of the interpretation of the physical data. Second, rather than remaining at this level, this book contextualized the study of the archaeology-ideology-politics connection within contextual constructionism and, more specifically, within the context of manipulations and deceptions, of truth and that which is not. This particular orientation facilitates a new and fresh understanding of the connection.[23]

Two recent cases continue to testify how formulating an archaeological past can be engineered by political and national motivation. One case occurred in China, the other in Japan.

Recent years witnessed a titanic Chinese size effort whose aim it was to prove an uninterrupted history of five thousand years of Chinese culture. The main problem seems to be that the first two thousand years in that chain are shrouded in a fog. Thus, a Chinese

> government-sponsored research program . . . using "the superiority of socialism to develop a multidisciplinary approach" has filled in key gaps in the ancient record of China's first kings and dynasties. The project, which mobilized more than 200 scholars for five years, has been hailed for shedding light on the murky origins of Chinese civilization. But it has also raised questions about the role of nationalism in scholarship. . . . [T]he Xia-Shang-Zhou Chronology Project, named for the three early dynasties under study, "has been able to solve a series of longstanding questions about early Chinese civilization." The project had yielded the most reliable time line yet for these dynasties, the earliest of which is said to date back more than 4,000 years. (Eckholm 2000)

The project apparently raised some eyebrows regarding the motivation to do it as well as the findings, and the sequence of dating the project used.

The Japanese case is even more interesting because it involves fraud. Japanese prehistoric research is a sizzling hot bowl because in theory it may hold the key to unlock the solution for a long-lasting debate in Japan about the origin of the Japanese people and culture. In November 2000 it was found that a famous Japanese archaeologist—fifty-year-old Shinichi Fujimura (deputy director of the Tohoku Paleolithic Institute)—has planted "ancient" stone tools in archaeological sites. Fujimura admitted that he buried stoneware in late October to make up the finds at the Kamitakamori ruins. He also said he similarly planted stoneware at the Soshinfudozaka ruins in Shintotsukawa, Hokkaido, but denied being involved in such activities in other archaeological sites. Obviously, Fujimura's activities caused much concern and some questions about the way archaeology supported the historical narrative of the development and continuity of Japanese culture. This fabrication was supposed to help support a theory that argued that Japanese culture began about 12,000 years ago when tribes from eastern Siberia entered northern Japan and gradually spread throughout the Japanese archipelago. Fujimura's forgery, evidently, cast some serious shadows on previous findings, and may necessitate a reexamination of these findings for signs of forgery, or authenticity.[24]

Summarizing the main features of Israeli archaeology, Kohl pointed out (1998) three particularly distinctive main features. First is the state significance accorded to and popular interest in certain archaeological remnants. Second is the selective past which is typically focused on the iron age and classical period or the periods of the First and Second Jewish Temples. Third is the way in which the selection of sites mentioned above was used to construct and support a specific type of nationalism.

This is perhaps the place to note that archaeology does not have to be cast into the direct role of mythmaking. Three illustrations will suffice. First is Fox's work (1993), which points out that careful archaeological work could show that the descriptive term "last stand," as attributed to Custer's battle at the Little Bighorn, was not appropriate because such a battle did not take place. In the case of the fateful events at the Little Bighorn, archaeology was very effective in helping to reveal the truth and dispel a myth.[25] A second, albeit less directly relevant work is by Vitelli (1996). There the authors discuss the complex issues involved in archaeological ethics. Most of the work centers on looting, burial, repatriation, occupation, and relations with native people. However, the main reason behind these deviances is the fact that archaeological artifacts are utilized in constructing specified pasts and therefore in molding national and personal identities. In this context, the meaning of stealing archaeological artifacts goes beyond personal loss; it is interpreted as stealing part of a nation's past. Indeed, many countries felt it was necessary to pass legislation on dealings with archaeological artifacts and creating rules as to who is authorized to deal in what type of artifacts. Thus, although not directly connected to the topic of this book, the issue of archaeological ethics in the context presented by Vitelli is relevant in adding another ingredient to our understanding of the complex relations between archaeology and politics.

Finally, one cannot finish this brief review without mentioning a relevant debate which raged in Israel in October–November 1999. On October 29, 1999, Ze'ev Herzog, an archaeologist from Tel Aviv University, was interviewed in the local daily *Ha'aretz*. There he stated that the biblical version about major historical events was not validated by the accumulated knowledge of seventy years of strenuous archaeological excavations. Moreover, archaeological evidence even contradicted it.

> Following 70 years of intensive excavations in the Land of Israel, archaeologists have found out: The patriarchs' acts are legendary, the Israelites did not sojourn in Egypt or make an exodus, they did not conquer the land. Neither is there any mention of the empire of David and Solomon, nor of the source of belief in the God of Israel. These facts have been known for years, but Israel is a stubborn people and nobody wants to hear about it.

The storm which this interview (and another relevant interview on Israeli TV) created was something to watch. The Israeli Ministry of Education even sponsored a seminar where Herzog was severely attacked (Segev 2000). The November 5, 1999, issue of the Supplement to *Ha'aretz* was flooded with responses, the most informed and devastating of which was by Hershel Shanks (editor of *Biblical Archaeology Review*). In a detailed rebuttal, Shanks responded to each and every one of Herzog's claims, not forgetting to point out what he felt was the political context of Herzog's work. Among other things, Shanks notes that

> just because we have not yet found hard evidence to support the veracity of the biblical narrative does not make it untrue. . . . Herzog [is a] serious scholar. . . . But [he] also [has] a political agenda . . . publicly described [by Avraham Malmat of Hebrew University] as "anti-Israel and anti-Bible." At the extreme, [he] can even be viewed as anti-Semitic. . . . Taken on its merits, Herzog's argument is simplistic and flawed. But it is also very clever and, as one might expect from such a distinguished archaeologist, based on an intimate knowledge of the facts on the ground. But the arguments are much more subtle than Herzog's quick-and-easy analysis recognizes. . . . All modern critical scholars recognize that the Bible['s] . . . purpose is primarily theological, not historical. And it is tendentious; it exaggerates to make a point. It often speaks metaphorically when it appears to a modern mind to be speaking factually. And, of course, given the fact that it is a human document, it can also be inaccurate. . . . It is in this context that we must ask whether there is any history to be found in it.[26]

IDENTITIES, THE PAST, AND ARCHAEOLOGY

Understanding the importance of the debate in Israel on the interpretation of the nature of its past is crucial. It is a heated debate, very much in the news, and involves strong emotions.[27] The major reason for the emotional involvement in, as well as the frequent media exposure of, this debate must be linked to the fact that the debate is intertwined with the national and personal identities which are the obvious outcomes of different constructions of the past. A strong sense of an imagined community (Anderson 1991) is created by utilizing the past for construction of nationality, and these constructions in turn also yield a strong sense of national integration and personal identities (Cerulo 1997).

Israel is a new country. Before its formal establishment as such in 1948, and thereafter, its continued existence depended—among such other factors as its military might, international support, and its economy—on the commitment, involvement, and willingness to sacrifice of its (usually—but not only—Jewish) citizens. To attain such commitment, one needs to create and sustain a strong and firm belief in the cause. Moreover, the massive waves of Jewish immigration to Israel created the need to socialize these new immigrants into a coherent and consistent culture sharing the same values, symbols, goals, past, and future.

A special type of identity was required to cope with the rough reality of Israel. That identity had to contend with a harsh terrain, poor economy, scarcity of resources, and a paucity of physical comforts. In addition, the clash with the Arabs created a situation where physical violence and wars became an integral part of existence. To survive this situation, specialized personal identities had to be carved. They had to be strong, demonstrate few weaknesses, be able to show restraint in facing some very challenging conditions, and endure hardships. Thus, a *sabra* (fruit of the prickly pear cactus) identity was constructed, conceptualized as maintaining all the above characteristics on the outside, but opposite traits in the inside.[28]

How does one create such an identity? It required a long and complex process of state-sponsored socialization (as well as similar sponsorship by family and peer groups). A useful term here is Gramsci's (1971) term "hegemony," which describes a situation where the social, political and stratification order is accepted as nonproblematic and legitimate. It did not take long to establish this hegemony, a key element of which was the establishment of science. The Hebrew University, supposedly the shrine of science on Mount Scopus, was certainly an illustration.[29] One reason for this is that an argument which utilizes what so many people accept as objective scientific truth can be a powerful tool in legitimizing political claims. It is then easier to accept such claims and their validity is less questionable. Supporting a specific historical hegemony can become very relevant for such scientific disciplines as history, anthropology, political science, and other disciplines, including archaeology. What looks like scientific support for a specific political order is a very powerful tool indeed. Stalin's use of the science of genetics as fabricated by Troffim D. Lysenko is an apt illustration.

The State of Israel used quite a few effective tools and symbols of socialization to help create this identity. The Holocaust and the Masada myth were most certainly utilized to help into being a new national and personal identity which could cope with the challenges of creating a new Jewish state. The social construction of the past in the process of shaping a collective memory and identity made that past extremely important.

Both history and archaeology must be viewed within this context in Israel. Both are professions that focus on exposing the past. However, archaeology attempts to uncover the physical remnants of ancient cultures. As such, and in a culture which is obsessed with discovering its past, archaeology's role should not be underestimated.

From its early days, Zionist lore emphasized that it had to create and solidify the links of Jews to the land. This land assumed some different (and morally and politically loaded) names such as Palestine, Zion, Israel, Eretz Israel. In its attempts to persuade Jews and others that the land later called Israel was the appropriate geographical location for the Jews, many Zionist scholars, politicians, and moral entrepreneurs searched for proofs for an eternal connection between Jews and this land. The Bible, of course, can be interpreted to provide such a link, but other periods could provide that as well. The interest of David Ben-Gurion (and others) in the Bible, as well as in biblical archaeology, is no mere coincidence. It was secular Zionism which adopted the Bible (not the Talmud) as an important element in the movement's attempts to shape a new personal and collective Jewish identity. Moreover, the Bible was taken as a validating source for geographical claims over the land.[30] The enigmatic and fascinating period of the Second Temple is another focal point. Showing that Jews always longed for this particular piece of land, that ancient Jewish warriors fought and died valiantly for it, can all be utilized in a moralistic-political discourse whose goal is to justify the return of Jews to Israel.

Archaeology can play a major role in this discourse. If archaeological excavations *can* in fact substantiate the moral-political arguments for the historical right of Jews to be in Israel, then clearly the importance of archaeology goes well beyond dry science. In order to legitimize one's claim to a land, simply take a shovel and start to dig. Legitimacy may rest just a few meters below ground surface. The way archaeological sites are stratified implies that the most ancient strata (cultures) are at the bottom, while the most recent cultures are located in the strata closest to the surface. Hence, theoretically, and under ideal conditions (e.g., no earthquakes, which shift strata), the deeper one excavates, the more ancient remnants one encounters. The question may thus become how deep is one to excavate in order to substantiate specific legitimacy claims. Moreover, an interesting dilemma may be created by the way excavations are carried out. Excavations mean going down from the top layer(s) to the bottom, that is, from the remnants of the more recent cultures to those of the more ancient ones. In a strange historical irony, as archaeologists dig their way into the more ancient remnants, they may be destroying the remnants of the more recent ones. If the excavations are conducted by professional archaeologists, care in documentation of the findings can reduce this problem, but not eliminate it completely, because the actual layer itself may vanish. Thus, if one wishes to see the remnants of a recent culture in its natural setting, for purposes of reconstruction, tourism, or moral-political claim-making activities, it will not be possible if the excavations go deeper into the site. Hence the problem of how deep one digs is a complex issue involving not only legitimacy claims, but issues of possible damage incurred to remnants of other cultures. The decision on what findings to focus upon, what to ignore, how to interpret findings, what constitutes a significant find, are all issues archaeologists deal with when they try to infuse meaning into physical findings. The contextual authenticity of the findings is another complex issue.

This analysis brings us back to the issue of the social construction of scientific explanations and hypotheses or, in other words, the question of social influences on the choice of research and the role of those influences in the crystallization of interpretations. Clearly, looking at the social construction of science is a recent phenomenon.[31] It means that investigators must pay attention to these issues in the formulation of what is defined as scientific knowledge. Moreover, we need to contextualize our analysis within issues of deceit, and hence a justification of the empirical phenomenon we are about to analyze is required.

MASADA—CHOICE OF THE EXCAVATION FOR THIS STUDY

Sometimes making distinctions between truth and that which is not is not simple or easy. This is typically the case if crucial information is missing, or if the parties involved are not clear about their intentions. There are, however, plenty of areas and cases where the dividing line between deception and truth is easier to establish.[32] One such area is science. However, rather than focus on deception in science generally, we concentrated on one particular scientific discipline, archaeology, and on Masada specifically.

NOTES

1. For a short review see Zerubavel 1995, pp. 28–32, 79–80.
2. See Lewis 1975, pp. 3–41; Chamberlin 1979, pp. 18–27; Benjio 2001. For more on archaeology and the Middle East see Meskell 1998.
3. See report in *Ha'aretz*, December 3, 1997, p. 5b.
4. See, e.g., Appleby, Hunt, and Jacob 1994; Ben-Yehuda 1995; Gillis 1994; Irwin-Zarecka 1994; Morris 1997; Olick and Levy 1997; Schwartz 1996a, 1996b, 1997; Sturken 1997; Zerubavel 1995. See also (in Hebrew) *Zemenin*, vol. 76, 2001.
5. Robinson 1996; Knightley 1975.
6. See Ben-Yehuda 1997.
7. For example, one expression of this debate regarding the issue of Zionism and post-Zionism was published in a special supplemental issue of one of Israeli daily newspapers in October 1995; see Sheleg 1995.
8. Vol. 7, no. 1 (spring/summer 1995).
9. See there particularly Kimmerling 1995 and Shapira 1995.
10. See, e.g., Hall and Du Gay 1996.
11. Anderson 1991; James 1996.
12. See, e.g., the *Evening Standard*, August 13, 1996, p. 2.
13. See, e.g., the *Guardian*, September 3, 1996, pp. 1–2; the *Times*, September 3, 1996, p. 7. See also Ash 1990.
14. Works such as those by Bodnar 1992; John R. Gillis 1994; Halbwachs 1980; see also Coser 1992; Hutton 1993; Iwona Irwin-Zarecka 1994; Le Goff 1992; Olick and Levy 1997; Schwartz 1982, 1990, 1991, 1997, 2000; Sturken 1997; White 1987, to mention only a few, are witness to this.
15. E.g., see Etzion 1992; Finkelstein and Silberman 2001; Marcus 2001; Niebuhr 2000.
16. In fact, he emphasizes the point made by many other researchers, which he seems to find agreeable, that archaeology helped bring into being a "new system of beliefs" (p. 27, first footnote).

17. See Yadin 1966; Ben-Yehuda 1995.

18. For a presentation of the accusations, and a counterargument, see Shanks 1986. One can very easily interpret the delayed publications about the Masada excavations as supporting Shanks's counterarguments. In this context, it is interesting to note that the editors of the first volume of the final report of Yadin's excavations note that it is quite obvious that Yadin did not leave a manuscript as the final report of the excavations (see Aviram, Foerster, and Netzer 1989a, pp. 1–2). For some sobering thoughts on archaeology's situation in Israel today see Hallote and Joffe 2002.

19. In a paper presented at the annual meeting of the Israeli Sociological Association, March 1998, University of Haifa. See also his 1997 paper.

20. The original Hebrew text can be literally translated as "archaeology's conquests 'presentize' our past and actualize (or ascertain) our historical continuity," assuming that one can turn the word "present" into a verb.

21. See also, e.g., Feige 1997.

22. See *Ha'aretz*, June 16, 1998, p. 2B.

23. See also Schrire's 1995 sensitive and revealing work.

24. See French 2000; Kovner 2000; Uranaka 2001. See also articles in the *Japan Times* from: November 6, 2000 ("Renowned Archaeologist Admits Planting Miyagi Finds"); November 9, 2000 ("Archaeological Hoaxes Spur History Text Rethink"); and December 21, 2000 ("Disgraced Archaeologist Denies Other Findings Were Also Faked").

25. See also the Open University's illustrative documentary video series on "Archaeology," chapter on the "Secrets of Little Bighorn."

26. See also Marcus 2000; Niebuhr 2000; and Finkelstein and Silberman's 2001 book which delves deeply into the issues and controversies created by the new confrontation of archaeological knowledge and the Bible. Obviously the 1999 controversy continued. See, for example, Bunimovitz 2001; Finkelstein and Silberman 2001; Mazar 2001.

27. See, for example, Benvenisti 1996; Katzman 1996; Koren 1996.

28. See Almog 1997.

29. And note the word "Hebrew" in the name (and not, say, "Jerusalem University").

30. See Aran 1993 on the interest in the Bible in modern Israel.

31. See, e.g., Cole 1992; Fuchs 1992; Knorr-Cetina 1981; Latour and Woolgar 1979; Pickering 1992; Zuckerman 1988.

32. Deception in military operations is a good example. For some illustrative works on military deceptions in World War II see Breuer 1988; Cruickshank 1979; Handel 1987; Howard 1990; Montagu 1953; Reit 1979; Wheatley 1980; Young and Stamp 1991.

ELEVEN

THE SOCIAL CONSTRUCTION OF CULTURES

This book is about distinctions between truth and fabrication, fact and fiction, particularly in the creation and presentation of false social realities.Our specific instance is the excavations at Masada.

Examining politics, ideology, and archaeology gave us some interesting and powerful insights into cultures and the ways in which the science of archaeology is used and abused. Looking at the Masada excavations in detail helped us shed light on how archaeologist Yadin (and others) constructed interpretations for the archaeological discoveries which conform with a fabricated national myth. It seems evident that while in the excavations of Masada the factual level was not altered, the interpretative level was drastically compromised (that is a case of interpretative deception).

The Masada story has two faces. There is Josephus's Masada, a historic account of a doomed revolt and the suicide of a desperate group of extreme and fanatical Jews, the Sicarii. Josephus's history revolves around the political and military failure of the Jews in their revolt against the Roman empire. Masada was the last gloomy chapter in his tale. Josephus's account is not a heroic tale. Secular Zionist moral entrepreneurs, however, managed to transform this tale of failure into a heroic mythical tale. The Masada mythical narrative was crystallized between the 1920s and 1940s, a time of personal, political, and social turmoil. At that time, the secular Zionist movement not only was trying to recreate a home for Jews, but also was attempting to create a new national and personal identity for those Jews (Ben-Yehuda 1995). Thousands of Jews were returning to what they viewed as their homeland. This return occurred on the background of fiercely growing Arab resistance, pogroms in Europe prior to World War II, the horrendous Holocaust, and a general anti-Semitic stereotype of Jews.

Adopting the Second Jewish Commonwealth as a period to identify with made sense because it was the last period in which the Jews had their Temple and during which a major revolt for political liberty and national sovereignty took place. However, it was also a period of a major military, political, and social disaster, with, at its nadir, the destruction of the Second Temple. The reckless, desperate Jewish revolt could not succeed when Rome was at the peak of its military power. The grim and bloody results of the revolt make the adoption of this period as a major symbol for heroism problematic. The Masada affair is an interesting instance of that turbulent period and the problematics involved.

In order to make this period appear heroic, it was necessary to introduce major changes into its interpretation. Moreover, the major historical source for these events is Josephus, who could easily be viewed as a Jewish turncoat and traitor and whose own interpretation of the Great Revolt is hardly complimentary.

The basic symbolic idea behind the Masada myth is that of proud Jews fighting for their own cultural identity and freedom, in their own land, to the bitter end. It is a narrative of the few against the powerful many, a struggle against tremendous odds. It is the tale of preferring a liberating and violent death to a despicable life of slavery or horrendous death in the Roman arena. The slogan "Masada shall not fall again" (in Hebrew: *Metzada lo tipol shenit*) can be taken to mean both that Jews shall not choose ways which might lead to Masada-like situations, and that fighting, at any cost, even in the face of tremendous odds, is always preferable to surrender. However, the slogan itself reflects the mentality of a besieged nation.

While for years the memory of the Sicarii and of Masada was repressed, the renewal of national Jewish life in Israel sparked an interest in both. The reconstructed positive memory of the Sicarii provided Jews who had lived for hundreds of years under foreign rule, far from their homeland, at times subjected to virulent anti-Semitic discrimination and persecutions, with a sense of belonging and the conviction that hundreds of years ago, and against tremendous odds, Jewish freedom fighters fought and died heroically in Israel. This powerful identification with the Sicarii gave these twentieth-century Jews a vigorous and vital sense of historical continuity and a shared and mystical feeling of transcendental integration. What was portrayed as the heroic calamity of Masada only strengthened these feelings. It is thus difficult and improper to downplay the role of the Great Revolt in the modern collective secular and national Jewish consciousness, particularly in the new twentieth-century era beginning around the twenties and thirties in British-occupied Palestine. During this time, the secular Zionist movement in Palestine was attempting to rebuild the Jewish culture, society, identity (Cerulo 1977), and nation.

The anti-Semitic image of the Jew, crystallized in Europe, implied that

Jews were afraid to fight, exploited their neighbors, and were eternally involved in questionable financial transactions (in particular usury, i.e., lending money at high rates of interest). Jews were despised, degraded, and described as lazy, mean, miserable people.

Zionism was conceived in the late nineteenth century by *secular* Jews against the background of anti-Semitic pogroms and various nationalistic struggles in Europe. Zionism's main goal was for Jews to return to Zion, their natural homeland and the place where they belong. It was aimed at changing this stereotype in the most radical and significant way. The intention was to create a new type of Jew, one who was willing to fight, who was proud, and who would work his/her own land. This modern experiment in identity formation reflected a sharp historical discontinuity between the cultural milieu of Jews in the "Galut" (Diaspora) and the newly emerging Jewish culture in Palestine, which denied much of the cultural existence of Jews in the Galut, but did not deny certain aspects of that existence which seemed to support what was felt to be the new type of Jewish consciousness. For example, acts of heroism were held up as symbols. Moreover, virtually ignoring almost two thousand years of Jewish history, the new Zionist resocialization emphasized biblical themes (as if the two millennia of Jewish life in the Diaspora did not and should not really count) and in particular the heroic aspect of that biblical past. This in itself provided a sharp discontinuity with Jewish existence in the Diaspora. Jewish religious scholarship for almost two thousand years was focused on the Talmud, the compilation of Jewish ritual laws; the new secular Zionism focused on the Bible. The Talmud was too reminiscent of a cultural existence which the new cultural entrepreneurs felt uneasy with. It is thus no mere coincidence that David Ben-Gurion's interest and support for biblical studies led to a biblical cult in Israel. Likewise, it is no coincidence that another famous military and political leader, Moshe Dayan, titled his 1978 book *To Live with the Bible*. When the original source itself was not heroic enough, a new narrative was concocted. The Masada myth fits this pattern well.

Thus the modern attempt to mold a new type of nationalistic, secular Jewish identity involved some profound changes in the personal and social consciousness of Jewish individuals. That attempt succeeded in creating such a new type of a secular Jew: the *sabra* (Almog 1997). A major part of this process was to deny the very legitimacy of the Jew who lived in the Diaspora. It needs to be added that in many cases the families of young Zionists were far from welcoming (and sometimes even hostile) to the ideological choice of their young Zionist family members (see, e.g, Rosenthal 1954).

At this point it is instructive to examine the words of Zalman Shazar, Israel's president in 1963. The aging president was flown to Masada by helicopter, and when he arrived there in time for the ceremony inaugurating the second season of the excavations, he said, "At this time, when we are trying to renew the heroic period of our nation's history, the story of Masada should penetrate every home in the country" (in Silberman 1993, p. 285). Thus Masada was used as both a powerful symbol and a physical site to visit (with an overwhelming experiential impact) in the socialization process of Jewish youth in Palestine and, later, in Israel. Masada was visited by almost every youngster in Israel, most of whom climbed to the top of the ancient fortress and heard the mythical narrative. It became a major formative symbol for Jewish heroism and martyrdom and crystallized the wish to be politically free and independent. Of course, all of the most unpleasant aspects of the Sicarii deeds and policies (including their very name) were repressed and expunged from the Masada myth.

The need for heroic tales for secular Zionism in the first half of the twentieth century was obvious. Moreover, the threat of a Nazi invasion into Palestine in the early 1940s considerably magnified the feeling of a dangerous external threat. In those years the Masada mythical narrative served as a guiding light, a genuine heroic story that people could look up to and be inspired by, and a possible guideline for potential action. Indeed, two of the prestate underground Jewish organizations, the Hagana and the Etzel, used the Masada mythical narrative as a basis for desperate plans to cope with Rommel's Afrika Korps if and when it invaded Palestine.[1]

In a strange parallel to the acts of the Sicarii, most of the political assassinations committed by the three prestate Jewish underground groups were aimed against other Jews. Most of these political assassinations were carried out by groups for whom Masada and the Sicarii were very central socialization symbols (see Ben-Yehuda 1993). Moreover, during the late 1980s and early 1990s, a mysterious group calling itself Sicarikin appeared in modern Israel. Its anonymous member/s made quite a few threats, and even committed a number of acts of violence (e.g., burning apartment entrance doors) against Israeli figures who favored, or were sympathetic to the moderate Arab-Palestinian position regarding the Israeli-occupied territories. It is also interesting to note that the Israeli Mossad's assassination unit was named Metzada, i.e, Masada.[2]

The Cultural Aspect

Culture is the sum total of the nonmaterial and material objects which define people's way of life.[3] In Howard Becker's (1986) simpler terms, culture consists of "doing things together." Cultures are socially constructed and typically consist of such building blocks as shared language, values, beliefs, and norms. Our everyday behavior both reflects and actualizes the culture of which we are part. Undoubtedly, language is a very major tool with which we construct the social realities which make cultures happen, prevail and persist. However, there is another way to look at cultures: viewing them in ideological and political terms.

Based on the writings of such scholars as Althusser (1971), Gramsci (1971), Hall (1980), and Mills (1956), we can argue that societies are controlled by the power of the political state, or by dominant groups. These groups develop and mold cultures which appear to be neutral, but which in fact serve, preserve, and replicate the ideology and interests of the dominant and powerful elites. It is not difficult to see that this view of cultures can easily become subversive. Taken literally, it implies that everything cultural is ideological, and that power dictates which ideology dominates. The question of how exactly that happens, or why, is more difficult to answer. The appeal of such a point of view to postmodernism is apparent.[4]

However, if we soften this view somewhat, it may become a useful tool. We can, without too many analytical difficulties, accept the approach that underlying cultures there is a strong ideological element which is typically coupled with the use of power, helping the basic worldview of particular ideologies to be dominant. In fact, the conceptualization that values are building blocks of cultures implies this. We need not assume a more paranoid and conspiratorial view that all aspects of cultures are dominated by some power elite which manipulates the masses into believing and acting according to its interests. Reality is much more complex, because conflicts and power exhibit fragile and strong coalitions. Some conflicts last longer than others; other conflicts need not be about power or economic issues.

Although the above discussion may give the false impression that conceptualizing culture is a rather straightforward task, it is not. Crane's review (1994) points out how fragmented and uncrystallized the sociology of culture is. However, Crane is very clear that

> the most profound change that the sociology of culture has brought about in the outlook of . . . sociologists is the idea that what they are studying is not necessarily an objective empirical reality but is instead a social construction . . . to a considerable extent, the sociology of culture has been concerned with demystifying and even debunking established cultures. (pp. 9, 17)

Swanson (1971) notes that we can conceptualize all societies as sharing two fundamental types of processes whereby individuals fulfill their roles in the social structure: those performed in the service of those individuals' own interests, and those performed by them as agents of the social system. Consequently we can ask to what extent individuals perform their roles with the expectation of personal gain, and to what extent they operate to further the good of the collective. In reality, of course, the differentiation between the two is not always that simple, and the debate of the public versus the private occupied some of the sociological dialogue in the 1990s. Yadin saw himself in a domain that mixed private and public interests. What may seem like a contradiction between Yadin's motivations and his falsifications can easily be resolved by understanding that these motivations were utilized to justify the falsifications.

This is the place to recall that in this book the accuracy of Josephus's writings is *not* being judged, tested, or challenged. This book simply contrasts the narrative provided by Josephus with the Masada myth. Had the myth been based on a careful and justified textual reexamination of Josephus, or on new evidence, I would have had to reevaluate my contrast. But the Masada myth most certainly was not based on such work. Yadin and the other archaeologists who participated in the fabrication of Masada deliberately chose to falsify interpretation of data (e.g., the cases involving locus 8, loci 2001–2002, the lots, the siege ramp).

Yadin's excavations of Masada were intended to provide scientific credibility for a mythical tale. Although the excavations did yield an impressive amount of discoveries, the excavators nevertheless did *not* find empirical support for the Masada mythical narrative. Indeed, they probably could not. The problem for them thus became how to utilize their findings to create the impression that indeed the Masada mythical narrative does have a scientific base.

The Social Construction of Scientific Knowledge

Science has become crucially important in providing us with our perception of reality. As such, socially constructed scientific knowledge may almost seem like an oxymoron. It is not. The debate between the two main perspectives which examine science—essentialism and constructionism—has raged fiercely in the sociology and philosophy of science.[5] While older formulations in the sociology of science emphasized the essentialist perspective,[6] the more recent approaches tend to emphasize the social construction of scientific knowledge. The idea of scientific knowledge as socially constructed is an intriguing and rewarding exercise in thought. After all, scientists are supposed to be engaged in a fierce endeavor to uncover truth, or so at least is the popular image of science. To view the process of creating scientific knowledge as a process of social constructionism is really to look at how scientists construct meaning out of facts, how they interpret facts, and how they weave meaningful frames of explanations.

Examining how science creates realities, what kind of realities it promotes and rejects, as well as looking at the nexus where ideology meets science enables us to comprehend how the two areas interact.[7] Indeed, relying on previous works by Erich Goode, Hills pointed out that:

> Increasingly in modern societies, scientists are contributing—sometimes unwittingly—to . . . ideological struggles. Interest groups use scientific research data as moral armaments to bolster their contention that there is only *one* possible view of the world—the *real* world. . . . In so doing they mystify human behavior by imputing an *inexorability* and *inevitability* to those man-made social creations. . . . Scientists . . . have become our contemporary "pawnbrokers of reality." (1980, p. 44)

Some words about the sociology of science are called for at this point. Making philosophical, historical, and sociological observations of science, or of the more general category of knowledge, has become one of the more fascinating yet esoteric of academic activities.[8] We should pay attention to Shapin's observation that the

> sociology of scientific knowledge is one of the profession's most marginal specialities, yet its objects of inquiry, its modes of inquiry, and certain of its findings have very substantial bearing upon the nature and scope of the sociological enterprise in general. (1995, p. 289)

Older approaches, such as functionalism,[9] were eventually replaced by approaches which focused on the actual products of science[10] and on social interests. The more recent approach is that which focused on the social construction of science, or in its generic name, "laboratory studies."[11] This approach concentrates on studies about what scientists actually do in laboratories and why. It examines how scientists work, formulate hypotheses, interact, form theories, and why (Shapin 1995, p. 304). In this way the traditional philosophy of science which, following Plato's famous cave allegory, assumed that facts were some mirrors of reality, has become obsolete (Fuchs and Ward 1994). Scientific activities and knowledge are socially situated and contextualized (Shapin 1994, p. 485). This approach developed into a new focus of inquiry, asking how "nature and society were 'co-produced' " (Shapin 1995, p. 312). Indeed, Swidler and Arditi (1994) point out that the sociology of knowledge needs to examine "how kinds of social organization make whole orderings of knowledge possible."

The use of power in the generation and maintenance of knowledge is an intriguing subject.[12] In a long historical process, many scientific disciplines have managed to establish themselves at various times as the most powerful, perhaps most legitimate, pattern of knowledge. Science has now emerged as the main claimant to having the way to reach truth. While science at first tried to project an image that the knowledge it manufactures is free from social or historical influences, that claim has eroded. Science obviously can and should be seen as socially constructed, and as legitimizing itself by presenting its cause, methods, and results as "truth" (Aronowitz 1988). Moreover, Bourdieu's work (e.g., 1984) showed how different status groups define knowledge which they manufacture or maintain as valued or legitimate and consequently benefit their own causes.

Studying science from a social constructionist point of view[13] does not create any particular problem for the incorporation of the concepts of power, legitimization, and networking into the analysis. Much like "laboratory studies,"[14] the constructionist perspective examines the process through which facts are discovered and communicated and the process through which these facts are socially constructed as both relevant and meaningful, and the meaning of accepting or rejecting knowledge claims (Collins 2000). A novel approach in this context is the actor-network analysis,[15] which contextualizes the amount of "truth" in scientific statements, not in some objective process relating to the statement, but to the type and quality of the social network in which the scientist claim-makers are embedded. This new approach accords well with contextual constructionism. It does not deny the existence of any reality; rather, it attributes the generation of this reality to specified networks of scientists who process, negotiate, and create the interpretations and versions of reality.[16]

When we look at how scientific research is conducted, how facts are produced and interpretations generated, we need to be attentive to how these scientists debate and how they rely on local resources and circumstances (Knorr-Cetina 1981). Put differently, Knorr-Cetina draws our attention to the high degree to which scientific "truths" are contextualized, and to the ways in which scientists work and construct knowledge (1999).

The constructionist perspective requires that we pay very close attention to the actual work of scientists, their ideologies, motives, power, and networks, and be sensitive to the local context in which specified studies are carried out. A few prominent scholars[17] have even suggested that a sociological look at science requires that we examine the relations between scientific paradigms, ideas, and cultural images (see also Simpson 1997).

The excavations of Masada were not carried out for some compelling and tangible archaeological reason. These excavations, compared by Silberman (1989, p. 89) to the excavations of the tomb of Tutankhamen, cost a fortune and involved thousands of people and impressive national and international efforts. Did they "solve" any major historical or archaeological riddle? Certainly not. The ideological-political-cultural context in which these archaeological excavations took place was the crucible of the Masada mythical narrative. That myth was used for the creation of a new personal and national secular Jewish identity by secular Zionists from at least the 1920s. There can hardly be a doubt that the major figure in making the 1963–65 archaeological excavations of Masada happen, Prof. Yigael Yadin, was an enthusiastic supporter of the myth. Yadin's perception of what he wanted to believe took place in Masada (Jewish heroism) led him into particular deceptive interpretations of his findings. When there were no archaeological findings, he used his moral views of the Masada mythical narrative to guide his creative interpretations. As Lynch (1994) indicates for other contexts, the importance of ideology both for Yadin's choice of Masada as a site for archaeological excavation and for his interpretation of the empirical evidence provides no new revelations. Other scientists, working in other domains of science, are involved in similar processes. What gives archaeology (and to a lesser degree history) a definite edge in this context is its unique ability and potential to legitimize particular versions of the past by being able to provide scientific support for ideological claims centering on patriotic and national identities. But in terms of carefully drafting his account of the Masada mythical narrative, so as to maximize the drama and allure of his account, Yadin acted no differently than other scientists who give much weight to the way a study is presented: title, choice of terms, sequencing the tale.[18] The way Yadin presented the factual and interpretative aspects of his work was structured in such a way as to maximize the suspension of disbelief. He integrated a mythical tale together with the facts in such a manner that the facts were presented *as if* they supported the myth. The presentations of the siege ramp to Masada, the skeletal remains, the ostraca, the synagogue, the ritualistic immersion bath—all illustrate this process of creating deceptions. Yadin concealed contradictory, valid and competing interpretations, never explaining to his audience why he chose one particular interpretation over the others. In the case of the pig bones he even *concealed* a very relevant and important discovery.

Yadin's books (1966e, 1996h) on Masada helped solidify the myth and gave it strong scientific legitimacy. It was the "truth" that Yadin created, legitimized, and communicated to whoever cared to listen, a heroic myth embraced by millions. The fact is that to this very day the souvenir shop at the bottom of Masada sells Yadin's more than thirty-year-old book; other serious books on Masada cannot be found there.

Thus, on the one hand we have the Masada mythical narrative, and on the other hand we have the archaeological physical evidence from Masada, all within a political and ideological context which supported the Masada mythical narrative. The combination of these two ingredients in the hands and mind of Yadin helped manufacture a social reality in which the Masada mythical narrative received significant and powerful support, not because of the evidence, but despite the evidence.

Examining past cultures has become a way for modern cultures to legitimize their national, ideological, and political claims, that is, to socially construct "imagined communities." Moreover, the legitimization of these claims is utilized to forge new national and personal identities for cultures which seek ways to establish their ancient roots. True, archaeology is not the only or exclusive discipline to fall into this trap. Both history and sociology in Israel fell into this alluring trap as well.[19]

This book contrasts scientific objective archaeology with ideologically motivated (nationalistic) archaeology. At Masada people's belief in the valid and objective authority of the scientists, most certainly of Yadin as a credible and esteemed archaeologist, was utilized to give credence to an imaginary tale.[20]

We have to understand that the personal morality and beliefs of scientists can and sometimes does affect not only the choice of their studies, but the results as well. Such famous persons as Sigmund Freud (Masson 1984) and Carl Jung (Noll 1994, 1997) were also involved in such practices.[21] Yadin, like Kinsey, Blondlot, and a host of other scientists, let his personal beliefs affect and lead his research. However, unlike Yadin, some of the others (e.g., Blondlot, Lysenko) simply fabricated data. For example, Kinsey selected his samples in such a way that the evidence which he created and presented in public gave a "scientific" picture of human sexuality which may have been totally warped and skewed. Yadin did not touch or manipulate the level of data collection in such a manner; he used the archaeological discoveries as a basis for warped interpretations. But both did deceive their unsuspecting audiences. Both used science to define the boundaries of their respective "imagined communities." However, while Kinsey desperately wanted to change those boundaries, Yadin wanted to keep those boundaries intact. Both, one must add, were quite successful.

To Yadin's credit, one must emphasize that the untruths and deceptions were accomplished not by fabricating data, but by warping the interpretations. A comparative view compels one to note that warping interpretations so that they conform to prevalent world views is nothing new. In the past, in archaeology and in other disciplines (e.g., psychology, biochemistry, genetics, physics, astronomy), there have been well-publicized cases involving belief leading scientists to fabricate both data and interpretations in order to suit contemporary worldviews.[22]

CONTINUITY OF THE RESEARCH LINE

Conceptualizing social stability and social change in the way I have done enables us to examine such varied phenomena as witchcraft, the occult, science fiction, deviant sciences and scientists, moral panics, drug use and abuse, political deviance, political assassinations, the construction of collective memory, and mythmaking as bona fide phenomena for contrasting deviance and nondeviance and thus gain new insights into processes of change and stability.[23]

NOTES

1. For a more detailed description of these plans see Ben-Yehuda 1995, pp. 131–36, 137–38.
2. See Hoy and Ostrovsky 1990, pp. 34, 117–19.
3. E.g., see Macionis 1995, p. 62.
4. See, e.g., Rosenau 1992.
5. See, e.g., Gross and Levitt 1994. For viewing science in its context see Swidler and Arditi 1994.
6. See, e.g., Joseph Ben-David's works.
7. For an interesting recent such examination see Dolby's 1996 book.
8. See, e.g., Lynch and Woolgar 1990; Lynch and Bogen 1997; McCarthy 1997; Shapin 1995; Swidler and Arditi 1994.
9. Focusing on the organizational aspects, career patterns, and norms of science. See, e.g., Zuckerman 1988.
10. E.g., the so-called Edinburgh school. See Barnes 1977; Bloor 1976; Shapin 1982.
11. See, e.g., Knorr-Cetina 1983, 1994, 1999; Pinch and Bijker 1987.
12. See, e.g., Aronowitz 1988; Swidler and Arditi 1994, pp. 317–21.
13. See, e.g., Sismondo 1993, 1996.
14. See, e.g., Latour and Woolgar's 1979 study.
15. See, e.g., Latour 1983; Shapin 1995, p. 313.
16. See, e.g., Collins and Pinch 1993; Pickering 1992.
17. See, for example, the works by Ezrahi (1990), Martin (1991), Mendelsohn and Elkana (1981), Shapin (1994), and Swidler and Arditi (1994).
18. See, e.g., Law and Williams 1982.
19. See, e.g., my 1997 review.
20. See Robinson 1996, pp. 252–59.
21. For a short review of some more such cases, see Ben-Yehuda 1985, pp. 189–94.
22. See, e.g., my 1985 and 1986 discussions on deviance in science.
23. See Ben-Yehuda 1985, 1990, 1993, 1995; Goode and Ben-Yehuda 1994.

BIBLIOGRAPHY

NOTE: Transliterating (or translating) Hebrew names and terms into English is a thorny issue. In this book, Hebrew names of books and authors were translated into English. If these names appeared in the original in English, that English term was used instead. Hebrew books and articles are identified as such by using the expression: "(Hebrew)" at the end of the reference. The major guideline in this process was whether the identification of the author/term is such that no problems in identifying the person/term will occur.

* * * * * *

Almog, Oz. *The Sabra—A Portrait* [Ha Tsabar—Diukan]. Tel Aviv: Am Oved, Ofakim Library, 1997. (Hebrew) (A 2001 English translation is available from the University of California Press.)

Althusser, Louis. "Ideology and Ideological State Apparatus." In *Lenin and Philosophy and Other Essays*, 86–127. London: New Left Books, 1971.

Anderson, Benedict. *Imagined Communities: Reflections on the Origin and Spread of Nationalism*. Rev. ed. London: Verso, 1991.

Anderson, Myrdene. "Cultural Concatenation of Deceit and Secrecy." In *Deception: Perspectives on Human and Nonhuman Deceit*, edited by Robert W. Mitchell and Nicholas S. Thompson, 323–48. Albany: State University of New York Press, 1986.

Appleby, Joyce, Lynn Hunt, and Margaret Jacob. *Telling the Truth About History*. New York: W. W. Norton and Company, 1994.

Aran, Gideon. "Return to the Scripture in Modern Israel." In *Les Retours Aux Ecritures: Fondamentalismes Presents Et Passes*, edited by Evelyne Patlagean and Alain Le Boulluec, 101–31. Bibliotheque De L'ecole Des Hautes Etudes, Section des Sciences Religieuses, vol. 99, 1993.

Aronowitz, Stanley. *Science as Power: Science and Ideology in Modern Society.* Minneapolis: University of Minnesota Press, 1988.

Ash, Marinell. "William Wallace and Robert the Bruce." In *The Myth We Live By*, edited by Samuel Raphael and Paul Thompson, 83–94. London: Routledge, 1990.

Asimov, Isaac. "Alas, All Human." *Magazine of Fantasy and Science Fiction* 56, no. 6 (1979): 131–49.

Avigad, N., et al. *Masada: An Archaeological Survey during 1955–1956.* Jerusalem: Ministry of Education, Antiquity Branch, Hebrew University, Israeli Exploration Society, 1957. (Hebrew)

Aviram, Joseph, Gideon Foerster, and Ehud Netzer, eds. *MASADA I: The Yigael Yadin Excavations 1963–1965: Final Report.* Jerusalem: Israel Exploration Society and Hebrew University of Jerusalem, 1989a.

———. *MASADA II: The Yigael Yadin Excavations 1963–1965: Final Report.* Jerusalem: Israel Exploration Society and Hebrew University of Jerusalem, 1989b.

———. *MASADA III: The Yigael Yadin Excavations 1963–1965: Final Report.* Jerusalem: Israel Exploration Society and Hebrew University of Jerusalem, 1991.

———. *MASADA IV: The Yigael Yadin Excavations 1963–1965: Final Report.* Jerusalem: Israel Exploration Society and Hebrew University of Jerusalem, 1994.

———. *MASADA V: The Yigael Yadin Excavations 1963–1965: Final Report.* Jerusalem: Israel Exploration Society and Hebrew University of Jerusalem, 1995.

Avi-Tamar, Yoram (Yoram Tzafrir). *The Sign of the Sword.* Jerusalem: Carta, 1989. (Hebrew)

Ayalon, Amos. *The Israelis: Founders and Sons.* Jerusalem: Schocken Books, 1972. (Hebrew)

Bailey, F. G. *The Prevalence of Deceit.* Ithaca, N.Y.: Cornell University Press, 1991.

Barnes, Barry. *Interests and the Growth of Science.* London: Routledge and Kegan Paul, 1977.

Barnes, J. A. *A Pack of Lies: Towards a Sociology of Lying.* New York: Cambridge University Press, 1994.

Bartal, Israel. "Sixty Seconds about Judaism." *Ha'aretz*, June 5, 1992, 1. (Hebrew)

Bash, Harry H. *Social Problems and Social Movements: An Exploration into the Sociological Construction of Alternative Realities.* Amherst, N.Y.: Humanity Books, 1995.

Becker, Howard S. "Whose Side Are We On?" *Social Problems* 14, no. 3 (1967): 239–47.

———. *Outsiders.* New York: Free Press, 1963.

———. *Doing Things Together.* Evanston, Ill.: Northwestern University Press, 1986.

Ben-Dov, Meir. "In Contradiction to the Claim Made by Geologist Dan Gill, Archaeologists Claim the Masada Siege Ramp Is Man-made." *Ha'aretz*, August 13, 1993, p. 6. (Hebrew)

Ben-Itto, Hadassa. *The Lie that Wouldn't Die.* Tel Aviv: Dvir, 1998. (Hebrew)

Ben-Tor, Amnon. "Undermining the Foundations." *Ha'aretz*, November 18, 1994, 6–7. (Hebrew)

Benvenisti, Meron. "A False Mediterranean Port." *Ha'aretz*, March 21, 1996, 1B. (Hebrew)

Ben-Yehuda, Nachman. *Deviance and Moral Boundaries: Witchcraft, the Occult, Science Fiction, Deviant Sciences, and Scientists.* Chicago: University of Chicago Press, 1985.

———. "Deviance in Science: Towards the Criminology of Science." *British Journal of Criminology* 26, no. 1 (1986): 1–27.

———. *The Politics and Morality of Deviance.* Albany: State University of New York Press, 1990.

———. "Deviantization and Criminalization as Properties of the Social Order." *Sociological Review* 40, no. 1 (1992): 73–108.

———. *Political Assassinations by Jews: A Rhetorical Device for Justice.* Albany: State University of New York Press, 1993.

———. *The Masada Myth: Collective Memory and Mythmaking in Israel.* Madison: University of Wisconsin Press, 1995.

———. "The Dominance of the External: Israeli Sociology." *Contemporary Sociology* 26, no. 3 (May 1997): 271–75.

———. "Where Masada's Defenders Fell." *Biblical Archaeology Review* 24, no. 6 (November/December 1998): 32–39.

———. *Betrayals and Treason: Violations of Trust and Loyalty.* Boulder, Colo.: Westview Press, 2001.

Benziman, Yotam. "Like the Broken Ceramic." *Kol Ha'ir*, June 17, 1994, 54–59. (Hebrew)

Berger Peter L., and Thomas Luckmann. *The Social Construction of Reality.* Baltimore: Penguin Books, 1966.

Best, Joel. *Damned Lies and Statistics: Untangling Numbers from the Media, Politicians, and Activists.* Berkeley: University of California Press, 2001.

———. *Images of Issues: Typifying Contemporary Social Problems.* 2d ed. New York: Aldine De Gruyter, 1995.

Bloor, David. *Knowledge and Social Imagery.* London: Routledge and Kegan Paul, 1976.

Bodnar, John. *Remaking America: Public Memory, Commemoration, and Patriotism in the Twentieth Century.* Princeton, N.J.: Princeton University Press, 1992.

Bourdieu, Pierre. *Homo Academicus*, translated by P. Collier. Cambridge: Polity Press, 1984.

Breuer, William B. *The Secret War with Germany: Deception, Espionage, and Dirty Tricks, 1939–1945.* Novato: Presidio Press, 1988.

Broad, William. *Teller's War: The Top-Secret Story Behind the Star Wars Deception.* New York: Simon & Schuster, 1992.

Broad, William, and Nicholas Wade. *Betrayers of Truth: Fraud and Deceit in the Halls of Science.* New York: Simon & Schuster, 1982.

Brown, Anthony Cave. *Bodyguard of Lies.* New York: Quill/William Morrow, 1975.

Brown, David J. "The Battle of the Atlantic, 1941–1943: Peaks and Troughs." In *To Die Gallantly: The Battle of the Atlantic*, edited by Timothy J. Runyan and Jan M. Copes, 137–57. Boulder, Colo.: Westview Press, 1994.

Cerulo, Karen A. "Identity Construction: New Issues, New Directions." *Annual Review of Sociology* 23 (1997): 385–409.

Chamberlin, E. R. *Preserving the Past.* London: J. M. Dent and Sons, 1979.

Charters, David A., and Maurice A. J. Tugwell, eds. *Deception Operations: Studies in the East-West Context.* London: Brassey's, 1990.

Cohen, Adir. "Lies." In *Psychology, Politics, Love, Society, Business, Sex, Personal Life, Art, Literature, and Science.* Haifa: Amatzia, 1999. (Hebrew)

Cohen, Erik, and Eyal Ben-Ari. "Hard Choices: The Sociological Analysis of Value Incommensurability." *Human Studies* 16 (1991): 267–97.

Cohen, Yael. *Semantic Truth Theories.* Jerusalem: Magness Press, Hebrew University, 1994.

Cole, Stephen. *Making Science: Between Nature and Society.* Cambridge, Mass.: Harvard University Press, 1992.

Collins, Harry, and Trevor Pinch. *The Golem: What Everyone Should Know About Science.* Cambridge: Cambridge University Press, 1993.

Cotton, Hanna M. "The Date of the Fall of Masada: The Evidence of the Masada Papyri" (English). *Zeitschrift fur Papyrologie und Epigraphik*, Band 78 (1989): 157–62.

Cotton, Hanna, and Yehonatan Preiss. "Who Conquered Masada in 66 A.D. and Who Occupied It until It Fell?" *Zion* 55 (1990): 449–54. (Hebrew)

Coser, Lewis, ed. *Maurice Halbwachs: On Collective Memory,* translated and with an introduction by Lewis A. Coser. Chicago: University of Chicago Press, 1992.

Crane, Diana. "Introduction: The Challenge of the Sociology of Culture to Sociology as a Discipline." In *The Sociology of Culture: Emerging Theoretical Perspectives*, 1–19. Oxford, UK: Blackwell, 1994.

Cross, Robin. *Citadel: The Battle of Kursk.* London: M. O'Mara Books, 1993.

Cruickshank, Charles. *Deception in World War II.* Oxford: Oxford University Press, 1979.

Dolby, R. G. A. *Uncertain Knowledge: An Image of Science for a Changing World.* Cambridge: Cambridge University Press, 1996.

Doty, William G. *Mythography: The Study of Myths and Rituals.* University: University of Alabama Press, 1986.

Dunnigan, James F., and Albert A. Nofi. *Victory and Deceit: Dirty Tricks at War.* New York: William Morrow and Company, Inc., 1995.

Dupuy, Ernest R., and Trevor N. Dupuy. *The Encyclopedia of Military History from 3500 B.C. to the Present.* London: Macdonald, 1970.

Echolm, Erik. "In China, Ancient History Kindles Modern Doubts." *New York Times*, November 10, 2000.

Ekman, Paul. *Telling Lies: Clues to Deceit in the Marketplace, Politics, and Marriage.* New York: W. W. Norton & Company, 1992.

Eldar, Akiva. "Education and Lies: Who Got Control of the History Books?" *Ha'aretz*, August 24, 2000, 4B. (Hebrew)

Elgazi, Yoseph. "Without Parameters of Human Suffering." *Ha'aretz*, January 19, 1995, 2. (Hebrew)

Eilon, Giora. "Zahal Is Re-Writing History." *Jerusalem*, October 13, 1995, 14–17. (Hebrew)

Etzion, Yehoshua. *The Lost Bible.* Tel Aviv: Schocken Publishing House Ltd., 1992.

Ezrahi, Yaron. *The Descent of Icarus: Science and the Transformation of Contemporary Democracy.* Cambridge, Mass.: Harvard University Press, 1990.

Falk, Oren. "Psychiatric File: Israel 95." *Kol Hair*, no. 871, May 3, 1995, 34–47. (Hebrew)

Fedler, Fred. *Media Hoaxes.* Ames: Iowa State University Press, 1989.

Feige, Michael. "Archaeology, Anthropology and Developmental Towns: The Shaping of the Israeli Place." *Zion* 63 (1997): 442–59. (Hebrew)

———. "The Conferences of 'The Society for the Investigation of Eretz Israel and Its Antiquities' and the Attempt to Homogenize the Israeli Space." Paper presented at the 29th annual meeting of the Israeli Sociological Association, at the University of Haifa, February 24, 1998. (Hebrew)

Feldman, Louis H. "Masada: A Critique of Recent Scholarship." *Commentary* 53 (1973): 218–48.

Finkelstein, Israel, and Neil Asher Silberman. *The Bible Unearthed: Archaeology's New View of Ancient Israel and the Origin of Its Sacred Texts.* New York: Free Press, 2001.

Finley, M. I. "Josephus and the Bandits." *New Statesman*, December 2, 1966, 832–33.

Foerster, Gideon, with Naomi Porat. "Art and Architecture." In *MASADA V: The Yigael Yadin Excavations 1963–1965: Final Report*, edited by Joseph Aviram, Gideon Foerster, and Ehud Netzer. Jerusalem: Israel Exploration Society and Hebrew University of Jerusalem, 1995.

Fox, Richard Allan. *Archaeology, History, and Custer's Last Battle.* Norman: University of Oklahoma Press, 1993.

French, Howard W. "Meet a 'Stone Age' Man So Original, He's a Hoax." *New York Times*, December 7, 2000.

Friedman, Norman. *The Fifty-Year War: Conflict and Strategy in the Cold War.* Annapolis, Md.: Naval Institute Press, 2000.

Fuchs, Stephan. *The Professional Quest for Truth: A Social Theory of Science and Knowledge.* Albany: State University of New York Press, 1992.

Fuchs, Stephan, and Steven Ward. "What Is Deconstruction, and Where and When Does It Take Place? Making Facts in Science, Building Cases in Law." *American Sociological Review* 59 (1994): 481–500.

Gaon, Stav. "Exposing Network." *Kol Hair*, May 22, 1998, 24–25. (Hebrew)

Gardiner, Robin, and Dan van der Vat. *The Riddle of the Titanic.* London: Weidenfeld and Nicolson, 1995.

Gardner, M. *Fads and Fallacies in the Name of Science.* New York: Dover, 1957 (originally published in 1952).

Geertz, Clifford. *The Interpretation of Cultures.* New York: Basic Books, 1973.

———. *After the Fact: Two Countries, Four Decades, One Anthropologist.* Boston: Harvard University Press, 1995.

Geva, Shulamit. "Israeli Biblical Archaeology at Its Beginning." *Zemanim* 42 (1992): 93–102. (Hebrew)

———. "Biblical Archaeology." *Ha'aretz*, weekly supplement, November 11, 1994, 50–52. (Hebrew)

Gill, Dan. "A Natural Spur at Masada." *Nature* 364, no. 6438 (1993): 569–70.

Gillis, John R., ed. *Commemorations: The Politics of National Identity.* Princeton, N.J.: Princeton University Press, 1994.

Goode, Erich. "The American Drug Panic of the 1980s: Social Construction or Objective Threat?" *Violence, Aggression and Terrorism* 3, no. 4 (1989):

327–48 (reprinted in the *International Journal of the Addictions* 25, no. 9 [1989]: 1083–98).

Goode, Erich. "The Ethics of Deception in Social Research: A Case Study." *Qualitative Sociology* 19 (1996): 11–33.

Goode, Erich, and Nachman Ben-Yehuda. *Moral Panics: The Social Construction of Deviance.* Oxford: Blackwell, 1994.

Goren, Shlomo. "The Heroism of Masada in Light of the Halacha." In *Masada in a Historical View,* 41–46. A collection of articles from the conference "With Shmaria Guttman on Masada," Inner document, Kibbutz movement, Mador Leyediat Ha'aretz, 1985. (Hebrew)

Gramsci, Antonio. *Selections from the Prison Notebook.* London: Lawrence and Wishart, 1971. (Or, *Selections from the Prison Notebooks of Antonio Gramsci.* New York: International Publishers, 1971.)

Gross, Paul R., and Norman Levitt. *Higher Superstition: The Academic Left and Its Quarrels with Science.* Baltimore: Johns Hopkins University Press, 1994.

Guske, Heinz F. K. *The War Diaries of U-764: Fact or Fiction?* Gettysburg, Pa.: Thomas Publications, 1992.

Guttman, Shmaria. *With Masada.* Tel Aviv: Hakkibutz Hameuchad, 1964. (Hebrew)

———. "The Roman Siege." In *The Roman Period in Eretz Israel: A Collection of Lectures and Articles,* 179–93. The Kibbutz movement, knowledge of the country branch, 1973. (Hebrew)

Hadas-Lebel, Mireille. *Flavius Josephus: Eyewitness To Rome's First-Century Conquest of Judea,* translated by Richard Miller. London: MacMillan, 1993.

Halbwachs, Maurice. *The Collective Memory.* New York: Harper and Row, 1980.

Hall, Stuart. *Culture, Media, Language.* London: Hutchinson, 1980.

Hall, Stuart, and Paul Du Gay, eds. *Questions of Cultural Identity.* London: Sage Publications, 1996.

Hallote, R. S., and A. H. Joffe. "The Politics of Death, and the Death of Archaeology, in Modern Israel: Between 'Nationalism' and 'Science' in the Age of the Second Republic." *Israel Studies,* forthcoming.

Hamilton, Richard F. *The Social Misconstruction of Reality: Validity and Verification in the Scholarly Community.* New Haven: Yale University Press, 1996.

Handel, Michael, ed. *Strategic and Operational Deception in the Second World War.* Portland: Cass, 1987.

Harlow, John. "Scarred Family Reveal Flaws in 'Saint' du Pré." *Sunday Times,* September 14, 1997, 7.

Hazony, Yoram. *The Jewish State: The Struggle for Israel's Soul.* New York: New Republic/Basic Books, 2000.

Herzfeld, Michael. *Ours Once More: Folklore, Ideology, and the Making of Modern Greece.* New York: Pella Publishing Company, 1986.

Herzog, Ze'ev. "The Bible: No Actual Findings." *Ha'aretz,* weekend supplement, October 29, 1999, 36–38. (Hebrew and English)

Higham, Charles. *American Swastika.* Garden City, N.Y.: Doubleday & Company, 1985.

Hills, Stuart L. *Demystifying Social Deviance.* New York: McGraw-Hill, 1980.

Horsley, Richard A., and John S. Hanson. *Bandits, Prophets, and Messiahs: Popular Movements at the Time of Jesus.* San Francisco: Harper and Row, 1985.

Howard, Michael. *Strategic Deception in the Second World War.* London: Pimlico, 1990.

Hunt, Scott, Robert Benford, and David Snow. "Identity Fields: Framing Processes and the Social Construction of Movement Identities." In *New Social Movements: From Ideology to Identity,* edited by Enrich Larana, Hank Johnson, and Joseph Gusfield, 183–208. Philadelphia: Temple University Press, 1994.

Hutton, Patrick H. *History as an Art of Memory.* Hanover: University of Vermont, 1993.

Hurvitz, Gila, ed. *The Story of Masada: Discoveries from the Excavations.* Jerusalem: Hebrew University; Antiquities Authority; Society for the Exploration of Eretz Israel and Its Antiquities, 1993. (Hebrew)

Irwin-Zarecka, Iwona. *Frames of Remembrance: The Dynamics of Collective Memory.* New Brunswick, N.J.: Transaction Publishers, 1994.

James, Paul. *Nation Formation: Towards a Theory of Abstract Community.* London: Sage Publications, 1996.

Jones, James H. "Dr. Yes" *New Yorker,* August 25 and September 1, 1997, 99–113.

———. *Alfred Kinsey: A Public/Private Life.* New York: W. W. Norton, 1997.

Jones, Mark, with Paul Craddock and Nicolas Barker, eds. *Fake? The Art of Deception.* London: British Museum Publications, 1990.

Kashti, Or. "The Polish-Israeli Committee for the Coordination of School Textbooks Calls for the Removal of Rooted Stereotypical Approaches in the Two Nations." *Ha'aretz,* April 5, 1996, 1A, 12A. (Hebrew)

———. "Apprehensive about Confusing Adolescents with the Truth." *Ha'aretz,* February 6, 1997, 4B. (Hebrew)

Katzman, Avi. "Culture in a Pressure Cooker." *Ha'aretz,* February 6, 1996, 2B. (Hebrew)

Kav, Pnim, "The First Essene Settlement Was Exposed near Ein Geddi." Hebrew University, April 1998, 10. (Hebrew)

Kimmerling, Baruch. "Academic History Caught in the Cross-Fire: The Case of Israeli-Jewish Historiography." *History and Memory* 7, no. 1 (1995): 41–65.

Klosner, Yoseph. *The History of Israel.* Part 4, *The Jewish Revolt and the Destruction of the Second Temple.* Jerusalem: Published by Yahadut and Enoshiut. A. Eitan and S. Shoshani Press, 1925. (Hebrew)

Knightley, P. *The First Casualty.* 1975. Reprint, London: Prion in 2000.

Knorr-Cetina, Karin. *The Manufacture of Knowledge.* New York: Pergamon Press, 1981.

———. "The Ethnographic Study of Scientific Work: Towards a Constructivist Interpretation of Science." In *Science Observed: Perspectives on the Social Study of Science,* edited by Karin Knorr-Cetina and Michael Mulkay, 115–40. London: Sage Publications, 1983.

———. *Epistemic Cultures: How the Sciences Make Knowledge.* Cambridge, Mass.: Harvard University Press, 1999.

Kohl, Philip L. "Nationalism and Archaeology: On the Constructions of Nations and the Reconstructions of the Remote Past." *Annual Review of Anthropology* 27(1998): 223–46.

Kohl, Philip L., and Clare Fawcett, eds. *Nationalism, Politics, and the Practice of Archaeology.* Cambridge: Cambridge University Press, 1995.

Kohn, Alexander. *False Prophets: Fraud and Error in Science and Medicine.* Oxford: Basil Blackwell, 1986.

Koren, Yehuda. "There Is a Secular Israeli Culture." *Yediot Aharonot,* February 2, 1996, 28. (Hebrew)

Kossoff, David. *The Voices of Masada.* London: Vallentine Mitchell, 1973.

Kovner, Rotem. "The Distant Past Has Suddenly Become Closer." *Ha'aretz,* December 8, 2000, 6B. (Hebrew)

Ladouceur, David. "Josephus and Masada." In *Josephus, Judaism, and Christianity,* edited by Louis H. Feldman and Gohei Hata, 95–113. Detroit: Wayne State University Press, 1987.

Lankford, J. "Amateurs and Astrophysics: A Neglected Aspect in the Development of a Scientific Specialty." *Social Studies of Science* 11 (1981): 275–303.

Latour, Bruno. *Science in Action: How to Follow Scientists and Engineers through Society.* Cambridge, Mass.: Harvard University Press, 1987.

Latour, Bruno, and Steve Woolgar. *Laboratory Life: The Social Construction of Scientific Fact.* Beverly Hills: Sage Publications, 1979.

Law, John, and R. J. Williams. "Putting Facts Together: A Study of Scientific Persuasion." *Social Studies of Science* 12 (1982): 535–58.

Le Goff, Jacques. *History and Memory.* New York: Columbia University Press, 1992.

Lewis, Bernard. *History: Remembered, Recovered, Invented.* Princeton: Princeton University Press, 1975.

Liazos, Alexander. "The Poverty of the Sociology of Deviance: Nuts, Sluts and Perverts." *Social Problems* 20, no. 1 (1972): 103–20.

Livne, Micha. *Last Fortress: The Story of Masada and Its People.* Tel Aviv: Ministry of Defense Publishing, 1986. (Hebrew)

Lloyd, Mark. *The Art of Military Deception.* London: Leo Cooper, 1997.

Lynch, Michael, and David Bogen. "Sociology's Asociological 'Core': An Examination of Textbook Sociology in Light of the Sociology of Scientific Knowledge." *American Sociological Review* 62 (1997): 481–93.

Lynch, Michael, and Steve Woolgar, eds. "Introduction: Sociological Orientations to Representational Practice in Science." In *Representation in Scientific Practice,* 1–18. Cambridge, Mass.: MIT Press, 1990.

Lynch, William T. "Ideology and the Sociology of Scientific Knowledge." *Social Studies of Science* 24 (1994): 197–227.

MacDougall, Curtis D. *Hoaxes.* 1940. Reprint, New York: Dover, 1958.

Macionis, John J. *Sociology.* 5th ed. Englewood Cliffs, N.J.: Prentice-Hall, 1995.

Magness, Jodi. "Masada—Arms and the Men." *Biblical Archaeology Review* 18, no. 4 (1992): 58–67.

Malcolm, Janet. *The Journalist and the Murderer.* New York: Vintage, 1990.

Marcus, Amy Dockser. *The View From Nebo: How Archaeology Is Rewriting the Bible and Reshaping the Middle East.* Boston: Little Brown & Co., 2001.

Martin, Emily. "The Egg and the Sperm: How Science Has Constructed a Romance Based on Stereotypical Male-Female Roles." *Signs* 16 (1991): 485–501.

Mason, Steve. "Will the Real Josephus Please Stand Up?" *Biblical Archaeology Review* 23, no. 5 (September/October 1997): 58–65, 67–68.

Masson, Jeffrey Moussaieff. *The Assault on Truth: Freud's Suppression of the Seduction Theory.* New York: Farrar, Straus and Giroux, 1984.

McCarthy, Doyle E. *Knowledge as Culture: The New Sociology of Knowledge*. New York: Routledge, 1997.

Mendelsohn, Everett, and Yehuda Elkana, eds. *Science and Culture*. Dordrecht: D. Reidel and Company, 1981.

Meshorer, Ya'acov. "The Masada Coins." In *The Story of Masada: Discoveries from the Excavations*, edited by Gila Hurvitz, 133–37. Jerusalem: Hebrew University; Antiquities Authority; Society for Studying Eretz Israel and Its Antiquities, 1993. (Hebrew)

Mills, C. Wright. *The Power Elite*. New York: Oxford University Press, 1956.

———. *The Sociological Imagination*. 1959. Reprint, Harmondsworth: Penguin Books, Ltd., 1970.

Mitchell, Robert W., and Nicholas S. Thompson. *Deception: Perspectives on Human and Nonhuman Deceit*. Albany: State University of New York Press, 1986.

Moen, Doug. *The Big Book of Conspiracies: Allegedly True Tales From the Information Underground*. New York: Factoid Books/Paradox Press (imprint of DC Comics), 1995.

Montagu, Ewen. *The Man Who Never Was*. Harmondsworth, Middlesex: Penguin Books, 1953.

Morris, Richard. *Sinners, Lovers and Heroes: An Essay on Memorializing in Three American Cultures*. Albany: State University of New York Press, 1997.

Mure, David. *Master of Deception*. London: William Kimber, 1980.

Naveh, Yoseph. "Ostraca and Inscriptions on Clay in Hebrew and Aramaic from Masada." In *The Story of Masada: Discoveries from the Excavations*, edited by Gila Horowitz, 85–94. Jerusalem: Hebrew University, Israel Exploration Society and the Antiquity Authority, 1993. (Hebrew)

Negev, Avraham. "The History of the Kingdom of the Nabateans." *Mada* 6 (1965): 329–37. (Hebrew)

Netzer, Ehud. "Masada: The Survey, The Excavations, and the Reconstruction." In *The Dead Sea and the Judean Desert 1900–1967*, edited by Mordechai Naor, 185–97. Idan Series. Jerusalem: Yad Yitzhak Ben-Tzvi, 1990. (Hebrew)

———. "The Buildings Stratigraphy and Architecture." In *MASADA III: The Yigael Yadin Excavations 1963–1965: Final Report*, edited by Joseph Aviram, Gideon Foerster, and Ehud Netzer. Jerusalem: Israel Exploration Society and Hebrew University of Jerusalem, 1991.

———. "Masada Ramp Thesis Is Still as Firm as Bedrock." *Jerusalem Post*, December 21, 1994, 7.

Niebuhr, Gustav. "The Bible, as History, Flunks New Archaeological Test." *New York Times*, July 29, 2000.

Noll, Richard. *The Aryan Christ: The Secret Life of Carl Jung*. New York: Random House, 1997.

———. *The Jung Cult: Origins of a Charismatic Movement*. 2d ed. New York: Simon and Schuster, 1997.

Norris, Christopher. *Reclaiming Truth: Contribution to a Critique of Cultural Relativism*. Durham, N.C.: Duke University Press, 1996.

Ofshe, Richard, and Ethan Watters. *Making Monsters: False Memories, Psychotherapy, and Sexual Hysteria*. New York: Charles Scribner's Sons, 1994.

Olick, Jeffrey K., and Daniel Levy. "Collective Memory and Cultural Constraint: Holocaust Myth and Rationality in German Politics." *American Sociological Review* 62, no. 6 (1997): 921–36.

Paine, Robert. "Masada: A History of a Memory." *History and Anthropology* 6, no. 4 (1994): 371–409.

Pallone, Nathaniel, and James J. Hennessy, eds. *Fraud and Fallible Judgment: Varieties of Deception in the Social and Behavioral Sciences.* New Brunswick, N.J.: Transaction Publishers, 1995.

Parrish, Thomas, and S. L. A. Marshall, eds. *The Encyclopedia of World War II.* London: Secker & Warburg, 1978.

Perrett, Bryan. *Last Stand! Famous Battles Against the Odds.* London: Arms and Armour Press, 1991.

———. *Against All Odds! More Dramatic "Last Stand" Actions.* London: Arms and Arms, 1995.

Philip, Craig. *Last Stands: Famous Battles against the Odds.* London: Grange Books, 1993.

Pickering, Andrew. *Science as Practice and Culture.* Chicago: University of Chicago Press, 1992.

Pinch, Trevor, and Eiebe E. Bijker. "The Social Construction of Facts and Artifacts: Or How the Sociology of Technology Might Benefit Each Other." In *The Social Construction of Technology Systems: New Directions in the Sociology and History of Technology*, 17–50. Cambridge, Mass.: MIT Press, 1987.

Pipes, Daniel. *Conspiracy: How the Paranoid Style Flourishes and Where It Comes From.* New York: Free Press, 1997.

Podeh, Eli. *Denouncing Embarrassment and Acclaiming Plaster: The Israeli-Arab Conflict in the Mirror of Hebrew Textbooks for Studying History and Civility (1953–1995).* Jerusalem: Hebrew University, Harry S. Truman Research Institute for Advancing Peace, 1997. (Hebrew)

Potter, Jonathan. *Representing Reality: Discourse, Rhetoric, and Social Construction.* London: Sage Publications, 1996.

Rabinowitz, Abraham. "Lots of Controversy: Six Years after the Death of Yigael Yadin, His Colleagues Have Begun Publishing the Fruits of His Fabulous Archaeological Career." *Jerusalem Post*, weekend magazine, March 16, 1990, 6–9.

Rasberry, Robert W. *The "Technique" of Political Lying.* Washington, D.C.: University Press of America, 1981.

Raz-Krakotzkin, Amnon. "The Real Brain-Washing." *Ha'aretz*, October 6, 1992, 4. (Hebrew)

Reit, Seymour. *Masquerade: The Amazing Camouflage Deceptions of World War II.* London: Robert Hale, 1978.

Revel, Jean-François. *The Flight from Truth: The Reign of Deceit in the Age of Information*, translated by Curtis Cate. New York: Random House, 1991.

Roberts, David. *Great Exploration Hoaxes.* San Francisco: Sierra Club Books, 1982.

Robinson, Peter W. *Deceit, Delusion, and Detection.* London: Sage Publications, 1996.

Rodgers, William Ledyard. *Greek and Roman Naval Warfare.* Annapolis, Md: Naval Institute Press, 1964.

Rosenau, Pauline Marie. *Post-Modernism and the Social Sciences: Insights, Inroads, and Intuitions*. Princeton, N.J.: Princeton University Press, 1992.

Roth, Jonathan. "The Length of the Siege of Masada." *Scripta Classica Israelica* 14 (1995): 87–110.

Rotstein, Rephael. "The Bothering Myth." *Ha'aretz*, April 20, 1973, 16. (Hebrew)

Sa'ar, Rally. "History in a Mine Field." *Ha'aretz*, March 29, 1998, 3B. (Hebrew)

———. "The Regime Changes and with It the Historical Interpretation." *Ha'aretz*, March 18, 2001, 13A. (Hebrew)

Samuel R., and P. Thompson. *The Myths We Live By*. London: Routledge, 1990.

Schiff, Ze'ev, and Ehud Ya'ari. *War of Deception*. Jerusalem: Shocken, 1984. (Hebrew)

Schrire, Carmel. *Digging Through Darkness: Chronicles of an Archaeologist*. Charlottesville: University Press of Virginia, 1995.

Schultz, Duane. *Wake Island: The Heroic, Gallant Fight*. New York: St. Martin's Press, 1978.

Schwartz, Barry. "The Social Context of Commemoration: A Study in Collective Memory." *Social Forces* 61 (1982): 374–402.

———. "The Reconstruction of Abraham Lincoln, 1865–1920." In *Collective Remembering*, edited by David Middleton and Derek Edwards, 81–107. London: Sage, 1990.

———. "Social Change and Collective Memory: The Democratization of George Washington." *American Sociological Review* 56, no. 2 (1991): 221–36.

———. "Memory as a Cultural System: Abraham Lincoln in World War II." *American Sociological Review* 61 (1996a): 908–27.

———, ed. "Special Issue: Collective Memory." *Qualitative Sociology* 19, no. 3 (1996b).

———. "Collective Memory and History: How Abraham Lincoln Became a Symbol of Racial Equality." *Sociological Quarterly* 38, no. 3 (1997): 469–94.

———. *Abraham Lincoln and the Forge of National Memory*. Chicago: University of Chicago Press, 2000.

Schwarz, C., et al., eds. *Chambers English Dictionary*. 7th ed. Edinburgh: W & R Chambers, 1988.

Searle, John R. *The Construction of Social Reality*. New York: Free Press, 1995.

Segal, Avi. "It Is Not Allowed to Die in Defense of the Wailing Wall." *Jerusalem*, October 18, 1996, 10. (Hebrew)

Segev, Tom. "Decision in Ma'ale Hachamisha." *Ha'aretz*, January 21, 2000, 12B. (Hebrew)

Seligman, Adam. *The Problem of Trust*. Princeton, N.J.: Princeton University Press, 1997.

Sexton, Donal J. "The Theory and Psychology of Military Deception." In *Deception: Perspectives on Human and Nonhuman Deceit*, edited by Robert W. Mitchell and Nicholas S. Thompson, 349–56. Albany: State University of New York Press, 1986.

Shanks, Hershel. "Archaeology as Politics." *Commentary* 82, no. 2 (1986): 50–52.

Shapin, Steven. "History of Science and Its Sociological Reconstruction." *History of Science* 20 (1982): 157–211.

———. *A Social History of Truth: Civility and Science in Seventeenth-Century England*. Chicago: University of Chicago Press, 1994.

Shapin, Steven. "Here and Everywhere: Sociology of Scientific Knowledge." In *Annual Review of Sociology* 21, edited by John Hagan and Karen S. Cook, 289–321. Palo Alto, Calif.: Annual Reviews Inc., 1995.

Shapira, Anita. *Land and Power (The Sword of the Dove).* Tel Aviv: Am Oved, 1992. (Hebrew)

———. "Politics and Collective Memory: The Debate Over the 'New Historians' in Israel." *History and Memory* 7, no. 1 (1995): 9–40.

Shargel, Baila R. "The Evolution of the Masada Myth." *Judaism* 28 (1979): 357–71.

Shashar, Michael. "Masada, Moshe Dayan, and the Destruction of a Myth." *Yediot Ahronoth: Cultural, Literary, and Art Supplement,* October 28, 1983, 4. (Hebrew)

Shatzman, Israel. "The Roman Siege On Masada." In *The Story of Masada: Discoveries from the Excavations,* edited by Gila Hurvitz, 105–20. Jerusalem: Hebrew University; Antiquities Authority; Society for Studying Eretz Israel and Its Antiquities, 1993. (Hebrew)

———. "Panel Talk on the Roman Siege of Masada." In *Masada: Transcripts of Discussions about the New Reconstruction of the Site Ma'ale Hachamisha,* 40–41. Tel Aviv: Israel's National Parks Authority, Ministry of Tourism, Authority for the Development of the Negev, April 2, 1995. (Hebrew)

Shavit, Ya'acov. "Truth Will Rise from the Land: Points to the Development of Public Jewish Interest in Archaeology (Till the 1930s)." *Cathedra* 44 (1986): 27–54. (Hebrew)

Shea, Christopher. "Debunking Ancient Israel: Erasing History or Facing the Truth?" *Chronicle of Higher Education,* November 21, 1997, A12–A14.

Sheleg, Yair. "Zionism—The Battle for the Rating." *Kol Hair,* October 6, 1995, 57–71. (Hebrew)

Sheri, Merav. "Only 220 Bones: Who Is Really Buried in Masada? It Is Possible that the Answer Will Provide Another Nail in the Burial Coffin of the Masada Myth." *Ha'aretz,* February 18, 1998a, 4B. (Hebrew)

———. "Reifying Our Past, Said Ben-Gurion." *Ha'aretz,* March 18, 1998b, B4. (Hebrew)

———. "Archaeologist Claims to Have Found Remnants of an Essenes Sect Settlement in Ein Gedi." *Ha'aretz,* January 27, 1998c, 13A. (Hebrew)

Silberman, Neil Asher. *Between Past and Present.* New York: Anchor Books, Doubleday, 1989.

———. *A Prophet from Amongst You: The Life of Yigael Yadin: Soldier, Scholar, and Mythmaker of Modern Israel.* Reading, Mass.: Addison-Wesley, 1993.

Simpson, John. "Organized Disclosures in Contemporary America: The De-Differentiation of the Public Sphere and the Secularization of Modernity." In *Prophetic Religion in the Twenty-first* Century, edited by Anson Shuppe and Bronislaw Misztal. New York: Praeger, 1997

Sismondo, Sergio. "Some Social Constructions." *Social Studies of Science* 23 (1993): 515–53.

———. *Science Without Myth: On Constructions, Reality, and Social Knowledge.* Albany: State University of New York Press, 1996.

Smallwood, Mary E. *The Jews Under Roman Rule.* Leiden: E. J. Brill, 1976.

Snow, David A., and Robert Benford. "Master Frames and Cycles of Protest." In

Frontiers of Social Movement Theory, edited by Aldon Morris and Carol Mueller, 133–35. New Haven, Conn.: Yale University Press, 1992.

Stern, Menachem. "The Zealots and the Sicarii: Branches of a National Freedom Movement." In *The Great Jewish Revolt: Factors and Circumstances Leading to Its Outbreak*, edited by Kasher Arye, 380–83. Jerusalem: Zalman Shazar Center, 1983. (Hebrew)

Stone, Sir Roy. "How We Know Who We Are." *Daily Telegraph*, Arts & Books Section, September 7, 1996, A1.

Sturken, Marita. *Tangled Memories: The Vietnam War, the AIDS Epidemic, and the Politics of Remembering*. Berkeley: University of California Press, 1997.

Swanson, Guy. "An Organizational Analysis of Collectivities." *American Sociological Review* 36 (1971): 607–23.

Swidler, Ann, and Jorge Arditi. "The New Sociology of Knowledge." In *Annual Review of Sociology* 20, edited by John Hagan and Karen S. Cook, 305–29. Palo Alto, Calif.: Annual Reviews Inc., 1994.

Sykes, Steven. *Deceivers Ever*. Speldhurst: Spellmount, 1990.

Tevet, Maya. "Fighting to the Last Stone." *Jerusalem*, January 15, 1972, 36–39. (Hebrew)

Thomas, David Hurst. *Skull Wars: Kennewick Man, Archeology, and the Battle for Native American Identity*. New York: Basic Books, 2001.

Tomarkin, Yigael. "What Is There in Common Between Mahler and the Table-Desk in S.A.?" *Ha'aretz*, October 7, 1988, weekly supplement, 1988, 23. (Hebrew)

Tonkin, Elizabeth. "History and the Myth of Realism." In *The Myth We Live By*, edited by Raphael Samuel and Paul Thompson, 25–35. London: Routledge, 1990.

Trabelsi-Hadad. "Livnat Instructed to Shelve a History Book: 'A Moral and Zionist Failure.'" *Yediot Aharonot*, March 13, 2001, 14. (Hebrew)

Uranaka, Taiga. "Faked Digs Put Archaeologists on Defensive." *Japan Times*, January 28, 2001.

Urwin, George J. W. "The Defenders of Wake Island and Their Two Wars, 1941–1945." In *The Pacific War Revisited*, edited by Gunter Bischof and Robert L. Dupont, 111–37. Baton Rouge: Louisiana State University Press, 1997.

Vankin, Jonathan, and John Whalen. *The Sixty Greatest Conspiracies of All Time: History's Biggest Mysteries, Coverups, and Cabals*. Secaucus, N.J.: Carol Publishing Group,Citadel Press, 1997.

Vasek, Marie M. "Lying as a Skill: The Development of Deception in Children." In *Deception: Perspectives on Human and Nonhuman Deceit*, edited by Robert W. Mitchell and Nicholas S. Thompson, 271–92. Albany: State University of New York Press, 1986.

Vitelli, Karen D., ed. *Archaeological Ethics*. Walnut Creek, Calif.: AltaMira Press, 1996.

Weiner, J. S. *The Piltdown Forgery*. 1955. Reprint, New York: Dover, 1980.

Weiss-Rosmarin, Trude. "Masada and Yavneh." *Jewish Spectator* 31, no. 9 (November 1966): 4–7.

———. "Masada, Josephus, and Yadin." *Jewish Spectator* 32, no. 8 (October 1967): 2–8, 30.

Wheal, Elizabeth-Ann, Stephen Pope, and James Taylor. *A Dictionary of the Second World War*. 2d ed. London: Grafton Books, 1995.

Wheatley, Dennis. *The Deception Planners.* London: Hutchinson, 1980.

White, Hayden. *The Content of the Form.* Baltimore: Johns Hopkins University Press, 1987.

Wise, David A. *The Politics of Lying: Government Deception, Secrecy, and Power.* New York: Random House, 1973.

Yadin, Yigael. *Masada: First Season of Excavations, 1963–1964.* Preliminary Report. Jerusalem: Israel Exploration Society, 1965. (Hebrew) (Available in English, see below)

———. "The Excavations of Masada—1963/64 Preliminary Report." *Israel Exploration Journal* 15, no. 1–2 (1965e): 1–120.

———. Introduction to *Masada: The Israeli National Park Authority,* by Livne Micha and Zeev Meshel. Jerusalem: Israeli Government Printing House, 1966. (Hebrew)

———. *Masada: Herod's Fortress and the Zealots' Last Stand.* London: Weidenfeld and Nicolson, 1966e.

———. *Masada: In Those Days—At This Time.* Haifa: Shikmona Ma'ariv Library, 1966h. (Hebrew)

———. "Metzada." in *Encyclopaedia for Archaeological* Excavations in Eretz Israel, vol. 2, 374–90. Jerusalem: Society for the Investigation of Eretz Israel and Its Antiquity and Masada Ltd., 1970. (Hebrew)

———. "Nineteen Hundred Years to the Fall of Masada." *Ma'ariv,* April 16, 1973, 15, 33. (Hebrew)

Yadin, Yigael, and Gerald Gottlieb. *The Story of Masada by Yigael Yadin retold for young readers by Gerald Gottlieb.* New York: Random House, 1969.

Yadin, Yigael, and Yoseph Naveh. "The Aramaic and Hebrew Ostraca and Jar Inscriptions from Masada." In *MASADA I: The Yigael Yadin Excavations 1963–1965: Final Report,* edited by Joseph Aviram, Gideon Foerster, and Ehud Netzer, 1–70. Jerusalem: Israel Exploration Society and Hebrew University of Jerusalem, 1989.

Young, Martin, and Robbie Stamp. *Trojan Horses: Deception Operations in the Second World War.* London: Mandarin, 1991.

Zagorin, Perez. "The Historical Significance of Lying and Dissimulation." *Social Problems* 63, no. 3 (1996): 863–912.

Zebrowitz, Leslie. *Reading Faces: Windows to the Soul.* New York: Westview Press, 1997.

Zeitlin, Solomon. "Masada and the Sicarii." *Jewish Quarterly Review* 55 (1965): 299–317.

———. "The Sicarii and Masada." *Jewish Quarterly Review* 57 (1967): 251–70.

Zerubavel, Eviatar. *The Fine Line: Making Distinctions in Everyday Life.* New York: Free Press, 1991.

Zerubavel, Yael. *Recovered Roots: Collective Memory and the Making of Israeli National Tradition.* Chicago: University of Chicago Press, 1995.

Zias, Joseph. *Human Skeletal Remains from Masada: The Credibility of Josephus and Yadin: Has Masada Fallen Again?* Draft, courtesy of the author, 1998.

———. "Whose Bones?" *Biblical Archaeology Review* 24, no. 6 (November/December 1998): 40–45, 64–65.

Zias, Joseph, Dror Segal, and Israel Carmi. "Addendum: Human Skeletal Remains." In *MASADA IV: The Yigael Yadin Excavations 1963–1965: Final Report*, edited by Joseph Aviram, Gideon Foerster, and Ehud Netzer, 366–67. Jerusalem: Israel Exploration Society and Hebrew University of Jerusalem, 1994.

Zuckerman, Harriet. "Deviant Behavior and Social Control in Science." In *Deviance and Social Change*, edited by E. Sagarin, 87–138. Beverly Hills: Sage Publications, 1977.

———. "The Sociology of Science." In *Handbook of Sociology*, edited by Neil Smelser, 511–74. Newbury Park, Calif.: Sage, 1988.

INDEX